*This book is respected by professionals, commended by publications, treasured by parents.*

### Respected by Professionals...

"I have worked with children and parents for over forty years. Never have I seen or felt the intensity of their pain as now. *Relief for Hurting Parents* is extremely timely. It offers comfort, encouragement, and solutions."
**–Grace H. Ketterman, M.D., Child Psychiatrist and Pediatrician**

"This volume is a must for all parents because of the unusual insight and practicality stemming from the author's experience. I recommend and use it constantly in my counseling practice as well as seminars."
**–H. Norman Wright, Founder, Family Counseling and Enrichment**

"Your book is an excellent resource. You are right on target on the subject of teenagers."
**–Kirk Fordice, Governor, State of Mississippi**

"I want every one of you parents to get this book, *Relief for Hurting Parents, How to fight for the lives of teenagers.* God has raised up Buddy Scott because we can't do it alone."
**–Josh McDowell, Josh McDowell Ministry**

"This book will show you how to equip your child with a healthy conscience."
**–Wayne Shepherd, Moody Broadcasting Network**

"In *Relief*, Buddy Scott has captured the parenting skills and values that are passing away and placed them in one volume to be preserved for all time."
**–L. Duane Alcorn, Ed.D., L.P.C., L.M.F.T., Marriage and Family Therapist**

"Buddy Scott provides practical, proven solutions. He has been used by the Lord to knit many families together in a fabric of honesty, love, and mutual responsibility."
**–Robert S. McGee, Founder, Rapha Hospital Treatment Centers**

"I hope a lot of parents read this book. It is excellent."
**–Philip E. Batt, Governor, State of Idaho**

"We have found Buddy's book, *Relief for Hurting Parents*, an excellent complement to our program. It offers parents practical and effective tools for dealing with oppositional-defiant teenagers."
**–W. Tom Parker, Former Executive Director, Minirth-Meier Clinic Day Hospital**

"*Relief for Hurting Parents* certainly contains valuable insights and practical information for every family. I commend your efforts to help the many parents who may turn to your book as a last resort."
**–Don Sundquist, Governor, State of Tennessee**

"*Relief for Hurting Parents* is full of helpful clear directions for how to deal with struggling adolescents...Scott has a solid understanding."
**–Cliff Schimmels, Professor of Education, Lee College**

"You have great insights..."
**–Orrin G. Hatch, United States Senator**

"This book represents the best advice available for dealing with teenagers. It contains practical and easy-to-follow steps for maintaining order in your home."
**–Steve Underwood, Attorney, Tennessee Oilers**

## Commended by Publications...

"This parenting book means business. It's for the parent at the end of his or her rope, as well as for parents who haven't had to face serious problems yet. It's a unique book that offers firm solutions to tough problems."
**–*Atlanta Daily World* newspaper**

"*Relief for Hurting Parents* is an excellent resource for helping parents deal with teenage children."
**–UPDATE, Official Publication of the United States Air Force Chaplain Service**

"Buddy Scott's sound advice from the front lines combined with sincere faith are like lifelines for sinking families. I know it's a fact—*Christian Parenting Today* readers with teenagers look to him for help when the going gets tough."
**–David Kopp, Former Editor, *Christian Parenting Today* magazine**

"Through stories, illustrations and how-tos, Scott presents Christ-centered concepts and principles to help parents balance compassion and appropriate discipline with teenagers."
**–*Parents of Teenagers* magazine**

"Buddy Scott understands the pain of caring parents whose kids go astray and offers suggestions for persevering in love...This comprehensive book also teaches you how to head off problems before they begin. It's a valuable resource for any family—those in crisis and those who wish to avoid it."
**–*Focus on the Family* magazine**

"Buddy Scott restores parents' confidence in themselves and reassures them that kids can change. He clearly lays out how parents can reinforce the moral structure of their homes."
**–*Bookstore Journal***

"*Relief for Hurting Parents* helps Christian parents cope."
**–*Publishers Weekly* magazine**

"*Relief* is sincere, honest, encouraging, and hard-hitting... and good preventative medicine... I had a hard time getting it back from the hurting parents to whom I had loaned it."
**–*Youthworker* magazine**

"The book is based on sound principles that work."
**–*Southwestern Journal of Theology***

"*Relief* delivers...encouragement and practical strategies for coping with problem teen-age behavior."
**–*Campus Life* magazine**

"Scott gives help, hope, relief, and support to hurting parents."
**–*Quaker Life* magazine**

"This book is unequaled in its unique combination of strength and tenderness."
**–Victor Oliver, Oliver-Nelson Books, Thomas Nelson Publishers**
**(first publisher of *Relief for Hurting Parents*)**

# Treasured by Parents...

"As I read this book, I felt life flowing into me." —**Texas**

"Your book charged me with new hope and dedication." —**Utah**

"The book restored my confidence in myself as a human being." —**Texas**

"This book has been an anchor in my storm." —**Georgia**

"By reading *Relief for Hurting Parents,* I discovered I was doing a lot of things right, and I discovered new things to do. I feel better about myself as a parent." –**Washington**

"*Relief* is an answer to prayer." –**Florida**

"*Relief* changed my life." –**Louisiana**

"This is the help I've been searching for, for years." –**Minnesota**

"*Relief for Hurting Parents* was truly heaven-sent to me." –**Georgia**

"Your book is like a healing balm covering our wounds. Our daughter hid it for a time, but we found it, and now it goes with us everywhere again." –**Texas**

"Your book has brought direction and more peace into our lives." –**Colorado**

"I devoured the book. Nothing else comes close to helping like *Relief* does." –**Oregon**

"We were about burned out emotionally. Thanks for the much-needed help." –**Ohio**

"I carry your book everywhere I go. It has so much healing within it." –**Texas**

"I loaned *Relief* to a dear Christian couple. The mother came back clutching the book, asking if she could keep it. She said it was keeping them SANE." –**Missouri**

"My precious kids will have a better mother because of your work." –**Alabama**

"This book not only saved our child...it also saved our marriage." –**Texas**

"Through the principles we learned in *Relief,* our home and lives, that were once in chaos, are now in harmony." –**South Carolina**

"I've only read the 1st chapter, but I've mustered up more faith to carry on." –**Illinois**

"I'm reading *Relief* for the third time. Through it, I am finding inner peace." –**Utah**

"My wife and I bless you for writing such a helpful, intelligent, spirit-filled and honest book. We took turns reading chapters and discussing the book's concepts and our feelings. This proved to be therapeutic for us." –**Oregon**

"Your book is amazingly compatible with what we were doing, but gave us so much more in the way of specifics." –**Utah**

"I read *Relief* with a pad of stickum notes and pencil in hand. By the end of the book, the wall was covered in yellow stickums as far as my arm could reach!" –**Indiana**

"I have highlighted over half the book. It is full of information that *every parent* needs to know. I am going today and order 10 copies to give to friends." –**Tennessee**

"Our daughter has mental health problems, and the book has been a great help." –**Ohio**

"If I had purchased your book one week earlier, I would have read chapter 28 and known not to put my son in the treatment center I chose. They were doing what your book warns parents about. I had him transferred to another hospital. Thanks!" –**Georgia**

"I wish Buddy's book had been a prerequisite to Lamaze classes." –**Michigan**

"The Boy Scouts have a handbook; now parents have a handbook." –**Alabama**

"*Relief for Hurting Parents* is the book of instructions that should come with strong-willed children. It is the manual for our parent support group." –**Texas**

"Thank you for giving parents a place to go when all seems hopeless!" –**California**

"The support group enabled me to understand my childhood and dysfunctional family. It helped me deal with many issues that had been stuffed and ignored. It showed me there *is* a way to stop the cycle." –**Texas**

"I am sending you a picture of the children *Relief* helped raise. If you ever get a little discouraged, Buddy, dig out that picture and look at those healthy, smiling, bright faces and know that all your hard work and financial burdens are worth it! As a single parent, I could not have managed to keep my three children healthy, active, drug-free, responsible and aware of others without their other parent— had I not had your book." –**New York**

# DEDICATION

*This book is dedicated to and written for*
*all fair and reasonable parents—and those who aspire to be.*

❖

## A REQUEST FROM THE AUTHOR

The author requests that you refrain from using any information
in this book until you have read and understood the book as a whole.
He advises parental discretion in allowing children to have access to this book.

# RELIEF

# FR

Written in honor of parents who care so much they hurt

# HURTING

# PARENTS

## HOW TO FIGHT FOR
## THE LIVES OF TEENAGERS

*How to prepare younger children
for less dangerous journeys
through teenage years*

## BUDDY SCOTT

ALL⊕N
PUBLISHING

*Go to...*
# www.buddyscott.com

Originally published in 1989 in Nashville, Tennessee, by Oliver-Nelson Books, a division of Thomas Nelson, Inc., Publishers.

Published in Lake Jackson, Texas, by Allon Publishing, P.O. Box 804, Lake Jackson, Texas 77566, (979) 297-5700. (No unsolicited manuscripts accepted or returned.)

Unless otherwise noted, the Bible version used in this publication is the *New King James Version*. Copyright © 1979, 1980, 1982, Thomas Nelson, Inc., Publishers.

Scripture quotations noted TEV are from the *Good News Bible*—
Old Testament: Copyright © American Bible Society 1976;
New Testament: Copyright © American Bible Society 1966, 1971, 1976.
Used by permission.

Names and events have been changed for protection and privacy.

Printed in the United States.

Library of Congress Catalog Card Number: 93-72385

ISBN: 0-9637645-0-0

17 18 19 20 21 22 23 24 25—07 06 05 04

# CONTENTS

# PREFACE

Teenagers are going through the transition from childhood to adulthood, from dependence on parents to independence of parents. It is normal during this time for teenagers to elbow their way toward independence by being a little defiant at times. But their defiance should not register beyond 4.0 on the Richter scale. Families can't hold up against repeatedly severe homequakes and their aftershocks. Families must have help. Here's help.

Here's help also for parents of younger children. If the basic concepts and principles contained in this book are learned and applied early, parents will be more adequately prepared for their children's journey during the teenage years.

Parents have had a lot of experience in helping their children through difficult homework assignments, friend problems, or occasional bad grades, but certain irresponsible acts are in a different league altogether . . .

> being rebellious
> behaving violently
> screaming profanities
> committing crimes
> being sexually active
> viewing X-rated videos
> abusing alcohol
> abusing drugs
> selling drugs
> skipping school
> failing in school
> threatening teachers
> misbehaving constantly in school
> sneaking out at night
> using family cars without permission
> violating traffic laws habitually
> wrecking cars
> refusing to cooperate
> refusing to attend church
> disrespecting parents
> influencing siblings to do wrong
> attempting suicide
> partying in the home during their parents' absence
> having abortions without parental knowledge

involving themselves with the wrong crowd
lying constantly

These home-shaking disappointments make you understand why the word *rebellion* happens to contain the words *rebel* and *lion*. Living with an out-of-control teenager can be like living with a lion on a rampage!

These horrors are new to the family. They can be stubborn and be*wild*ering! So much so, in fact, that not even longtime psychologists and psychiatrists have mastered rescue techniques that work most of the time—yet parents by the thousands are being drafted to try to rescue their children from these problems.

I've served beside hundreds of these parents during the last ten-plus years, and together we have fought for the lives of their children. This book is a compilation of what I have learned on the front lines of domestic combat.

Many of the kids we fought to save in the early days are fine now—they are working in our businesses, attending our churches, and raising families of their own. A few have called and told me they would be happy to help me talk to others who are presently in the throes of teenage problems.

God has given me a new calling. I sense His call on my life to write, speak, and teach. This new calling calls me away from providing private counseling. I will, instead, be teaching others how to help the way we've learned to help. This support for hurting parents and their kids must spread across America like a warm quilt.

# PART I

## *Encouragement*

I asked twenty sets of parents of misbehaving teenagers where I should begin in writing this book. They quickly agreed that I should begin by offering some immediate pain relief. I took their advice, and this first part is for relieving parental pain.

You need to know that what you are feeling is likely very normal for what you're going through, that you are not losing your mind, that you are not alone, that someone understands and can put it into words for you, that God has not forsaken you, that you are not a failure (as self-doubt might tempt you to believe), that it's right for you to expect your children to live decent lives, and that there is still hope.

In the following chapters I will seek to ease your pain and help you overthrow your intimidations, revive your confidence in your ability to parent, renew your courage, and develop a proper posture for parenting. ■

# CHAPTER 1

# DEALING WITH THE PAIN

Hurting parents, God understands how you feel. God lost His kids . . . and no one can say He didn't raise them right, either. He loved them. He spent time with them. He gave them the best of everything. He carefully taught them what not to partake of or even touch. He made sure they understood that their futures depended on their choices. He warned them of the consequences if they strayed from their upbringing. Nevertheless, a bad influence pulled them away and involved them in wrongdoing.

God found out and confronted Adam and Eve, who acted somewhat like many of today's teenagers. They were evasive and placed blame elsewhere.

God's family was traumatized: Adam and Eve's original relationship with God and each other had been violated, and there were long-term ill effects. God was put on standby, and He watched His creation fall further and further away from Him.

Abused parents, God understands how you feel! *God has been where you are!* Just as the Son understands what it's like to live in our dangerous environment, the Father understands what it's like to be abused by those you have created.

## Abused parents hurt in nearly every way possible.

I have referred to hurting parents as abused parents because so much of what I've seen kids do to their parents is nothing less than parent abuse.

We have Children's Protective Services for helping abused kids; abused parents need some help, too! I want to offer some relief to good parents who are being abused. As parents of misbehaving children, you hurt in about every way possible.

You hurt . . .

- because the children you love have turned toward self-destruction.
- because your children stand in grotesque defiance against you.
- because your megacontribution to the lives of your kids is not being appreciated by them.

You hurt . . .

- because you feel like failures as parents.
- because you are haunted by your thoughts, *If only we had done this or not done that.*
- because other parents—some with younger children or some fortunate enough not to have had severe problems with their teenagers—look at you like you are failures.
- because you are frustrated from going behind your kids cleaning up their messes.
- because you have to mix with people at work, at community functions, or at church who know about your children's problems.
- because you wonder if you ought to give up your positions at church or in the community.

You hurt . . .

- because you don't know for sure how to help your children.
- because you don't know what to do or how to think.

## Good parents can have trouble with their teenagers.

Some parents who ask for help are among the finer people of their communities, and their adolescents' problems aren't always the parent's fault.

Please hear me, readers: Good parents, successful parents, can have trouble with their children. The wrong crowd—be it the movie screen crowd, the music crowd, the TV crowd, or a group of peers—can lure kids away from good parents.

The majority of influences beamed at our children today are contrary to their moral and spiritual health and, thereby, their social and emotional health. Think about it.

## Abused parents are more numerous than you would like to believe.

Abused parents, hurting in secret, are sprinkled all over America. You are hurting in secret because family problems aren't something you want to publicize.

Only a few years earlier, the children were playing Little League; you were making every game. You thought your children would never treat you like so-and-so's kids. You watched your children hit and run, and your hearts swelled with pride and expectancy.

A couple or so years later, however, your children are still hitting and running, but now it's of a sordid sort: They hit you with a miserable disappointment and run to something worse.

### It hurts s-o-o-o bad!

Again last week, like most of my weeks, a mom and dad cried beside me. They said, "We've spent all our money on him, and he's still into drugs." Their vitality had been siphoned to a critical level. At middle age, their dreams had begun to shrivel. Their son, their most precious investment, had abused them and had turned to those who don't care about him or anybody else. Such brokenhearted parents often begin to wonder . . .

> What is life all about anyhow?
> Why keep on trying?
> Why work?
> Why stay moral?
> Why do anything?
> Why not avoid the pain with booze?
>   Or with prescriptions from a doctor?
> Why not sleep all the time?
>   Or eat all the time?
> Why pray?
> Why go to church?
> WHERE IS GOD?

Excuse me, readers, but I'd like to venture away from the subject for a few moments to make a request of you.

*Please don't be disappointed with God.* Apparently, it's easy for people to be disappointed with God at this point. They pray and pray and pray for God to change their children, and He doesn't. And some parents feel abandoned by Him.

God is at the same place you are. He is agonizingly watching your children (*His* children) hurt themselves and others. Neither you nor God can storm their control centers and legislate their improvement. God has given your children the same freedom He has given you, the freedom of choice, acceptance or rejection, as they so choose.

I courteously seek to help parents remember that God has promised that, as a rule, He will not interfere with people's choices. Yet, that is precisely what you may be asking Him to do when you pray for Him to change your sons or daughters. (Remember, God didn't interfere with Adam and Eve's choices when their choices would mess up the whole world!)

We pray astray when we ask God to take command of someone's control center by force. He will not make robots out of people. Your children, like you, have been entrusted by God to shape their own destinies.

Then, should we not pray at all? Certainly we should!

*How should we pray?* Feel free to pray for your children's eyes to be opened . . .
to the deceptions going on around them,
to the fat self-concern of their "friends,"
to what they are doing to their families,
to how their sins are also against their God,
to what they are sacrificing to the wrong crowd and pleasure gods,
to the *saving* nature of the *Savior.*

Pray that God will put someone in your children's pathway who can win their friendship and offer them help . . . help that they *can receive.* Pray that you will not compromise your own values so that your children will continue believing in your integrity.

And as you pray, remember that God knows how you feel. He's been where you are. And now *you* know how He feels. You are where He's been and where He still is. You and God have so much in common that your communication ought to be improving! Let your children's pressure press you toward Him, and He will share His healing with you.

Back to the subject, pain.

Abused parents have learned the meaning of the word. To be abused by your own offspring is to experience torturous pain.

You can understand why it's so painful when you realize that you may be living under the threat of a divorce and a funeral occurring at the same time. One of your children may be threatening to divorce you—and that could include the death of your present relationship with that child and the death of your future hopes and dreams for him or her. Without quite realizing it, you may be involved in the stages of grief outlined by Elisabeth Kübler-Ross in her book *On Death and Dying:* denial and isolation, anger, bargaining, depression, and acceptance.

Abused parents, *you are overdosing on pain!* And as I'm sure you already know, your anxiety level is hazardous to your health. Fair and reasonable Christian parents need and deserve some relief. I would like to help.

Parent, do you feel guilty and feel like you may have failed? Do you wonder if outsiders are forming similar opinions of you? I urge you to invite those outsiders—the ones who are important to you—to read the first two chapters of this book. Doing that will help them revise their opinions.

Read and review them yourself. You will feel better.

Further, I would like to present you with a line of reasoning that will help you cope better.

Adopting "Encouragement" (see box) will help you maintain confidence in yourself and in your parenting skills when battle fatigue begins to threaten your poise. Read it every day if you need to.

## Encouragement for fair and reasonable Christian parents—and for those who aspire to be

The misbehaviors of our children do not necessarily indicate that we are failures as parents. Our worth as parents does not hinge on the choices of our children.

We remember that God raised Adam and Eve, and both made bad choices.

Other influences are competing against us for the health and well-being of our children. These influences can include peer pressure, pleasure pressure (the intense desire for euphoria), TV, movies, music, and certain celebrities, among others.

Our children are free moral agents, and they can make their choices independently of our moral standards, just as Adam and Eve chose to ignore God. And that may explain what's happening.

Like God, we must maintain our balance of being understanding and compassionate while demanding respect from our children. We deserve respect. We are the ones who are trying to save our children from damaging themselves morally, spiritually, emotionally, socially, and physically.

Our children absolutely must learn to respond appropriately to authority, or they will be ill-prepared to face the real world when we parents are replaced by employers, driver's licensing officials, insurers, credit managers, university officials, apprenticeship officials, the Better Business Bureau officials, military officials, police officers, and government agency personnel. We must hold our positions for the sake of our children's futures.

Just as God has never backed off and compromised His values, we should never back off and compromise ours. This faithfulness will keep our children in touch with where to return. We should never compromise ourselves into root rot. Our children desperately need wholesome roots to look back to. So long as our root system is healthy and strong, our kids have something to be tethered to while they explore wrong. If we develop root rot by compromising our own integrity, it severs their tethers.

And yet, we can never forget that we are responsible before God's authority to be fair and reasonable in disciplining our children, to set a proper example before them. Like Christ, we will seek to do the healing things for our children and not discipline them out of avenging hostility.

If we are seeking to heal our children, *we are decent parents*.

Copyright 1989 by R. A. "Buddy" Scott • Allon Publishing

## But what about those parents who have been doing wrong?

There are more problem parents now than ever before because traditional moral values have been and are being desecrated. The "new morality's" children are now parents. The children of yesterday's drug abusers are now parents. I am not blind to those issues. The following example illustrates what I've recommended in such cases.

Some time ago, a frustrated father contacted me about his daughter's promiscuity. During our visits, the fact surfaced that the father was living with a woman who was not his wife. I asked this father to join with his daughter in a remake, to say to her . . .

*Sweetheart, as you know, I haven't been living like I should, either. Your trouble has reminded me of my own problems. I, also, need to make a course correction. We will do this together.*

### But what about kids who are living in tough situations?

Children in homes where marital fighting is the norm, or where one parent has rejected them, or where they don't get along with the new stepparent, or where there's one live-in and then another, or where parents have bullied them all their lives and now they're big enough to defy the brutality, ad infinitum, their rebellion may be their only hope for survival. These children need individual counseling, and they may need to be rescued. They certainly don't need more pressure put on them. This book is not for their parents, unless it is used to help them become fair, understanding, loving, and repentant.

To parents who have been fair and reasonable Christian parents, I urge: Be careful and thorough in watching for difficult situations. For example, a child's problems at school may not be his or her fault. Your child's problems could well be the teacher's fault or the peer group's fault or the result of other problems. Investigate and make your assessments fairly and with caution. Never instantly decide that it must be the child's fault.

### But what about those parents who are doing wrong and couldn't care less?

Children of parents who refuse to clean up their own acts must make it *regardless of their parents' behavior*. Therefore, as an outside counselor, I often say something like this:

> *I want to challenge you to grow a new limb on your family tree, to veer away from your family's trend toward excessive drinking, drug abuse, affairs, and so forth. I'll be happy to serve as your coach for this, and I'd love for you to come back and see me in a few years and shake my hand and say, "I have a family of my own now, and we are doing just fine at growing a new limb on my family tree." I'll be looking forward to that day.*

## Abused parents can reduce the pain by dealing with in*timid*ation.

Learning to cope with in*timid*ation will help you become more confident of the direction you have chosen for helping your children.

Think of the word in*timid*ation. I've emphasized the word *timid* to help you realize where confusion can lead. Your obnoxious teenagers and the ugly messes they make can dis*courage* you. They can take away your *courage* and cause you to be too *timid* to take action.

### Abused parents often experience feelings of intimidation.

Parents of defiant, misbehaving adolescents are often feeling . . .

> angry
> guilty
> helpless
> drained
> embarrassed
> humiliated

threatened
defeated
depressed
blamed
defensive
fearful
nervous
anxious
ill at ease
*intimidated*

These feelings are normal for what you are going through.

You are in*timid*ated because you often don't know for sure what you should do or how you should think about your children's problems. Members of certain psychological circles make you feel inadequate and ill-equipped to do anything at all about the problems. You are in*timid*ated because of your insecurity about the unfairness of demanding change if the child can't help what he or she is doing.

And you are in*timid*ated by the feeling that it's all your fault. You keep asking, *How can we come down on them if it's all our fault?* Or maybe you're in*timid*ated because you are not in agreement with your spouse about what should be done.

But perhaps the scariest in*timid*ation is the risk involved in demanding appropriate behavior. You may be afraid that your action might cause your children to . . .

run away
drop out of school
fail to graduate from high school and college
lose their jobs
talk against you to significant others
report you to child welfare for child abuse
turn further away from you and toward the wrong crowd
get deeper into drugs
get someone pregnant or get pregnant
and so forth

Defiant and rebellious kids become aware of your dreadful anxieties and use them against you. They will sometimes grab hold of your fears and use them as tools of manipulation to further intimidate you. *They threaten to make your worst fears come true if you continue to interfere in their lives.* You may be left shivering in swamps of despair.

### Abused parents can be benched by the anxieties that spew from intimidation.

Abused parents are often benched by anxiety attacks. You sometimes sit with your head in your hands bewildered about what to do. You feel powerless, confused, and guilty.

It's as if you have become an invalid parent. Just think of what the word *invalid* means: "Having become incapable of caring for oneself, sick." Another meaning of *invalid* is "nonvalid, not worth anything." What on earth is happening to parents?

How terribly sad that good parents can be reduced to pose in such a humiliating portrait! Enough! ENOUGH!!

## Parents can deal with intimidation in four ways.

### 1. Understand that most professional counselors don't have all the answers.

Effective professional counselors are returning to *common sense* in counseling. They have begun to advise parents to parent like good parents already parent.

Dr. William Glasser, author of *Reality Therapy,* is a prime example. Dr. Glasser was head psychiatrist for the Ventura School for Girls in California when he had the opportunity to set up and display his conversion to common sense in counseling.

Ventura has been described as the last stop for girls before adult prison. Dr. Glasser became so disappointed in the ineffectiveness of traditional psychological techniques that he took a new direction. He decided to return to reason and morality in counseling. Dr. Glasser came up with his three *R*'s: (1) reality; (2) responsibility, and (3) right-and-wrong.

He wrote in his book, *Reality Therapy: A New Approach to Psychiatry:*

> To be worthwhile we must maintain a satisfactory standard of behavior. To do so we must learn to correct ourselves when we do wrong and to credit ourselves when we do right. If we do not evaluate our own behavior or, having evaluated it, if we do not act to improve our conduct where it is below our standards, we will not fulfill our needs to be worthwhile and will suffer as acutely as when we fail to love or be loved. Morals, standards, values, or right and wrong behavior are all intimately related to the fulfillment of our needs for self-worth and [are] . . . a necessary part of Reality Therapy.

And Dr. Glasser wrote about the girls at Ventura:

> We accept no excuses for irresponsible acts. Students are held responsible for their behavior and cannot escape responsibility on the plea of being emotionally upset, mistreated by mother, neglected by father, or discriminated against by society.

Dr. Glasser reported that this method worked in 80 percent of the cases at Ventura. It has become one of the more widely applied therapeutic techniques for the rehabilitation of teenagers in America.

Of course, I am not saying that all other counselors are ineffective; what I am saying is that the incompetence you may be feeling because you're "just a parent" is highly exaggerated. I am also saying that if you take your sons or daughters to a counselor, be sure the counselor has a commonsense approach. In a later chapter, I'll give you some guidance for selecting a counselor.

### 2. Have your doctor check for physical causes of uncivilized behavior.

It is wise to take your children to the doctor for thorough checkups to determine possible physical causes for the uncivilized symptoms you've observed. Receiving clearance here will reassure you that it's okay to be forceful in disciplining your children, and a physical examination will catch the unusual cases where deviant behavior is caused by physiological problems.

Be sure to tell your doctor exactly what you are seeking. Say something like,

> *Doctor, I would like for you to see if you can find any physiological reasons for my daughter's defiance and misbehavior. Here's what she's been doing that we object to.*

And give him or her the list.

A word of clarification: I am not talking here about behavior (like hyperactivity in the classroom) that can be modified with medication. I am talking about stubborn misbehavior that is irresponsible, illegal, un-American, and self-destructive. In fact, you could simply ask your doctor to check for any physiological causes of uncivilized behavior.

A word of caution: Some doctors are still adherents of the psychological approaches that Dr. Glasser and others left behind. Some will urge you to go that route. The decision is yours, of course, but I'd urge you to finish reading this book before you do so.

A word about your decision: Your decision on what is causing the irresponsibility—sickness or purposeful wrongdoing—decides the route you will take to try to solve the problem.

Something to think about: If it's sickness that always causes uncivilized behavior, then the thousands of people in your state prisons are in the wrong institutions. They should be in hospitals, instead. Do be careful.

### 3. Realize the best thing you can do is to raise your children consistent with the real world.

Continue to demand that your children act like they will have to act to be successful in future relationships. Future employers, future coworkers, future families, future neighbors, and God Himself will not put up with . . .

> rudeness
> selfishness
> extreme sloppiness
> dishonesty
> disloyalty
> irresponsibility
> tantrums
> chemical abuse

and with those who are often . . .

> searching for loopholes
> refusing to listen
> refusing to follow instructions
> sneaking around

> fudging on the rules
> hiding to avoid doing their part

and with those who are hateful to their providers.

*And if you allow these things, you are helping your children prepare to fail and be rejected throughout their lives.* That's as big a risk as the risks mentioned earlier. You are right if you keep positive pressure on your children to act responsibly.

Be strong! Be consistent! *It is not best for your children that you indulge them like no one else will ever indulge them again.*

*Mis-be-have:* Think of the word. It's made up of "miss *being*" and "miss *having*." Since you want your children to *be* okay and to *have* good things, you must raise them consistent with the real world and help them to not misbehave.

### 4. Recognize that if your children seek to hide wrong, they know to do right.

The biggest clue that your children are capable of doing right and avoiding wrong, and that you are correct in demanding that they do right instead of wrong, is in front of you. If your children know to hide to do wrong and to lie to evade getting caught, they clearly know right from wrong—and they are setting goals and making choices designed to get them to their goals.

This means that what they need for positive and constructive behavior is already in place and working within them. It further means that *if* they choose to change their goals from destructive ones to constructive ones, *they will change their behavior*—and their destinies. This line of logic should serve to confirm your correctness in demanding that your children behave themselves.

Misbehaviors indicate, with very few exceptions, that children have been attracted by the wrong influences and have begun to make self-destructive choices. (Misbehaviors do *not* normally indicate mental incompetence.) If children change their choices and their crowd (the group who supports them in defying what is right), they can change their direction. They really can.

Refuse to be benched by in*timid*ation, refuse to be *invalid*ated, gird your common sense about you, and confidently perform as parents. You're on!

In summary, four ways parents can deal with in*timid*ation are . . .

*First,* understand that most professional counselors don't have all the answers. Effective professional counselors are returning to common sense in counseling.

*Second,* have your doctor check for physical causes of uncivilized behavior.

*Third,* realize the best thing you can do is to raise your children consistent with the real world.

*Fourth,* recognize that if your children seek to hide wrong, they know to do right.

# CHAPTER 2

# DEVELOPING A PROPER POSTURE

've encouraged you pain-ridden parents to shed your intimidations, avoid invalidation, and stand before your children demanding that they not destroy themselves by being out of sync with you, their God, their country, and their own successful futures.

In later chapters, I'll give you specific suggestions on how to be more effective in taking your loving but firm stand before your children. But first, I would like you to check your posture as parents. You are obligated to have a good posture if you are going to be forceful about requiring your children to do well.

I've hesitated to write about how to pressure (discipline) kids to do better. I'm concerned that parents whose common sense is warped by their own problems will use this material to justify their unreasonable actions toward their children. I pray that I will never help unreasonable parents become meaner.

Our counseling agency has worked with our county's Children's Protective Services unit for years, and I've seen a great deal of child abuse. In fact, six columns I wrote on child abuse were selected as the most outstanding series written on that subject that year in the state of Texas for our size newspaper.

This intense awareness of the child abuse problem has made me concerned about the potential danger of the misuse of the contents of this book. I pray that people who are hateful, or people with control problems, or people who are already too rigid, or people who misquote the Bible to justify their extreme harshness will not use excerpts from this book out of context to support their meanness. I've consciously sought to avoid this tragedy.

### Good posture is extremely important.

Your posture is extremely important because you have little right to demand more of your children morally or in the area of self-control than you are producing yourself. To paraphrase the Bible: You must first get the 4×4 out of your own eye before you try to take the splinter out of your child's eye.

If you have done wrong in the past, you need not be benched. You can change, too, and it's good to be open with your children about it. You can say . . .

*You've watched me do wrong. You have seen the messes that my problems have caused. I have committed myself to changing, and I am going to do everything within my power to keep you from messing up like I have.*

I have a warning for abusive parents. To those who push their kids around physically or emotionally, I would like to remind you that you are also under authority, and your actions are also being scrutinized by your Parent—by your heavenly Father! You, like each and every one of us parents, will stand before God and give account for the way you have parented. Imagine yourself there, and imagine giving God your rationalizations. What would His response be?

Parental actions that violate God's laws and also violate the personhoods of children include such insults as . . .

- labeling them stupid, disgusting, lazy, bad, fools, bungling idiots, sluts, creeps, or otherwise putting down their value as persons
- using vulgar words to describe them
- attacking them with curse words
- slapping them
- returning evil for evil (like smashing their radio because you found it tuned to hard rock again)
- gossiping about their faults and offenses to relatives and friends
- showing a lack of confidence in their ability to do better
- proclaiming doom on your children by saying something like, "You're just like your Uncle Joe. He's never changed and you won't either!"

### God applies the golden rule to parenting.

Parenting is covered by the golden rule. We are required by God to do unto our children as we would have them do unto us, if the roles were reversed. We should be as polite and considerate of our children as we are of our adult friends.

I'll write about this plainly: It is not right for you to make a habit of speaking rudely to your children while demanding that they talk with respect to you. It is not right for you to hang out at the lounges while demanding that your children not use pot. "But lounges are legal and pot is not," someone might object. Kids don't buy that. To them, chemicals are chemicals. Besides, we adults know that alcohol is responsible for 100,000 deaths per year in our country. Beer parlors can hardly have one-upmanship over pot parties, regardless of what the law says.

If the rules don't apply to everyone, the rules aren't fair and equitable. If things are unjust, *your kids will rebel* in one way or another if they have any spunk at all. All humans—especially children—have a built-in cry for justice, one of the ways I think we were created in the image of God.

I would rank the drive for being treated justly above the intensity of the sex drive in young people. If we aren't just with our children, it will be nearly impossible for us to command their respect and obedience.

Counseling won't help the teenager much if the parents are unwilling to readjust their slouchy posture, unless the counselor takes the approach of helping the young person do well in spite of his or her parents (without criticizing or condemning the parents).

## Observe the seven commandments for developing the proper posture as parents.

Your every attitude, action, and reaction will originate from the posture you assume before your children. Consequently, your posture has to be correct if your behavior toward your children is to be correct. If your posture is improper, you will more likely misinterpret the recommendations contained in the remainder of this book.

My observations in counseling and my own experiences as a parent tell me that we all need help with our postures. This is why I'm requesting that you live loyal to the seven commandments for developing the proper posture as parents. Please memorize them.

### 1. Thou shalt monitor your attitudes and actions toward your children with the Good Shepherd by always asking, "Will this heal?"

You should submit your attitudes and actions as parents to the Good Shepherd. Christ is the Good Shepherd (the Good Supervisor). You can harmonize your supervision with His Super Vision by checking your attitudes and actions with this question: "Will this heal?"

This will do wonders for your posture as a parent. It will convert your common sense, if need be, to something even better—*uncommon sense* (a conscience chaperoned by Christ).

I developed the question "Will this heal?" as I searched for a way to know for sure what Jesus Christ would do in difficult and confusing situations. I had always heard people say that we should do what Jesus would do; but how do you know what Jesus would do in parent-teen struggles?

I studied the Gospels to see if I could find a way to know what Jesus would do, and I discovered that He always did the healing thing. Healing was and is His very essence. He healed nature, attitudes, diseases, sin, unbelief, ignorance, misunderstanding, hypocrisy, demon possession, and even death.

I developed a logical sequence of truth that put my thoughts into words . . .

Jesus Christ was a healer.
He still is.
Since I am to follow Him, I must be a healer, too.
Therefore, I will monitor my every thought, attitude, and action with this question: *Will this heal?*
    Will this help?
    Will this inspire improvement?
    Will this preserve good?

Testing your parental decisions with "Will this heal?" will help you parent as Christ would have you parent, because He always did the healing things. He never went for revenge against anyone.

You must understand, however, that sometimes it takes pain to heal, like receiving medication in the form of a shot to get well. Jesus brought healing to Peter by allowing him to sink. He brought healing to Thomas by confronting him about his doubting.

And, while I'm on the subject, I'd like to urge each parent to apply the question "Will this heal?" to your own life:

- Will wallowing in guilt heal?
- Will self-hatred heal?
- Will putting yourself down heal?
- Will blaming yourself and others heal?
- Will worrying yourself sick heal?
- Will closing yourself off from the world heal?
- Will contemplating suicide heal?
- Will losing your marriage over your child's problems heal?

If not, then these attitudes, actions, and thoughts are not God's will for you. There is no virtue in them.

Then what will heal?

- Receiving God's forgiveness and trusting His competency to completely forgive.
- Forgetting those things that are behind (the mistakes of the yesteryears) and focusing on the present and the future.
- Meditating upon "whatever things are true, whatever things are noble, whatever things are just, whatever things are pure, whatever things are lovely, whatever things are of good report," as the Bible encourages.
- Learning to pray and not faint.
- Learning to trust God and to relax in that trust.
- Getting yourself some help, if need be.

### 2. Thou shalt discipline rather than punish. (Be a shepherd, not a cow puncher.)

Understand the difference between discipline and punishment, and choose to discipline rather than punish.

*Punishment* has to do with getting even ("I'll get you for this!"). *Discipline* has to do with turning the child away from impending danger.

The word *discipline* means "to disciple." The following statement is suggestive of both the quality and the mood of our discipline: We are to disciple our children.

Punishment might say, *Go get me my belt. You chopped up the water hose with the lawnmower.*

Discipline would say, *I know you didn't do it on purpose, but you cut the water hose with the lawnmower. It needs to be spliced back together. Acme Hardware has a splice. You'll need to purchase one and repair the hose.*

Discipline has healing qualities; punishment rarely does.

### 3. Thou shalt not discipline for immaturity as you would for defiance.

Dr. James Dobson taught me the concept of distinguishing between immaturity and defiance in one of his film series. To honor this commandment, you must begin to consciously differentiate between *immaturity* and *defiance,* a judgment called too frequently by reaction rather than deliberation. Assigning the undesirable action to one of these categories should always be done before deciding how to respond. If you decide your child couldn't help what happened because of his or her stage of development, you will handle the situation differently than if you decide your child acted out of rebellion.

A child's clumsiness, for example, likely means that his or her mental habit patterns have not caught up with the new lengths of the legs, arms, and fingers. This is immaturity rather than defiance.

Bed-wetting in the teenage years is a physical problem and not a problem of the will. It should never be ridiculed.

Unauthorized use of a family car, however, is a problem of outright defiance, not immaturity. That act should be seen as a breach of trust, and discipline should be exacted accordingly.

A child's bad grades may be the result of bad study habits (immaturity) and may not be an indication that he or she doesn't care what you want (defiance). And stay alert for other causes: Bad grades could result from inability to concentrate in the midst of parental fighting. The cause may be outside the child.

### 4. Thou shalt not make giant hassles out of normal teenage problems.

You must recognize normal teenage problems for what they are and not overreact to them. Remind yourself that you are dealing with developing children, even though they are teenagers.

Parents of teenagers who keep on doing wrong stay generally frustrated, and you can easily fall into the trap of reacting just as negatively to normal teenage problems as you do to dreadful ones. You may misread your teens' actions and jump to the conclusion that things are as bad as ever.

This is not good, because kids who "always get it" are likely to develop the "why try?" attitude. And you can see why they would give up if they get screamed at either way. *Doing better has to have its attractive rewards—or kids will get discouraged and give up trying.*

Listen! Listen! Listen! Your child is going to have many normal teenage problems, regardless of whether he or she has been misbehaving. Underwear left on the bathroom floor or a wet towel left on the bed is not proof positive that your teenager doesn't care about what you want.

Emotionally charged parents need to be reminded of what normal teenage problems look like. Reviewing them can help you take care not to overreact to normal hassles and discourage your children from trying.

Here's a partial list of normal teenage problems:

- not wanting to do chores for the family
- enjoying doing the same chores for other families

- putting off chores
- doing chores just good enough to get by
- forgetting to weed-whack one side of the house
- maintaining an unkept room
- putting off homework
- not wanting to go to bed
- spending too much time in front of the TV
- staying on the phone forever
- hating to get out of bed
- forgetting to brush
- losing the retainer
- making an occasional bad grade
- having occasional trouble with teachers
- leaving candy and gum wrappers in your car
- failing to maintain his or her car properly
- getting a traffic ticket
- hating things loved yesterday
- failing to select a career
- bouncing in and out of a commitment to go to college
- spending some money carelessly
- holding the refrigerator door open while deciding what to eat
- being unsatisfied with what parents are providing
- going through a stage of being ashamed of parents
- teasing brothers and sisters
- demanding more independence by relating how good other kids have it
- resisting going to church at times
- forgetting to thank people for gifts

Understanding that these are normal kinds of problems will help you react more reasonably. Of course, you have to discipline your children and help them grow beyond these problems, but it's out of order to use the same fervency of discipline as you would for such things as the following:

- staying out past curfew
- running away from home
- skipping school
- failing classes
- taking or selling drugs
- drinking underage
- running with a bad crowd
- shoplifting
- exhibiting an ugly attitude

In some cases, though, some "normal" teenage problems are tied in with defiance. When that's the case, their occurrence must be handled with more sternness.

The point is this: Don't get just as upset when a kid forgets to feed the dog as you do when a kid curses a teacher. If you're hot and heavy on a kid's case about everything, he or she develops the "why try?" attitude—because the kid gets it one way or another. Be more friendly when dealing with the normal teenage problems.

There are other normal problems of which you should be aware. You and your teenager are at different and conflicting phases in life. Your natural desire to be heard and respected by your teenager normally conflicts with your teen's natural desire to flap wings of independence. Your natural desire to be loved and appreciated by your teenager normally conflicts with your teen's natural desire to discover the rest of the world (ignoring you to a painful extent).

As a mother, you may be entering menopause and trying to deal with your own hormonal changes; as a father, you may be trying to deal with your own mid-life struggles. Those problems naturally conflict with your teenager's *ram*bunctious phase of breaking away from the nest, proving that he can make it on his own, and making the point that he or she doesn't need to be told what to do any more. Seeking and abiding by your advice may remind your teenager of childhood, and that if your advice is sought and not taken, you will be mad; consequently, it's best to stay clear of that risk. This frustrates you to the maximum, because you want to save your teenager from making the mistakes you made, from the hurt you still feel, and you want to pass along the benefit of the knowledge you've gleaned. But your gift is rejected because the teen won't listen. You naturally feel rejected, too.

In some family situations, parents have found it helpful to sit down with their children and explain the natural conflicts that tend to happen. This can relieve pressure as family members become aware of what is going on. They are able to stop misreading the natural conflicts to mean lack of love, lack of respect, and rejection. They are able to develop ways of coping with the naturally conflicting phases of life. Continuing to have frequent family meetings can keep things "talked out."

### 5. Thou shalt remember thine own struggles as a child and be reasonably patient with your children.

Remembering how you chopped up a water hose when you were a teenager will help you feel less hostile while you're staring at the remains of your brand-new one.

Remembering how you used to leave a ring around the bathtub will help you decide not to wring your child's neck over it.

Remembering how you used to hate to go to church at times will help you understand why your teenager would resist attending at times.

Remembering how you looked at a *Playboy* magazine a couple of times will help you respond reasonably if you find one between your teenager's mattress and springs, when it hasn't been a problem in the past.

Remembering how you became aware of your sexual parts will help you respond without disgracing your teenager if you walk in while he or she is touching his or hers.

Remembering your own struggles as a child will help you be reasonably patient with your children and not have needless conflict with them.

### 6. Thou shalt build your children's self-concepts by genuinely appreciating their good attitudes and actions.

The absolute best way to encourage change is to give honest praise when improvement is shown. You've just got to nurture your children's self-esteem, confidence, and courage. The will to try hard and stick to it is only as healthy as the self-esteem. You must be sure that there are rewards for doing good. Kids must know that they really, really will get to enjoy admiration from their parents and a better relationship with their parents as they do better.

### 7. Thou shalt not disallow or put down your children's unique styles of personality.

Parental suppression of children's unique styles of personality has been cited as a major cause of problems. I believe it has caused more rejection by parents and more rebellion by children than any other single factor.

More often than not, a naturally tidy mother can't stand a naturally sloppy child, and a scholarly father can't stand a son or daughter with a moderate interest in intellectual pursuits. The mother might moan, "How could you have possibly come from me? Maybe a hobo left you at our door!" The father might loudly declare, "You could make *A*'s like I did if you weren't so disgustingly lazy! I'm ashamed of you!"

Be fair. Line up with reality. There's nothing deadly about sloppiness, and there's nothing wrong with making average grades when it's the best one can do.

Why de*valu*ate your children? Why communicate: "You are not okay because you are not like I want you to be"? Please don't.

Having children is a blind date. Mismatches sometimes occur; conflicting styles are thrown together. Unfortunately, you can't take your kids home, tell them goodbye, and walk away if the date wasn't what you expected. But it helps to remember that if your children seem foreign to you, then you seem just as foreign to them. They can't change their style any easier than you can change yours.

You need to declare one another's styles okay and learn how to handle it when you clash. Disallowing or putting down your children's styles of personality can inflict critical emotional damage.

The seven commandments are among the most basic. Memorize them! Make them a permanent part of you! That will do wonders for your posture as a parent.

---

### The seven commandments for developing the proper posture as parents

1. Thou shalt monitor your attitudes and actions toward your children with the Good Shepherd by always asking, "Will this heal?"
2. Thou shalt discipline rather than punish. (Be a shepherd, not a cow puncher.)
3. Thou shalt not discipline for immaturity as you would for defiance.
4. Thou shalt not make giant hassles out of normal teenage problems.
5. Thou shalt remember thine own struggles as a child and be reasonably patient with your children.
6. Thou shalt build your children's self-concepts by genuinely appreciating their good attitudes and actions.
7. Thou shalt not disallow or put down your children's unique styles of personality.

# PART II
# Towers of Conviction

Imagine that your home is a fortress and that the exterior walls of your home are fortress walls, built to protect and fortify your home. Your fortress should provide a safe setting for nurturing and maturing your children and for rescuing and recovering any you may be losing.

To accomplish these awesome purposes, you need some powerful convictions. Therefore, in the next eight chapters, you'll learn how to erect fifteen towers of conviction along the fortress walls surrounding your home. Memorize each tower as you imagine it erected into place.

In later chapters, you'll learn how to develop enough strength to keep your towering convictions in place.

*A note to parents of children who aren't misbehaving:* What applies to rescuing teenagers also applies to putting forth your best parenting effort toward helping your children stay out of trouble. You need the same parental posture, the same convictions, and the same strength. Be cautious of feeling that you don't need this information. Most traumatized parents once felt exactly like you may feel. They, too, felt that their presently rebellious child could never turn against them. ■

CHAPTER **3**

# ACKNOWLEDGING
# THE SITUATION

In this chapter, you'll erect the first four towers of conviction. These towers will establish and guard your position as parents as you begin to apply them to your everyday parenting situations.

**Tower of Conviction 1: We are breaking through denial
and admitting that our child is, in fact, ignoring our
guidance on purpose.**

Denial is a great problem. By refusing to own up to the seriousness of your teen-ager's problems, you put off serious rescue attempts until behaviors degenerate to desperate, stubborn levels. You won't be able to meet the problem head-on until you've worked through denial.

### Breaking through denial is hard.

A set of parents told me recently that their son had lied, sneaked out of the house, read pornography, cursed his mother, and been arrested a couple of times. Then one of them said, "But we don't want you to think he's a bad kid or anything."

Another parent said her son had just gotten out of jail and was still hanging out with the wrong crowd and doing pot. Then she followed that with, "But I'd say he's doing pretty well."

Those parents haven't come to terms with the fact that their children are acting terribly. And until they do, they will not get serious about launching an all-out attempt to rescue their children. The children will remain unchallenged and become even more entrenched in their self-destructive lifestyles. This is awful. Parents *must* break through denial in order to save their children!

One mother broke through denial with a flash of insight. She suddenly exclaimed, "My son is not only *running* with the wrong crowd, he *is* the wrong crowd! Other parents ought to keep their kids away from him!"

Tower of Conviction 1 is: We are breaking through denial and admitting that our child is, in fact, ignoring our guidance on purpose.

Or if you want to say it a little stronger: We are breaking through denial and admitting that our child is, in fact, acting terribly on purpose.

This tower is first because it is precisely what you have to do first.

## Tower of Conviction 2: Our child does wrong because of his or her choices, not because of mental illness or physical problems.

Once you've admitted that your teenager has a serious problem, you must assess the nature of the problem. Your decision will determine how you seek to help your child.

*Is it mental illness?* If you think it is, you will likely enlist the services of a psychiatrist and, possibly, a psychiatric unit. (Please read chapter 28 before you pro-ceed with mental health professionals. It's an expensive jungle out there.)

*Is it physiologically based?* If it is, you will need to choose a primarily medical route.

*Is it a family problem?* If it is—if the teenager is living in a war zone and is rebelling for survival—then you will want to pursue family counseling. If all parties aren't willing to participate in counseling, you will at least want to get those unjust pressures off your child.

*Or does he or she prefer to do wrong?* If you become convinced that this is the case, erect the second tower in good conscience and begin to discipline more force-fully.

You can use a process of elimination to assess the nature of your child's problem. Your family doctor will help you eliminate mental or physical sources of the problem.

A routine test for drugs, as part of the physical examination, is often advisable. You can make arrangements for this without your minor child's knowledge if you wish to avoid the negative impact of doubting that he or she is drug free. So far as psychological testing is concerned, your doctor can help you make this decision. Although test results may be helpful at times, they don't usually change the bottom line very much.

You likely know the answer to the third possibility, whether the teenager's problems are the result of a family problem or not.

If you are able to eliminate the first three, you'll know that you can erect the second tower of conviction: Our child does wrong because of his or her choices, not because of mental illness or physical problems.

In this world we all have to be in control (civilized) or we have to face the consequences of being out of control (uncivilized). If we do not control ourselves, we must be controlled by someone else. *As parents, we must pressure our kids to control their behavior.* Self-control is the only way for them to secure independence.

Let me reassure you further with Scripture. The Bible promises that your son or daughter has the power to refuse to do wrong and choose to do right:

> God is faithful, who will not allow you to be tempted beyond what you are able, but with the temptation will also make the way of escape, that you may be able to bear it. (1 Cor. 10:13)

### Tower of Conviction 3: Our child can change, and it's our responsibility as parents to give him or her a decent opportunity to improve.

The whole Bible radiates the single message that people can resurrect their lives from wrongdoing, even if it's habitual. If your child quits giving in to temptations and takes the ways of escape that God provides, the wrongs will stop and most of the consequences will coast to a halt and begin to heal.

If you buy into a philosophy that people can't change, you proclaim Jesus to be a charlatan and His Truth to be a hoax. The whole purpose of Christ's life, miracles, message, death, resurrection, and ascension was to make it possible for people to change, to convert. The third tower of conviction is supported by the whole message of salvation—the message of *salvag*ing people, including teenagers, from their sins. We're talking Easter here.

Cold shoulders, exclusion from family activities, caustic remarks (to him or her or to other members of the family about him or her), and prophecies of failure can work against your child's efforts. Your child will not change until somewhere along the way he or she is provided with a decent opportunity to change.

You will probably get what you expect. If you expect failure, your teenager will pick up on that intuitively and will more likely lower himself or herself to meet your expectations. If you expect success, your teenager will be more en*courage*d to succeed and will more likely raise himself or herself to meet your expectations. In psychology, this process is called scripting. Be extra careful what script you hand your teenager.

*Compass*ionately scrutinize your child's world and demand that the environment offer a re*assur*ing and supportive atmosphere favorable for success. A decent opportunity includes a decent atmosphere in which to change. You are responsible only for the setting, however, and not for the outcomes. When you've done your best to provide a nurturant setting, you've done well and can feel good about it.

You'll receive abundant help in this book for building the third tower of conviction. Your commandments for developing the proper posture, your other towers of conviction, your towers of strength, your allies, and your renewed understanding of forgiveness will help you know how to do your best in erecting this tower.

### Tower of Conviction 4: We have the right and are responsible before God to require our child to live as an American citizen in our home—to live a decent, legal, cooperative, and productive life.

There may be times when you begin to doubt yourself. You may think, *Maybe it's me. Maybe I'm the problem. Maybe I'm expecting too much.* Likely not.

You're not expecting too much if you require your children to be American citizens in your home. You are merely wanting your children to be decent, legal, cooperative, and productive. That's all. Isn't that the least you should desire for them?

You won't be aiming at family happiness with this tower—perpetual ecstasy is too hard to hit. You won't even be aiming at the restoration of affection—you'll most likely have to put that off until your teenagers become adults and have been on their own for a while. You will only be setting the goal of nurturing decent, law-abiding, and courteous citizens who do their parts in the world. Nothing less will suffice at home or at any other place in the future.

With this tower of conviction, you are setting standards consistent with the real world. When your kids grow up to be adults, they will never find a place where indecency, lawlessness, poor attitudes, and irresponsibility will be tolerated.

Why, then, should you let them do calisthenics for failure in your home? You shouldn't! You won't! You will build and maintain this tower of conviction with all your strength, for your kids' sake.

Notice the words "responsible before God." See it this way: You are *response able* before God to require your children to live decent, legal, cooperative, and productive lives.

### What are some dangers of assuming defensive positions?

I've thought about titling this book *How to Parent Nondefensively* or *How to Parent Without Yelling So Much.* You don't want to parent defensively (a position of I-must-win-and-you-must-lose). Digging into defensive positions always causes a no-man's-land to form in between, and a standoff is the result. For one side to win, the other side must give in and lose.

Giving up one's position—surrendering and losing—goes against all the survival instincts in human beings. I really suspect that when parents assume a defensive position toward their teenager, they subconsciously trigger the teen's instinctive struggle for survival. The teenager will sense the emergency status of fight or flight—to survive by fighting or to survive by flying away.

I recognize that sometimes you can't help getting into a defensive position but try to avoid it if at all possible. If it does happen, try to get out of it as soon as practical. Try to project a win win atmosphere:

*I love you. For me to win is for you to win, and we will be winning together.*

Instead of maintaining defensiveness, with all its bad side effects, use the towers of conviction to hold the child responsible for his or her own behavior and to help him or her see that the positive (constructive) or negative (destructive) consequences are flowing, quite naturally, from individual choices.

The first four towers of conviction concern themselves with the stance *you* take. The remaining towers concern themselves with the approach you are going to use with your children.

CHAPTER **4**

# PREPARING FOR SUCCESS

**Tower of Conviction 5: We must raise our child consistent with how he or she will have to become to be successful in the real world.**

C hildren must comply with rules of social order to be civilized. I have included some of the most basic rules here and have called them catchy concepts. These catchy concepts accomplish the following: (1) They give you relaxed ways of guiding your children; (2) they put more responsibility for the outcomes on your children; and (3) they keep your children consistent with how they will have to become to be successful in the real world.

**Catchy Concept 1:** *If you are rude to the suppliers, you shouldn't expect new supplies.*

This concept is a fact of life out in the real world. To be consistent, it should be a fact of life in your home as well.

If your children grow up and act rudely toward the employers who supply them with jobs, they will be strongly chastised or fired (left without jobs supplied).

If your children grow up to be rude to the neighbors who supply them with loaned tools, the tool supply will be shut off.

Logic says, "If you are rude to the producers, production will stop." Then stop producing if your kids are rude to you!

Don't set your kids up to fail later in the adult world by allowing them to succeed while being rude. Don't be bullied. Return to reason and trust your common sense.

But you don't have to get defensive. If your teenager has been abusive to you, you can quietly and courteously say . . .

*If you are rude to the suppliers, you shouldn't expect new supplies. You have been rude to me, and therefore I will not be supplying you with* _____.

Calmly state what supplies will no longer be available, and courteously give the conditions that will have to be met to restore the flow of supplies. Don't argue; arguing only creates defensive positions.

For example, a teenage boy who had told his mother the night before that her supper was gross found his cereal bowl upside down on the kitchen table the next morning. The father simply said, "If you are rude to the suppliers, you don't get new supplies."

The son replied, "I don't care. I'm not hungry anyway."

His father responded, "Good. I won't have to feel bad about you missing a meal."

A more effective approach would have been to excuse the boy from the meal he called gross and not allow him to snack later. But the parents found themselves so taken aback that they didn't immediately think of the best way to respond. Later, they thought of the right way and gave their response at breakfast the next morning.

Notice that these parents cut off only the supply of the particular thing about which their son was rude, and only withheld supplies for one meal. They might have also included refusing to supply between-meal snacks for a full day. Afterwards, the supply was reestablished, and conditions were normalized.

### Catchy Concept 2: If you don't do your part in the family, you don't get family privileges.

By law, all that parents are required to do for their children is not to neglect them, not to abuse them, and to put them through school. Almost everything else is family privilege and should be related to performance within the family.

Telephones, televisions, stereos, snacks between meals, desserts after meals, allowances, new clothes, the swimming pool, the trampoline, the Jet Ski, freedom to go out, taxi service, car usage, cosigning of notes, and the like are all privileges your children receive because they are *your* children. These things are gifts from you.

*They are not things you are obligated to always produce because you unconditionally love your children.* A better proof of your unconditional love is that you will lovingly and consistently discipline your children. Withholding from those you truly love is ten times harder than freely giving. It takes a lot more love!

Besides, in most of the cases I've dealt with, teenagers didn't see family privileges as one of their parents' ways of saying, "I love you." Their response to me has been, "The stuff they give me doesn't show me they love me. They are *supposed* to do that. All parents do that for their kids." Or "I didn't ask to be born." Or "They had me. They're obligated to take care of me."

So, establish this concept within your home: If your children don't do their part within the family, they don't get to enjoy all the privileges of the family. You may calmly say,

*No, you may not use the car tonight. You must do your part in the family to get to enjoy family privileges.*

I've been astounded a few times by how some parents will put up with their children's rudeness and defiance and keep on abundantly producing for them. I distinctly remember a fourteen-year-old girl who told her mother how she hated her and how stupid she was. As they left my office, I overheard the mother tell my receptionist, "I'm in a hurry. I've got to go to the mall and buy her five pairs of jeans for school before I can start supper." She bought designer jeans, too.

I've developed a saying to describe that kind of situation: "The parents are in the habit of giving. Their kids are in the habit of taking." And the kids will likely not stop being on the take unless the parents wake up and set out to modify and balance both habit patterns.

This reminds me of a joke I saw in *Reader's Digest:*

"I'm really worried," said one teenager to another. "Dad slaves away at his job so I'll never want for anything and so I can go to college. Mom spends every day washing and ironing and cleaning up after me, and she takes care of me when I'm sick."

"So what are you worried about?"

"I'm afraid they might try to escape!"

(*Reader's Digest* was quoting Jack Moore with Universal Press Syndicate.)

### Catchy Concept 3: Mess it up. Clean it up.

There's no need to yell when your teenager drops a jar of honey and breaks it on the kitchen floor. Just presume that he or she will clean it up (don't forget to differentiate between immature clumsiness and defiance). Cleaning up a mess is normally discipline enough for children since they hate to work so much.

- If they leave the bathroom a mess, they clean it up.
- If they throw their clothes in the hamper to keep from having to hang them up, they launder their own clothes.
- If they break a neighbor's window, they face the neighbor and make things right on their own.
- If they get into trouble with the police, they deal with the situation on their own (with parents serving as supportive bystanders).
- If they do wrong with another child, they apologize to the family of the other child.

This concept is so very important that it should be kindly taught from the beginning. Kids really will be much more careful if they know they have to clean up their own messes. You should be aware that your complaining does not change behavior, but their work of cleaning up after themselves does.

If your family hasn't been operating this way, however, it is only fair for you to have a family conference and carefully explain to your children how things are going to be handled differently in the future. If you just spring this new approach on them, they will probably be extremely reluctant to cooperate.

### Catchy Concept 4: Abuse it. Lose it.

Teach your children that if they abuse something, they will lose that something. This, too, is a fact of life. Notice how it will work later in the real world:

- If they abuse their supervisors after they enter the adult world, they will lose their jobs.
- If they abuse their credit cards, they will lose their cards and a good credit rating.

- If they abuse their driving privileges, they will lose their insurance and their licenses.
- If they abuse their spouse and children, they will lose their families.
- If they abuse a friend, they will lose that friend.

Being consistent with the real world today means that if your children abuse something, they lose that something:

- If your children abuse the privilege of going out by not keeping the family values, then they lose the privilege of going out and are grounded until a relationship of trust can be reestablished.
- If they hot-rod the family car or drive while using drugs or alcohol, they lose access to the car.
- If they defy you and tune their TV's to shows with immoral themes, they lose their TV's.
- If they use the phone to plot wrong, they lose their phone privileges.

Without assuming a defensive posture, make the statement:

*Since you and Susie chose to sneak out of the house when you spent the night with her, you have chosen for us to not let you spend the night with Susie again until you teach us to trust you again.*

Or you may choose to separate the two of them permanently. (See chapter 8 on the wrong crowd.) Notice the wording: "Since you . . . chose . . . you have chosen for us to . . . ."

### Catchy Concept 5: Waste it. Replace it.

This catchy concept comes in very handy when your teenagers have squirted out all the shaving cream in a fun fight or when they have used a whole bottle of disinfectant to clean the bathroom.

There's no need for a big scene. In a friendly matter-of-fact manner say something like . . .

*You guys were really having a blast. I got into shaving cream fights at college. I'll never forget the time we soaped up the dorm prankster. Another thing I still remember clearly is that we had to purchase our own ammunition and clean up our own messes. Do you want me to take the cost of the shaving cream out of your allowance, or do you want me to give you a couple of jobs to earn it?*

### Catchy Concept 6: Want more? Pay the extra.

You'll be thankful for this concept when your teenagers want designer clothes or tennis shoes with a prestigious name brand. You can say . . .

*It's okay with us if you want designer clothes. We will be happy to pay the amount we would normally pay for your clothes, and you can make up the difference.*

Don't say it smugly. Say it in a warm and friendly manner.

This kind of approach is highly preferable to barking, "Paying $95 for tennis shoes is the stupidest thing I've ever heard of! No! You're not going to have 'em! Don't ever mention it again!"

Although your kids may frustrate you at times, they are still your precious, irreplaceable children, and these catchy concepts will help you do unto them as you would have them do unto you in harmony with the golden rule.

## Parents have no right to bully children.

You should not talk to your children with any less respect than you talk to your adult friends.

Parental rudeness often occurs as a result of the aggravations that are not even related to the home. Parents have to discipline their anger when they're working with superiors, coaching soccer, or participating in a board meeting or a public meeting, and feelings get all bottled up. Sometimes, parents release all that anger when their children misbehave and the adult peer pressure is off the parents. What the parents wouldn't do to their peers is done to their bewildered children in the privacy of their own homes.

Such behavior is inexcusable! The golden rule says to do unto your children as you would like them to do unto you, if the roles were reversed. Remember to check your attitude and responses toward your children with "Will this heal?"

Parents are just people, and there are times when we simply get out of sorts, irritable, and snappy. In times like these, I've taken a note card and written on it in large letters: OUT OF ORDER. Then I've paper-clipped it to my shirt pocket. My sign served to clue the whole family in on my bad mood and to warn them to keep their distance (although I felt like a broken pay phone with that sign hanging on me). Something novel like this can help a lot.

I remember a time when I had gotten irritable without realizing it. One of my young children took me by the hand and, without speaking, led me to the bedroom. There I saw the covers pulled back and a note pinned to my pillow. It read: OUT OF ORDER. I got the message, laughed with him, and went to bed.

To get the most mileage out of your catchy concepts, you need to learn to let the inconvenient consequences teach your children. Ranting and raving allow your teenagers to dodge the lesson of the pain. They can transfer their anger to you and be mad at you for the way you've reacted to what they have done. Your aggravating reaction takes away the punch from the lesson that could have been learned.

On the other hand, if you remain matter-of-fact about their misbehavior and its correction, there is nothing for them to get upset about—except that they are having to suffer the consequences of *their* errors. This is best. Your mood for applying the catchy concepts should be one of kindness, with as much empathy as is merited, without the dreaded I-told-you-so attitude.

Tower of Conviction 5: We must raise our children consistent
with how he or she will have to become
to be successful in the real world.

The following catchy concepts will help us erect this tower:

1. If you are rude to the suppliers, you shouldn't expect new supplies.
2. If you don't do your part in the family, you don't get family privileges.
3. Mess it up. Clean it up.
4. Abuse it. Lose it.
5. Waste it. Replace it.
6. Want more? Pay the extra.

## Put realism into action.

These catchy concepts will help you put into action the fifth tower of conviction. But you must develop emotional readiness before you are prepared to carry through. You've got to muscle-up emotionally before you can take this on.

# CHAPTER 5

# AVOIDING MANIPULATION

**Tower of Conviction 6:  We refuse to be conned by our child.**

**D**o not cooperate with disgraceful in*timid*ations and manipulations. I use the word *disgraceful* on purpose; a teenager can take the gracefulness out of parenthood by insulting parents with con jobs.

According to the *American Heritage Dictionary,* one meaning of *manipulation* is "to manage shrewdly or deviously." In our context, it would mean that teenagers are managing their parents shrewdly or deviously. Parents must refuse to be managed this way.

I asked the participants in our parent support group, Parenting Within Reason, how their kids have tried to manipulate them. Here's the list they compiled.

Manipulative children try to get what they want by . . .

> lying
> arguing
> griping
> crying
> throwing tantrums
> whining
> pouting
> withdrawing
> boycotting parents or families
> cursing parents
> criticizing parents to other adults
> threatening to call Children's Protective Services

They make statements like . . .

- "You don't trust me!"
- "Everybody's doing it!"
- "You don't love me!"
- "I'm going to end up hating you!"
- "You're too strict!"
- "You're too old-fashioned!"

- "None of my friends' parents treat their kids the way you treat me! They're nice!"
- "My friends think you are gross!"
- "I'm going to quit school!"
- "I'm going to run away from home!"
- "When I turn seventeen, I'm getting out of this prison, and you can't do anything about it!"
- "I'm going to get deeper into drugs!"
- "I'll kill myself and then you'll be sorry."

### Refuse to cooperate with kids doing absurd things.

When you stop and think about it, some of the behaviors and comments listed are absurd.

What I mean here is like when you've done something ridiculous, and you've put the back of your hand against your forehead and moaned, "Good grief! I can't believe I did that. That was absurd!" That's the kind of thing I'm talking about.

If your kids are doing or saying things to intimidate and manipulate you and you allow them to, you are cooperating with absurdity! That is not what you want to do, is it? Then erect Tower of Conviction 6: We refuse to be conned by our child. In other words, We refuse to cooperate with our kids' absurdities. (This might be a good time to reread the section on withstanding intimidation in chapter 1.)

### Never issue negative challenges.

We've already established that you try not to scream so much at your children or assume a defensive posture. I need to add that you shouldn't challenge them to do negative things.

If a young person says, "I am going to kill myself," *don't* say, "Go for it!" Or "Go ahead! That'll be one less mouth to feed." Or "You don't have enough guts to kill yourself!" Or "Shall I pour the hemlock for you?"

*Think!* You don't challenge a person to commit suicide! Don't do something absurd yourself. Your response might cause the teen to become emotionally confused and actually carry through on the threat.

Instead, say something like,

*I love you and I trust you won't hurt yourself, but you can't do what you've asked to do.*

This answer, on the one hand, does not submit to intimidation or cooperate with manipulation. On the other hand, you hold your ground without issuing a negative challenge.

Here's another example. Rather than issue a negative challenge by saying, "You say you're gonna run away! There's the door! Go for it," courteously say . . .

*I love you and I don't want you to leave home, but still you can't go cruising with Bill. Also, I need to remind you that if you choose to run away, you choose for us to report it to the police as we have promised we would. Because we love you, we can't leave you out there without our protection or supervision.*

Again, notice the wording in the reply: "If *you choose . . . you choose* for us to. . . ." This wording helps the teen see that he is designing his own consequences.

If you issue a negative challenge to your children, you are putting them in a needless and useless bind. They can rise to meet your challenge (leave home, quit school, etc.), or they can give in and endure you and your hateful approach.

Caution: Saying to teens, "Do as I say or hit the door!" is like saying, "Stay under my dictatorship or go for *freedom!*" The choice comes out that way to teenagers because they have never experienced the adult world, and with that inexperience, they think that living independently of parents is a breeze.

You'd be wiser to make it a choice of your home, a foster home, or an institution (like a Christian school designed to deal with troubled kids). The foster home would be one chosen by you that understands what you are seeking to accomplish in your child's life, one willing to be consistent with your family values.

### Tower of Conviction 7: We will cause our child's tools of intimidation and manipulation to become useless.

It's much easier to accomplish this than you might think. You cause those tools to become obsolete. Here is an analogy to help you understand how to do this.

What if you need to remove a hex nut and you find a wrench that barely grips the corners, although it's actually too big? You will likely go ahead and try to use it even though you know you aren't using the proper tool. So, you crank the nut a couple of turns. Aaah! It works!

But, oops, it slips and rounds the corners of the nut. You try again; but the tool has become useless.

You toss it aside and try something else *because nobody keeps trying to use a useless tool.*

Since this is true, you can indirectly get your kids to put down their tools of intimidation and manipulation by causing them to quit working. Your kids know they are not using the proper tools, and if they quit working, they will put them down.

For example, if you become a sufficiently investigative parent so that you catch your kids in almost every lie, lying will have become too big a gamble, and they will eventually stop trying to use the *obsolete* tool. If you stop giving in to whining, pouting, and tantrums, these tools will become *obsolete,* too, and your kids will likely put them back in their toolboxes for a while (they'll try to use them again later).

#### Cause the tools of intimidation and manipulation to bring an undesired outcome.

Take this idea one step further and get an even stronger effect: Cause the improper tools to bring your children something they *don't want* rather than what they do want, and they will toss them aside even faster.

Say something like . . .

*Your mother and I have been talking, and we've decided that we are going to respond differently to any lying that you might do in the future. From now on, if you lie to us, you'll not only miss out on what you lied to try to get to do, but you* will be grounded *for two weeks so that we can supervise you more closely and give you the opportunity to teach us to trust you again.*

Another possibility is to say . . .

*Your father and I have decided that if you get a friend to ask us if you can go somewhere,* the answer will always be no. *We feel very strongly that family decisions need to be made with only family members present.*

Another situation might call for a comment like . . .

*We have decided that there will be* no chance for an appeal *of our decisions if you throw a tantrum to show your dislike for them. From now on, a tantrum is going to make us feel that you need closer supervision because you are having a hard time controlling your behavior.*

Still another situation might demand something like . . .

*Your mother and I are very troubled about your mention of suicide, and* we have scheduled you an appointment with your doctor. *We are asking him to examine you to see if hospitalization or psychological evaluation is needed. We love you very much, and we could never take a chance on anything happening to you.*

Another effective approach might go like this:

*You keep saying that you hate living here. Your father and I have decided to help you find another place to live. We have written for information on homes for troubled adolescents.* We will help you find another place *if you truly feel that it's impossible for us to make it together. We love you very much, and all that we want is for you to do well. We will help you every way we can.*

These remarks make it clear that the alternative home is not going to be a place of the teen's own choosing. (You will learn other ways to cause tools to become obsolete when we get to Tower of Conviction 9.)

### Use Towers of Conviction 6 and 7 to cope with the problem of lying.

Tower of Conviction 6 (We refuse to be conned by our child) provides the resolve you need for remaining unaccepting of lying. Lying is a special problem, and you have to know a few facts about it before you can begin to solve the problem.

*Lying is a form of gambling.* If the teenager tells the truth, she's going to get it. If she lies, there's a chance she won't.

People who gamble in casinos in Atlantic City and Las Vegas have only a 7 percent chance of winning. This is what I was told when I interviewed the director of an Atlantic City rescue mission for a radio program and newspaper article I was doing. Think of it: Gamblers in those casinos have a 93 percent chance of losing and yet they gamble by the millions.

Teenagers have a much greater chance of "winning" with a lie, so why wouldn't they gamble by lying? Sometimes, teenagers know it would be impossible to lose the gamble, so why wouldn't they lie with such favorable odds? It beats getting yelled at or being punished or having to make restitution. It also beats disappointing their parents or being humiliated in front of them. Coincidentally, a seventeen-year-old guy told me yesterday, "My parents only catch me one out of ten thousand times."

*Children who are punished harshly lie more than others.* Most adults would lie, too, if it were a choice between lying with a chance of escaping or telling the truth and being severely punished.

*Children who respect their parents a lot will lie to try to keep from harming their relationship with them.* They don't want to disappoint their parents and stand "naked" before them.

*Children who have watched their parents lie will lie more quickly than others. Lying is a habit.* Habits have to be broken; lying doesn't disappear overnight.

Let's put all these points together in an example:

*Ginger, we've found out that you've lied to us again. We love you, and we want to help you stop lying. We've got to help you stop before you become an adult, or you'll suffer some embarrassing failures. Here's what we've decided to do for you.*

*First of all, you're going to need to be grounded for a few weeks so that you can teach us to trust you again. We'll talk about the grounding structure in a few moments. [I'll cover how to structure grounding in chapter 6.]*

*Second, your lying has taught us that we need to check out what you say. Beginning today, any time there's a question about anything, we're going to be calling and checking with the other people involved. We know this will be embarrassing to both you and us, but we are willing to do this to help you tell the truth.*

*Third, since we'll be checking on things, you'll not know when we already know the truth before we ask you about it. This means it may be hazardous to your freedom to lie in the future.*

*Fourth, we have developed two levels of discipline. If you tell us the truth, there will be less discipline. If you lie, there will be more discipline. If you lie, Ginger, you will be automatically grounded for at least two weeks.*

*Fifth, we understand that lying seems to have become a habit with you. So here's how we're going to help you break your habit. We're going to give you a one-hour grace period to return to us and correct anything you've lied about. This will give you time to reconsider what you've done and correct it before it's counted against you. If you come to us and make it right, we'll not count it against you at all. We'll do this for a month or so.*

*Do you understand everything, Ginger? Just to be sure, let's go back over each point one more time. First, . . . ; second, . . . ; third, . . . ; fourth, . . . ; fifth . . . . Good. Now if you need additional help or just want to talk, always feel free to let us know. We love you, and we want to help you.*

Handling the lying problem this way drastically reduces the odds of "winning" by gambling with a lie. The parents may know the truth before they ask, they will be checking the child's reply, and the cost of "losing" is greatly increased.

Tower of Conviction 7 (We will cause our child's tools of intimidation and manipulation to become useless) enhances this effort. You simply cause the lying tool to quit working; and worse than that, you cause it to bring something they dislike rather than something liked.

Lying has to quit working. You've got to catch them in every lie and cause the lies to bring uncomfortable consequences, such as two weeks of grounding. Accept it as your challenge to be "in the know" so that lying never works.

*Important note:* It's better not to confront an issue if you can't know the truth about it than to confront it and give your teenager a chance to "succeed" by lying. For example, asking, "Who punctured the seat cover in my car?" clues the guilty party in on the fact that you don't know and you can't know who did it, unless he tattles on himself. The wording of the question assures him that he can "safely" escape by lying.

# CHAPTER 6

# ENFORCING NATURAL CONSEQUENCES

**Tower of Conviction 8:  We will be sure the discipline we choose to use is a natural consequence of the offense.**

lements of this conviction are contained in the responses quoted with Tower of Conviction 7. We'll be expanding it further with this tower because young persons must recognize that the consequences they are experiencing (and hating) are the natural results of their own wrong choices!

*You* are not doing anything to them. It's not your fault. *They* are doing it to themselves. It's their doing. The dreaded disciplines they undergo are the natural outcomes of their own wrong choices.

In being sure the discipline you choose to use is a natural consequence of the offense, you are keeping your children consistent with how they will have to become to function successfully in the real world. Yet you are not being defensive, and you are not constantly yelling at them.

The more consequential you can make the consequences, the more obvious it's going to be to your teenagers that they are causing the consequences and have control over them. The more logical and reasonable the discipline, the more nonsensical their excuses for objecting to it have to be.

**Choose the discipline that is appropriate to the offense.**

So, how do you make the right choices? You make sure the consequences are logical results of the misbehavior. The following two situations illustrate this.

1. Misbehavior or unkind attitude:
   *Son skipped school.*
   Natural result of the misbehavior:
   *He is not fully trustworthy.*
   Natural consequences:
   • *He has taught school personnel to trust him less.*
   • *He has taught parents to trust him less.*
   • *He has assigned himself to the needing-discipline category.*

2. Misbehavior or unkind attitude:
   *Daughter screamed, "I hate you!"*
   Natural result of the misbehavior:
   *Parents' feelings are deeply hurt.*
   Natural consequences:
   - *The family won't feel as close.*
   - *The parents will be out of the mood to want to take her places and to do things for her.*
   - *She has assigned herself to the needing-discipline category.*
   - *The parents will want to talk more and resolve it.*
   - *The family will need some recovery time.*

Several other examples of misbehaviors and disciplines are presented here. Observe that each begins with "Children who *teach us* . . . ."

Children who *teach us* that we cannot trust them out of our sight must remain in our sight (grounded and more closely supervised).

Children who *teach us* that they will throw a party in our home when we parents are out of town must no longer be trusted to stay by themselves.

Children who *teach us* that we cannot trust what they say must understand that we'll be checking almost everything they say.

Children who *teach us* that we cannot trust them to remain sober must no longer be allowed to drive the family car (or the car for which we have cosigned).

Children who *teach us* that they will let their grades fall must be more closely supervised in their studying, must watch TV and play video games less, and must be checked on at school more frequently.

Children who *teach us* that they do not know how to take care of doors because they are always getting mad and slamming them may lose their bedroom doors for a week or so.

Children who *teach us* that they will use their privacy to plot things against the family's moral values must have their privacy interrupted so that they can be watched more closely.

Children who *teach us* that they will use the phones in their rooms to converse with the wrong crowd will have their phones removed from their rooms. (Shepherds can't protect the sheep if they have direct lines to the wolves in sheep's clothing.)

Children who *teach us* that they need counseling will be provided with counseling.

Children who *teach us* that they aren't putting forth an effort to remember to get their lunch money must solve their own hunger pangs without mom or dad making a trip to the school.

Children who *teach us* that they aren't putting forth an effort to put their dirty clothes in the hamper must do their own laundry that week.

Children who *teach us* that they aren't taking their chores seriously must put off their own activities (family privileges) until their chores are completed.

As you reread these statements, note that the consequences are exactly matched to the offenses. That is as it should be.

Also, observe how the statements make it clear where the responsibility lies for the outcomes. In a home with fair and reasonable parents, the outcomes are shaped by the children. You do what they teach you to do. They are the *teachers,* and you are the *responders.* Your suspicious attitude or your trust is a response to what they have taught you about themselves. (The *teacher-responder* concept will be thoroughly explained when we erect Tower 9.)

Once again, let me remind you that the consequences are not punishments. Punishment implies revenge, and revenge won't pass the test of "Will this heal?" Your goal is to rescue and preserve your children.

**Avoid the discipline that is an unnatural consequence of the offense.**

To see how *not* to discipline, let's look at three examples of *un*natural consequences:

- "Jim, I can't believe you got in trouble at school for being a smart mouth! Go copy five pages out of the dictionary!"
  (Copying five pages out of the dictionary has no logical connection with the misbehavior in school. Therefore, it is an unnatural consequence.)
- "Elaine, you did it again! You left before your chores were done! Just for that, you are going to have to spend an extra weekend with your father and that witch he married."
  (That is nothing less than an act of revenge on the part of the mother. She would not have responded that way if she had checked her response with "Will this heal?" before proceeding. Again, this is an unnatural consequence.)
- "Jeremy, I told you not to ride your bike in the street; you're getting a whipping!"
  (A whipping is unnatural to the offense.)

Wait! Don't make a move until you have all the other towers in place. They work together to protect your family fortress. If you are presently in a crisis, say to your teenager . . .

*We need time to think. We are not going to respond to what you've done until a week from now. Oh yes, and you're grounded while we do our thinking* [if appropriate].

This approach is better than reacting before you are fully prepared. Use your week to absorb this material.

### Tower of Conviction 9: We are *responders,* and our child is the teacher. We will *respond* fairly to what our child *teaches* us.

You, as parents, are *responding* to what your children are *teaching* you. Therefore, you are *responders* and your children are *teachers.*

If your children teach you to trust them, you respond by honoring them with more freedom and privileges and appropriate appreciation (the natural result of trusting).

If they teach you to be suspicious, you respond by asking them more questions and watching them more closely (the natural result of suspicion).

If your children teach you not to trust them, you respond by limiting their freedoms and privileges (the natural result of loss of confidence).

It's up to them. Your children are the teachers, and their great responsibility is to teach you to trust them.

You are just responders. Your great responsibility is to respond fairly and consistently.

These labels can help you identify what is actually happening in most American homes. From now on, think of children as teachers and of parents as responders.

Now we are ready to use the *teacher-responder* concept in our example situations.

1. Misbehavior or unkind attitude:
   *Son skipped school.*
   What did he teach school personnel?
   *He taught them to trust him less.*
   How did they respond?
   *They gave him zeros for the day and assigned him to three days in an alternate classroom setting.*
   What did our son teach us?
   *He taught us to trust him less. He taught us that we allowed him to start taking his car to school prematurely.*
   How shall we respond to what our son has taught us?
   *"Since you taught us that we weren't able to trust you to have your car at school, we'll not allow you to drive it to school until trust can be reestablished."*

2. Misbehavior or unkind attitude:
   *Daughter screamed, "I hate you!"*
   What did our daughter teach us?
   *She taught us that we need to work on our relationship with each other, and that we need to establish boundaries for rudeness and hostility.*
   How shall we respond to what our daughter has taught us?
   *"Since you've told us that you may have serious doubts about your love for us, we are hurt enough that we don't feel that we can drive the hundred miles to purchase your formal this Saturday. You'll remember that we have a saying in our family: 'If you're rude to the suppliers, you shouldn't expect new supplies.' We need to get our relationship problems resolved before we take on anything else. Our love for each other is most important. If it becomes necessary, we'll secure the services of a family counselor to help us. We care that much. We love you, and we will always love you."*

## Move ahead with caution.

The towers of conviction are beliefs that you need to erect and honor as parents. The eighth, ninth, and tenth towers (the tenth to be discussed in chapter 7) are very closely related, and they must all be constructed in your mind before you act on them with your children. Together, these towers state that your children will be exposed to natural consequences, that the burden is on them to *teach* you how to *respond* to them, and that you are going to allow them to be fully responsible for what they do or neglect to do.

Each of these towers is going to require you to make careful explanations to your children. You are about to reconstruct the way those in your family relate to one another, and you must carefully prepare your children to understand how things are going to be different. For many years, your children have gotten used to things being one way, and now you are going to arrange things another way.

You are changing the game plan. You are going to add new order, discipline, consistency, predictability, and follow-through based on your towers of conviction. Be fair and carefully teach your children the new way before you institute it and then *don't compromise it!*

### Build the teacher-responder relationship.

When you are ready to construct the eighth tower, you need to sit down with your children one at a time and explain the *teacher-responder* relationship so that they can understand what is about to happen in their home and how they have the power to make things better.

You will want to say something like . . .

> *Dave, your mother and I have figured out how to label what's been going on in our home. You are a teacher, and we are responders. We are responding to what you've been teaching us with the attitudes and actions you've been showing us.*
>
> *Now, we both want the same thing. You want more freedom and privileges, and we want those things for you. We want to be able to trust you enough to give you more independence. Our dream all these years has been to raise children worthy of trust.*
>
> *As the teacher, Dave, it's up to you.* If you choose *to teach us to trust you, we will respond by trusting you.*
>
> If you choose *to teach us to be suspicious of you, we will respond by asking you a lot of questions and checking up on things.* If you choose *to teach us not to trust you, we will respond by grounding you so that we can supervise you more closely and give you the opportunity to teach us to trust you again.*
>
> *We will do whatever you teach us to do. We will be responsive.*

You may want to give an example or two of recent actions and reactions to help your teenager understand more clearly. You could say something like . . .

> *Dave, last week we trusted you to take our boat out by yourself. We got word from two different sources that you guys didn't wear life jackets as you promised and that one of your friends had beer in the boat. Dave, you chose to teach us that we couldn't trust you at that time to take the boat out with your friends, and therefore we responded by not letting you take the boat out without us anymore until you teach us to trust you with it again.*

The basic outline for constructing what you will say is this:

Since *you have chosen to teach us* _____, *you have chosen* for us to respond by _____ (natural consequence).

Try to vary how you present it so that you won't wear your children down with repetition.

While you are setting up the *teacher-responder* understanding, it is always appropriate to warn of natural consequences and to promise appreciation. Say something like . . .

> *We want to be sure that you understand what we mean. If you choose to teach us that you will tell us the truth, you will have chosen for us to respond by feeling no need to call around and verify what you say. We will respond by trusting you more.*
>
> *If you choose to teach us that you will be with friends who have good reputations, you will have taught us to respond by not hassling you about your friends. We will respond with admiration for your choice of friends.*
>
> *If you choose to teach us that you can handle your school scene on your own, you have chosen for us to respond by relaxing and growing in our respect for your sense of responsibility.*

### Grounding is an important tool in the teacher-responder relationship.

Many of you may ask, "But how do we respond if our teenager has already taught us not to trust him?" Grounding is the tool you'll need.

*Grounding is not punishment.* If you're used to lashing out with, "I've had it with you; you're grounded for six months!" STOP. "Thou shalt discipline rather than punish" (Be a shepherd, not a cow puncher), according to the second commandment for developing the proper posture as parents. You are out to disciple, not to play the hurt exchange.

Think of grounding as an opportunity you are providing your teenager for teaching you to trust him or her again. You can get more mileage out of grounding if you'll think of it this way. Here is an example of how to present grounding to your teenager:

> *Greg, I'm very sorry you chose to tell us you were going one place and went another instead. You've taught us that we can't be sure where you're going when you leave home. Therefore, we are going to respond by keeping you at home where we can give you closer supervision for a while.*
>
> *You used our phone to make the arrangements with your friends; and as you know, in our home, if you abuse a privilege, you lose that privilege. This means you'll be grounded from the phone as well.*
>
> *You and your friends have taught us that you don't make good music when you band together. Therefore, we are going to respond by warning you that another problem like this will cause us to believe that you and those friends are not good for one another. As for now, we'll call their parents and explain to them what happened and inform them of the stand we're taking.*

*And while we're dealing with problems, Greg, your grade card came this week. It wasn't good news. We were especially disappointed because you kept telling us that things were going well at school. It seems that you need to study more, that you need to be supervised more closely in your studying, and that we need to stay in closer touch with the school. We'll be careful to provide better supervision.*

*Greg, our trust has been damaged, and more than anything else, we want to trust you. Therefore, we are going to give you a way to teach us to trust you again. We are going to set up a thirty-day grounding schedule for you for this purpose. This is not punishment and we're not trying to get back at you; we just want to provide you with a way to reestablish trust. Incidentally, you won't be grounded from your weekly Explorer meetings since we try not to take positive things away from our children.*

*Your part, Greg, is to teach us to trust you again. Our part is to respond to whatever you teach us.*

*If all goes well for ten days, you'll have earned the privilege of having trust-worthy friends over once each week.*

*If all goes well for twenty days, you'll have earned the privilege of using the phone again for preapproved calls.*

*If we get a good report when we check with your teachers, you'll have earned the privilege of studying thirty minutes less per evening.*

*And if after thirty days you've continued to teach us to trust you, you'll have earned the privilege of going out again—provided we know where you're going and who you'll be with. You'll be ungrounded.*

*Greg, if you do well for an extended period of time, for two full months, we'll be so happy that we'll want to celebrate. We'll all go to White Water in honor of your success. Each of our children will be able to take a friend.*

I'd like to point out some of the significant elements in this example . . .

1. Grounding is presented as an opportunity for *reteaching* trust, not as punishment, providing a better atmosphere in which to improve.

2. Grounding is presented in a friendly manner without unduly projecting defensiveness or daring defensiveness.

3. Grounding is presented from the point of view of what it can accomplish *for* the teenager rather than what it will do *to* the teenager.

4. It is clear that grounding is the natural consequence of the teenager's misbehavior.

5. It clearly places the responsibility for good outcomes on the shoulders of the teenager (and his friends).

6. The grounding is for a specific amount of time. Grounding for an *unspecified amount of time* often causes despair in teenagers. They aren't able to see any hope on the horizon.

Grounding for *extended periods of time* is inadvisable since six months seems like an eternity to teenagers. Thirty days is more palatable to them. The time can be extended if trust has not been reestablished.

About five years ago, a despondent teenage girl reached out to me for help because her parents had grounded her for her entire senior year. In family counseling I showed them how to structure grounding for the purpose of teaching trust. Together, we taught their daughter that being grounded was her opportunity to teach her parents to trust her again

We renegotiated the time period from eight months to eight weeks, provided she retaught trust during that time. We helped her see how she had control through her attitudes and behaviors of whether or not grounding would need to be extended beyond eight weeks. (Incidentally, I see attitude as a choice, and a bad attitude is a willful misbehavior.)

7. This type of grounding does not take positive things away from the teenager. The teenager in the example was to be allowed to continue attending his Explorer meetings.

I persuaded one set of parents to reconsider taking participation in the swim team away from their daughter. It was the single activity that gave her a measure of success to enjoy and boosted her self-esteem.

I persuaded another family not to take the church youth group away from their son.

An exception would be if the swim team and the youth group were means for being with the wrong crowd.

8. This type of grounding builds incentives and rewards into the grounding structure. The example illustrates these motivational factors: Relief is in sight; incentives for staying true are spaced throughout the grounding schedule; and a big reward is waiting at the end of the difficult journey. The big reward is two months away to provide an incentive for an extended period of time to stabilize the improvement.

Please handle your kids with care. Appreciate them. Don't depreciate them!

Be quick to compliment and slow to criticize. Love your children in the way you speak with them. You are one of the primary sculptors of their self-concepts. Be an artist—not a bull in the china shop. To be right before God, you must envelop what I've written within the golden rule.

CHAPTER **7**

# ALLOWING THE PAIN OF WRONG CHOICES

**Tower of Conviction 10: We will allow our child to experience the pain of his or her own wrong choices.**

I n many instances, stubbornly defiant teenagers do the wrong and their parents wear the pain. What an awful way for parents to be treated! Their hearts are being broken by their children's disregard for them. They are being traumatized by seeing their kids make giant mistakes. And on top of it all—wounded and grieving as they are—they drag themselves up to stand in front of their children to try to shield them from the pain their kids are causing themselves. These are abused parents!

Such an arrangement is destructive to both parents and children. Parents are afflicted with pain they don't deserve while their kids are allowed to escape the pressure they truly need, the pain naturally caused by their own wrong choices.

The painful consequences of wrong choices are supposed to pressure offending children into realizing the wrongness of their wrongs so they will finally understand that they need to return to doing what's right. Instead of that desirable outcome happening, parents often shield misbehaving teenagers from the pressure.

### Parent abuse catches parents by surprise.

The problem is that parents are suddenly being forced to perform in an area they've never experienced before. Their kids were so neat only a couple of years ago; they just didn't know to prepare for what they are facing now.

These parents usually react the only way they know to react. They try to protect their children from being hurt, just as they always have. They use their wits and influence to get the kids out of trouble, and they do it as a natural reflex.

But your reflexes have to be retrained. What worked before doesn't work now that your child has begun . . .

> to be secretive
> to avoid you
> to lie

to look for every loophole
to manipulate
to intimidate
to run around with the wrong crowd

You have to learn new response patterns.

Here's your tower for doing that. Tower of Conviction 10 is: We will allow our child to experience the pain of his or her own wrong choices.

### Tower of Conviction 10 is the toughest of all to erect.

This tower is the most difficult one to build and maintain because it asks you to control your lifeguard instincts and stand by and watch your children suffer from what they have done.

You may think that you could never do that. But consider this: It really boils down to where you want to fight the battle for the lives of your children. Do you want to fight it at an early phase, or do you want to wait until their entanglements are more *entrenched?* Since you love your children, you are going to fight for their lives—no doubt about it—so it just becomes a question of when and where you want the crisis.

Perhaps I should explain what I mean by their entanglements becoming more entrenched. Rebellious children become more integrated into the wrong crowd and more segregated from the right crowd. They become less and less attractive to straights, and straights become more and more boring to them. They develop greater appetites for low adventure—for sex, alcohol, drugs, escape from responsibility, the party scene in general.

The further they drift, the more the way back begins to look as foreboding as a journey from another solar system. Putting things back together again begins to look completely impossible. They sometimes despair of trying.

Then they get arrested and may have negative experiences with some of the adults in positions of authority. Perhaps an officer shoves him around, or the court-appointed attorney doesn't care enough to understand her case and pleads her out to get rid of her. Maybe the judge is rude. And while she is in jail, the chaplain says she'll be back to talk but never returns. Fellow inmates laugh at him for being naive enough to believe the people in authority would care about him.

They find it easy to come to the conclusion: "The people who are supposed to be the good guys are worse off than I am! At least I'm not a hypocrite! I'd rather be like I am than like they are! I used to admire policemen, attorneys, judges, and ministers when I was growing up, but these people are complete disappointments! Nobody's any good! When I get out of here, I'm going to get bombed!"

I've seen all these things happen, and they indicate something of what I mean when I say that the entanglements of the misbehaving child become more entrenched as time passes.

Now, I'll repeat my question: Do you want to fight an all-out war for the life of your child at an early trench, or do you want to wait until your child's entanglements become more entrenched?

*You have to become convinced of Tower of Conviction 10,*
*or you will let it crumble.*

Your only hope for building Tower of Conviction 10 and keeping it from falling apart is to become convinced of its conviction. You must give your children *the privilege* of feeling the pain of their own wrong choices (within reason).

This tower is so-o-o tough because it goes against your nature, your reflexes. You are used to kissing your kids' hurts and making things okay again. Now I am urging you to stop doing that (if their hurt is a result of their own wrong choices). If you continue to do that, you are just keeping your children from coming face-to-face with how wrong their wrong is. The faster they can face up to how wrong their wrong is, the greater will be the chance for them to change before too much permanent damage is done.

You may think you are doing the right thing by shielding your children, but you must recognize this extremely important fact: The stuff kids can get into today can turn out their lights forever! Drugs can blow their mental circuits beyond repair. Certain diseases that they might catch can injure them permanently (like genital herpes) or even kill them (like AIDS). Their offspring can be born afflicted due to genetic damage from drugs, or they can be born with AIDS. *It is urgent* that self-destructive teenagers come face-to-face with how wrong their wrong is just as soon as possible!

If you help your children get away with doing wrong by helping them get by with it, you are actually helping them do wrong. *You are enabling them to continue to do wrong* apart from the impact of bad consequences. Your help is putting off their realizing how badly they need to change. Changing doesn't have to be important to them because somehow, some way, everything turns out okay; they see no need to change!

You are getting in the way of cause and effect, in the way of nature running its course. Your difficult child is not experiencing the potholes in the road of hard knocks if you are letting him or her walk on you instead of on the road itself!

One of the most effective teachers is the road of hard knocks. For *good*ness sake, you must let this stern substitute teacher—natural consequences—teach your children. This teacher is for those kids who refuse to learn by listening to their parents, teachers, and church leaders. They relegate themselves to learn by experience.

Parents can unwittingly become a part of their teenagers' successful-system-for-doing-wrong-and-getting-by-with-it. Their kids turn them into their safety net. They know that if they get into serious trouble, their parents will always be there to "catch" them—to talk to school officials, to pay their fines, or to get them out of jail.

I've even known some of the more hard-core, wrongdoing teenagers to come out of jail angry with their parents for taking so long to get them out! They would like their successful-system-for-doing-wrong-and-getting-by-with-it to work a little smoother.

If parents bog down, these kids know how to work on them. They've informed me of how they do it. "All I have to do is cry and look desperate, and Dad'll break down and give me what I want," a girl told me. A guy said, "I just get in Mom's face and threaten to go live with my dad!"

They've learned what works, and they use these tools of manipulation and in*timi*dation for successfully maintaining their self-gratifying lifestyles. Those who have ears to hear, let them hear!

*Sometimes self-concerned kids set up parents in "the grandparents' trap."*

Things get even worse. The grandparents' trap happens when a precious grandchild is born and the new grandparents are trapped into helping their prodigal child like never before. I've been beside many of these grandparents, and I've listened to them describe the nature of their trap. It's intimidation at its worst!

They've said, "They'd take our granddaughter right into the drug party if we didn't baby-sit her for them."

They've said, "We pay their rent because if we didn't they'd have to live with a bunch of other lowlifes and no telling what our grandbaby would be exposed to."

They've said, "We buy all the supplies for the baby, or he wouldn't have clean diapers and proper food."

They've said, "Sure we get him out of jail. If he stays in jail, he'll lose his job, and then how will they provide for the baby?"

They've said, "We've lost a son; we can't stand the thought of losing a grandson. The only spiritual training he gets is when he's with us. We've just got to stay close to them."

They've said, "We know they're using us, but that's the only way we get to help with the grandbaby."

Believe me, most of these grandparents would advise you to be swift in your attempt to rescue and recover your child before a grandchild enters the picture and you get into the grandparents' trap.

### You should take a stand as early as possible.

As soon as you discover that your child's life has begun to revolve around life-threatening problems, you can say . . .

*We won't house, feed, and clothe you* [we won't give you a stable base of operation] *so that you can keep on destroying yourself. We will not continue to produce for you while you use our supplies to help you and your friends destroy you. We will always help you up, but we will never keep you up while you are going down.*

This philosophy is needed by parents of drug abusers, for example, but it also applies to parents of kids with other problems. Drug abusers get with the drug crowd and stay at it for so long that they become physically and economically exhausted. Then they bring their pitiful-looking remains home to their parents and promise to change (and they are probably sincere at the time).

Their parents' hopes soar, and they take them in and nurse them back to health. But these abused parents don't know that their children are just vacationing with them from doing drugs. More often than not, they'll go back to it as soon as they're up to it again (because they almost never can change by themselves, no matter how good their intentions are).

That is why in most cases I urge parents to make the rule that their children can return home only through a drug treatment program. Providing transportation to a treatment program can be the parents' most effective response to the drug-dependent person who is requesting help. This alleviates one of the greatest fears of parents: They fear refusing to take in their child when he or she has no other place to go, especially if it's wintertime.

Parents can say . . .

*We love you with all our hearts, but we know that taking you back into our home is not what you need right now. You need a treatment program. And if you are ready to get well, we'll take you there. We've already made arrangements with the hospital, and their help is waiting for you. It'll be warm and safe there. After you complete the treatment program, we'll receive you back into our home if that's what's best for everyone concerned.*

### Watch out for superguilt!

Trying too hard to help your kids can be counterproductive. Your efforts can impose so much guilt on them that they will stay on drugs to keep from feeling it.

A woman called me long distance a few years ago and told me that she and her husband were selling their home to get the $15,000 it would take to pay their son's attorney. Their son was in jail for selling drugs.

After discovering that he had been into drugs for a long time, I urged her not to lose their home and their life savings on the attorney's fees.

I reasoned . . .

*If you do this, you will impose what I call superguilt on your son, and it will lock him into doing drugs. He will just about have to do drugs to handle the guilt over the damage he has caused his family. Damage so big, in his mind, that trying to undo it will be too overwhelming to him, and he'll stick to drugs instead.*

I asked this mother to let her son handle the situation himself, even if that meant using a court-appointed attorney. I went to the jail and spoke to this man through the bars. He had learned of his parents' intentions. He asked me not to let them do that. I assured him that I had done my best to prevent it. As it turned out, the parents still have their home and their life savings, and the grown child doesn't have superguilt to contend with.

### You need to learn a new reflex.

Your *new reflex* should be to allow your children to untangle their own tangles and to clean up their own messes. As one of our catchy concepts states: Mess it up. Clean it up.

Here is a formula for change: Change occurs when the pain of doing a wrong becomes greater than the pleasure received from doing the wrong. Realize this: The highs kids are experiencing from doing wrong feel s-o-o good and are s-o-o magnetic that the consequences have to be nearly nuclear to blast them away from misbehaving. (And they also have to have a strong support system for staying away from it.)

Pain pries kids away from wrong! Do your kids a big favor: Compassionately step aside (while still reassuring them of your love), and *let pain pry!*

Pain can be one of your greatest allies. You are telling your children that certain things are wrong to do, and pain proves it to them.

Wrong is supposed to hurt! Wrong is supposed to turn out wrong! That's what you've been saying all these years. So, be very reluctant to interfere with what you've been saying. Otherwise, you make it possible for your kids to believe that wrong can turn out okay, and that's the very last thing you'd ever want.

The pressure of pain can alert your kids to the fact that they have taken a wrong turn in life and they desperately need a course correction. Don't lose this ally by standing in its way.

### Think about the role of pain in your life.

Most of what you do is to relieve pain, avoid pain, or enjoy the opposite of pain.

You endure the pain of going to work every day because it is less painful than seeing your family go without necessities.

You do housework because it is less painful than living in a messy house.

You do yard work to avoid the pain of looking like a slob or being bored. Or you do it because you enjoy it. (Pleasure is the opposite of pain.)

You eat to avoid hunger pains.

You rest to relieve the pain of being exhausted.

You are cautious around fire because you remember the pain of being burned.

You are careful about speeding because you don't want to pay a ticket or see your insurance costs increase.

Pain is often a friend; it helps you take good care of yourself.

For years, people thought Hansen's disease caused fingers, toes, and other extremities to decay. Modern medicine has discovered that the belief is not true. Sufferers lose feeling in their extremities, and therefore pain cannot warn them that their extremities are being destroyed in some way.

Pain can protect and heal. You need to let pain motivate your children to take better care of themselves. Let the pressure of pain push your kids away from wrong and press them toward right.

### Don't get in the way after your pray!

One of the most tragic things I observe is good parents praying for their kids to break free from the wrong crowd and the stuff they're into while they're standing in the way of their kids' learning that doing wrong naturally causes nasty consequences.

The Bible is very clear on that point. Romans 6:23 says, "The wages of sin is death, but the gift of God is eternal life in Christ Jesus our Lord." The natural consequence of doing wrong is *degenerative,* and the supernatural consequence of living for God and good is *regenerative.*

The Bible further warns:

Do not be deceived, God is not mocked; for whatever a man sows, that he will also reap. For he who sows to his flesh [sinful desires] will of the flesh reap corruption, but he who sows to the Spirit will of the Spirit reap everlasting life [everlasting wellness]. (Gal. 6:7–8)

Good brings good. Bad causes bad. The bad consequences of being bad are supposed to pressure offenders back toward good. Parents must *get out of the way and let pain do its job.*

*Don't short-circuit nature's way of requesting a course correction.*

Feelings of guilt and the pain of uncomfortable consequences are two primary ways that a course correction is requested. Parents who shield their children from the consequences of their wrongs are often unkindly extending the amount of time it will take their kids to realize how messed up they are becoming. So, again, I suggest you pray and get out of the way.

Go ahead and stand beside your defiant young person and continue to assure him or her of your love and concern, but don't be too quick to stand in front of him or her to ward off the pain.

*But always be fair.*

To be fair in this new approach to your children, you will courteously warn them, in advance, that from now on they must untangle their own tangles. You will warn them that if they walk over their parents, their God, their church, and their country to do wrong, they will have to right their own wrongs.

- If they get fined, they will handle their fines on their own.
- If they recklessly wreck their car, you will not provide them with another car.
- If they get into trouble at school, you will not automatically take their side.
- If they offend other families by involving their children in something wrong, you will send them or you will go with them to apologize to the parents of those families.
- If they shoplift, they will have to deal with the store managers on their own.
- If they get in jail, you will not normally bail them out. (Jail can be safer than the streets.)
- If they flunk out of school, you will expect them to go to summer school or go for a GED.
- If your son gets a girl pregnant, you will strongly urge him to pay child support until his child turns eighteen.

From now on, the natural consequences of doing wrong will belong to those who do the wrong. Your children will be responsible to bear the pain of their own wrong choices or enjoy the rewards of their right choices.

Will it heal for your children to be allowed the privilege of suffering from their own wrongdoing? Yes, my experience tells me that it is the best available therapy when done in a compassionate spirit, apart from vengeance or rejection, without an I-told-you-so attitude or a holier-than-thou attitude, and without conveying all the details to relatives and friends. As Jesus instructed His disciples, we are to "be wise as serpents and harmless as doves" (Matt. 10:16).

Tower of Conviction 10 is: We will allow our child to experience the pain of his or her own wrong choices.

*You're still not ready to act.*

You are not yet ready to implement this tenth tower of conviction. I've requested that you read and understand this book as a whole before you use any of these concepts and principles of parenting.

Also, what you choose to do is your own responsibility. You are responsible to look at your situation and apply only what applies. You are responsible to compare what I have written to what others have written and then design your own strategies. I encourage you to get professional help in determining your individual course of action.

## You need balance in parenting.

An example will illustrate what I want to communicate about balance in parenting, which allows for pain but monitors the situation.

I know a teenager whom any parents would be proud to have in their home. He is more like a well-adjusted college student than a high schooler. His room is usually neat and clean, his grades are $A$'s and $B$'s, and he has the courage to stand up for his principles.

Recently, his father began to notice that the teen was losing interest in things, his room got messy, and he began to be ill-tempered with his parents and siblings.

His father could have gone off on a tirade about the new slouchiness. Instead, he asked himself, *Will that heal?* He decided that grouching at his son wouldn't be the healing thing to do. He remembered the seven commandments for parental posturing (see chapter 2).

In harmony with the commandments, he decided on this approach with his son, "Bob, you are normally a neat and highly motivated person. But lately I've noticed that you are letting things go. Is there something wrong that I can help you with?"

Bob confided, "Something's been wrong for several weeks."

They weren't able to talk then because his dad was taking him to school. That evening, though, they talked for a couple of hours. Bob (not his real name, of course) told his dad that he was tired of not having a close friend. He had just not met a person that he could feel close to and trust. They prayed together that God would help him find a close friend.

Dad got an $A+$ on this one. The last thing Bob needed—this son who was feeling left out of the mainstream of companionship—would have been for his dad to have seemed against him, too.

I know this illustration is off the subject of defiant and rebellious kids. I use it because it shows so clearly how you have to be sensitive and not just strike out with tough tactics.

Avoid two extremes when you consider your adolescent's attitudinal or behavioral problems. At one extreme is the school of thinking that says adolescent problems are due to heredity, bad environment, poor socialization, traumas from the past, physical problems, and other similar considerations—someone or something else's fault rather than the fault of the person misbehaving.

At the other extreme is the school of thinking that says it's all the kid's fault. This school gives little slack on behalf of the above-mentioned considerations or present parental problems.

Balance means maintaining the stand that since no teenager can act uncivilized and make it in society, every teenager is obligated to at least be a decent, legal, cooperative, and productive American citizen, no matter what has or hasn't happened to him or her.

At the same time, you must be *patiently understanding* of problems within the environment, or from heredity, or from past traumas, or from present physical problems, or from whatever other causes without allowing them to become excuses for rude, indecent, or illegal misbehaviors.

Less-fortunate adolescents should not chain themselves to excuses for not doing well. That would be self-imposed retardation. They must break free, be civilized, and learn how to be significant. America gives them that great potential! Parents need to help them *realize their potential*.

Parents should look for causes of unattractive behaviors, and they should help their children fix such things while they continue to demand decent behavior.

# CHAPTER 8

# RECOGNIZING THE ENEMY

### Tower of Conviction 11: We will see the wrong crowd as family enemy #1.

*How bad is the wrong crowd?*

Consider what I've learned in my experience on the front lines of rescuing and recovering teenagers: Every teenager who gets into trouble is, almost without exception, with the wrong crowd! I have found this to be 99 percent true.

Furthermore, I have never seen a youth counselor help a teenager who remains actively involved with the wrong crowd. The wrong crowd keeps the teenager defiant of receiving help and feeds his or her selfish attitudes and behaviors. The wrong crowd can be as dangerous as blood clots in the brain and can distort thinking as much.

Our agency alone works with three hundred families a year who are trying to redeem kids from the wrong crowd. Ours is one of seven counseling agencies in the county, and the others also deal with a lot of families. Hundreds of other families are trying to pull their kids away from the wrong crowd on their own. Obviously, it's a mammoth problem; the wrong crowd seems to terrorize most families to some degree at one time or another.

Without a doubt, the wrong crowd is the greatest threat to the safety and security of your children, and that makes it family enemy #1.

☐ *Each person in the wrong crowd is an enemy of Easter.*

Listen to the Bible:

> There are many whose lives make them enemies of Christ's death on the cross. They are going to end up in hell, because their god is their bodily desires. They are proud of what they should be ashamed of, and they think only of things that belong to this world. (Phil. 3:18–19, TEV)

You had better see the wrong crowd as family enemy #1 and fight to rescue your children from its carnivalistic and cannibalistic magnetism.

### Who or what is the wrong crowd?

The wrong crowd includes anyone who influences your child to do wrong or who does wrong with your child. There are two identifying characteristics of wrong-crowd-type kids: (1) They are sneaky and phony, and (2) they are proud of what they should be ashamed of, as the Bible says.

They sneak because what they are doing is unacceptable to decent people. They are doing things behind the backs of parents, teachers, police officers, Sunday school teachers, youth ministers, pastors, and their country. They sneak around because what they're doing is wrong *and they know it.*

They are phonies because they behave acceptably in front of people while behind their backs they are busy setting up themselves and others for self-destruction (the worst of all deceptions) while bragging about their evil adventures. They are actively or passively rebellious via . . .

using and abusing alcohol
being sexually active
taking drugs
sneaking out of the house
skipping school
shoplifting
running away

These people are hypocrites, but you can't tell by looking. The wrong crowd has so successfully infiltrated the youth scene that its members cannot always be identified by how they look. They have become good at being phony. I've known members of the wrong crowd to be student council representatives, cheerleaders, sports figures, class officers, and class scholars.

### "You will know them by their fruits."

You will *not* know them by how courteous they are. Parents especially get fooled by polite kids. These are the kids who are overzealous to say "yes sir" and "yes ma'am." For some reason, parents equate courtesy with good morals. But doing that is not wise. Of course, not all courteous young people are phonies. Take some time with your teenagers' friends and acquaintances. Chances are, it won't be long before you can discern the ones who are not genuinely courteous.

One set of parents learned this the risky way. They were so impressed with a polite teenage boy they had just met that they let him take their daughter for a Sunday afternoon cruise. He took her to a park and right away asked if she wanted to get in the backseat and fool around. She refused and reported what happened to her surprised parents.

Don't you think people of the wrong crowd learn how to get what they want? Don't you think they have learned that parents are impressed by courtesy? Sure they have, and that tool of manipulation is in their toolbox. Learning to be efficient phonies is their best survival technique.

*You can detect your children's involvement with the wrong crowd.*

Twenty parents in our parent support group, Parenting Within Reason, developed a list of symptoms to watch for. The presence of a few of these symptoms may not indicate that your children are in the wrong crowd, but if several are present, and especially if these symptoms are radical *changes from how your children have been in the past,* you should find out what's going on. It's better to be too cautious than too blind. The symptoms are as follows:

- Emotionally pulling away from the family
- Resisting family rules and values
- Being dissatisfied with how much freedom is allowed
- Becoming friends with kids you've never heard of
- Ceasing to bring friends home
- Becoming defensive about friends
- Beginning of unusual phone calls (the caller hangs up; kids won't identify themselves or will give only their first names)
- Always taking phone calls in private
- Hiding letters and other belongings
- Being evasive about where he or she goes and what he or she does
- Being careless about curfew but always having a good excuse
- Wanting to cruise and hang out at the "in" places
- Going straight to their rooms and holing up there after being out with friends
- Changing appearance to identify with kids who are into the wrong things
- Developing appetites for unacceptable things
- Asking for contraceptive devices
- Becoming dissatisfied with what you have provided: clothes, room furnishings, spending money, and the car
- Becoming excessively selfish
- Beginning to exhibit a negative personality change
- Lying and searching for loopholes
- Receiving grades that are much lower than usual
- Being absent from school or tardy without your knowledge (with evidence showing up later on report cards)
- Balking about going to church (unless the wrong crowd is part of the youth group)
- Being critical of straight kids

If you see these symptoms developing in your teenagers, be on guard. Someone from the wrong crowd is spreading the contagion. Family enemy #1 is in contact with your children!

I helped a family interpret the symptoms. A couple visited with me recently about their daughter. They described some of these symptoms and couldn't figure out why she had begun to act "differently." I offered an observation, "Your child is in contact with the wrong crowd."

They objected, "That couldn't be true! They're all such nice kids! They all go to our church!"

I asked for names. One parent said, "I'm sure you won't know any of them." I knew three out of five of the kids from hearing their names mentioned in connection with problems in other families.

I picked up the phone and called one of my teenage friends who had gotten out of the wrong crowd. He verified that the friends in question had been viewing porno videos and skipping school to go for joy rides (without driver's licenses).

### God, please help parents to be careful!

The wrong crowd is in disguise, luring kids away from good parents, and these "trusting" parents most often don't know it's happening!

The wrong crowd is made up of sneaks and phonies who are deceived into being proud of what they should be ashamed of. They are the support group, the companions, for thinking wrong thoughts and for doing wrong things. Furthermore, they are the ones who have the power to deprogram your children's moral and spiritual values.

I can't begin to tell you how much damage I have seen the wrong crowd do to adolescents. The range of damage goes from turning children against their families to turning them on to life-sapping addictions to turning them off to life through accidents, overdoses, and suicides.

Tower of Conviction 11 is: We will see the wrong crowd as family enemy #1.

### But how about the electronic wrong crowd?

I believe we agree that the wrong crowd is lethal and that you cannot afford to get comfortable with your children's hanging out with that crowd.

But have you? Maybe you have without realizing it.

Think about the TV shows and the movies that you let your children watch. Do those shows and movies agree with your traditional Christian values?

If they don't, you are allowing your children to hang out with the wrong crowd via TV and movie screens. You are allowing those programs to deprogram your children from what you've lovingly taught them and to reprogram them against you in your own home and community!

If you are going to protect your children from the wrong crowd, don't forget those elements that are with them electronically. They are the most impressive and persuasive of all! They show your children more electrifying sexual situations, alcohol use, selfishness, materialism, and violence than their peers ever will. And they have your children's undivided attention much, much more of the time than you do. (Remember when you've tried to get their attention while they were absorbed in a TV program? Pretty all-consuming, isn't it?)

How about some of the rock or country singers? Do their lifestyles and lyrics agree with your love of the Ten Commandments? If not, then look at your children under those headsets. They are being programmed against you and your principles, and they are being reprogrammed. It's like a scene from a science-fiction movie; alien forces are at work in your home!

*The Bible says that no child is immune to the evil influence of the wrong crowd.*

Maybe you think that because you've done such a good job in raising your children they will be able to mix with the wrong crowd and not be influenced. The Bible disagrees. It says, "Do not be fooled. 'Bad companions ruin good character.' Come back to your right senses" (1 Cor. 15:33–34, TEV).

### What is today's wrong crowd doing?

The wrong crowd has changed a great deal from what it was like when you and I were kids.

Its members are going to local theaters to see what I call playteen movies, which are about teenagers entertaining themselves with their reproductive systems, the boys making sexual targets out of girls.

I spoke to several home and family classes at a couple of high schools some time ago, and I asked the students how many of them had seen *Porky's*. Over two-thirds had. I encourage you to rent the *Porky's* video (or *Fast Times at Ridgemont High*), and you'll find that I'm not exaggerating about the content of such films.

Many teenagers have unlimited access to R-rated movies through cable TV, and some have access to X-rated shows via satellite dish. Some pass around X-rated videos and magazines.

As I was writing this chapter, I counseled with one of a group of fourteen-year-old girls who were gathering after school at the home where one of them baby-sat to watch X rated videos owned by the family. The girl I saw had gotten involved sexually with her boyfriend.

Yet, much of the pornography seen by young people is viewed in front of parents who have bought into the psychological idea that pornography doesn't influence behavior. That's especially amazing in view of the fact that media impressions work everywhere else! I wonder why corporations purchase thirty-second spots on Super Bowl telecasts at the unbelievable price of $500,000 each if media impressions don't affect behavior? We need to return to reason!

Teenagers are mixing alcohol with their carnal knowledge. Inhibitions are reduced, synthetic well-being is produced, birth control and disease control are ignored, and dis*grace*ful things happen.

And if you analyze the situation, you realize that the kids have merely modeled the "adults" they've been watching via TV, movies, concerts, and magazines. *Negative adult role models are one of the biggest problems kids have today!*

Anxiety attack! How can you know if your son or daughter is dating someone who has been pornographically programmed? Over half the kids have been to some degree.

The most popular event among the wrong crowd is the party scene. The primary activities include emptying kegs of beer, dancing, and making out. These parties usually involve up to thirty or more young people.

Worse parties most often occur at a teenager's house when the parents are out of town for the weekend. There are mixed drinks and mixed drugs, porno videos or satellite, the hot tub, the swimming pool, and bedrooms for loan.

Two of the finer parents I know found that their daughter had thrown such a party. They accidentally discovered Polaroid pictures of their fourteen-year-old in various sexual poses with a guy in her bedroom.

Another set of parents heard that their daughter was at a local party, and they went to get her. They forced their way into the apartment to find forty kids doing drugs and drinking alcohol. After a thorough search, while kids scattered, they finally found their daughter standing in a closet drugged, nude, and used.

Over 50 percent of American teenagers drink alcoholic beverages occasionally, and around 35 percent use drugs at least once a month.

☐ *Be advised that the sneaks are really sneaky.*

One of the things we frequently hear about is guys sneaking into the homes of thirteen-, fourteen-, and fifteen-year-old girls and having sex with them while their parents sleep one wall away. Or girls spend the night with girlfriends and have sex or do drugs with older brothers or other friends.

I worked with a youth minister to get a young girl into church so that she could be with the right crowd. She and a guy in the youth group sneaked into an empty Sunday school room, and she became pregnant. I felt so bad about it.

**You have to come face-to-face with the seriousness of these problems.**

I don't like writing about these events, and you don't like reading about them. But these things are happening in America right where we live. Families must become aware of how serious the problems are and realize the importance of monitoring their children's friends.

You have to parent defensively (without appearing defensive), because the world is poised against your raising morally and spiritually healthy children. This is why I refer to your home as a family fortress. The wrong crowd is just about everywhere.

**How can you know if new friends are from the right crowd or the wrong crowd?**

Parenting defensively concerns itself with investigative parenthood. I know some parents will be uncomfortable with that idea. I don't like it, either. But since the risks are of such a deadly nature, parents are placed in uncomfortable positions.

In most of the cases I've seen, the parents had to make a choice between cooperating with teenagers' right to privacy while they continued on a self-destructive course *or* invading their privacy to begin the desperate struggle to save their futures.

*1. Listen in on one side of phone conversations.* You can often "read" the whole conversation by hearing only half of it. This is why I'm so opposed to private phones in kids' rooms.

For example, if your teenager replies with a lot of one-word answers like "yes" and "no" and says, "I can't talk right now," while the body language speaks of uneasiness, it is time to be concerned.

*2. Check with other parents and adult youth leaders.* Call parents you are close to and ask if they know anything about the names that you are beginning to hear. Coaches, Sunday school teachers, youth ministers, schoolteachers, and other youth leaders may also be able to give you a clue or two. They love young people, and they don't want a sidetracked kid to derail others.

3. *Notes left in dirty clothes can be a source for clues.* This invasion of privacy might bother you a little more. However, some parents have saved their children by reading such notes that have revealed involvement with drugs or alcohol; sexual relationships; ducking out of PG-rated movies to slip into R's; shoplifting and other crimes; and contemplations of suicide.

One set of parents found a note in which their teenager's boyfriend was asking her when he was going to get to undress her. The parents were able to intercede before he defiled her with his lust.

I hate the thought of reading notes. But while some parents are busy honoring the privacy rule, their children are becoming more entangled and entrenched with the wrong crowd.

4. *Room searches are also in order when you're struggling to preserve the lives of your children.* This invasion of privacy might bother you even more; it certainly bothers me. But all is fair in love and war when the war is being compassionately waged to save your children's lives and when it is being monitored by "Will this heal?"

**Privacy is an earned privilege for teenagers, not an inalienable right.**

I recommend that you handle the privacy issue with this kind of common sense. Say something like . . .

> If you choose *to teach us to be worried that you may be harming yourself, our intense love for you will cause us to respond by looking for every clue we can find to discover if you really are involved in something that will end up hurting you. Privacy is a family privilege that comes with teaching us to trust you, and maturing toward adulthood. Small children have no privacy at all.*

After you've stated your reasonable position, use one of the catchy concepts you've learned to reiterate how things naturally work in your home.
Say something like . . .

> *And as you know, in our home if you abuse it, you lose it; that's the way it is here. If you abuse privacy, you lose privacy.*

Next, remind the teen that his or her goals and yours are exactly the same (you have a lot in common) and offer some fresh encouragement.
Say something like . . .

> *We want to trust you completely. We want you to begin to stand as an adult beside us. We want to give you more and more freedoms and privileges. Teach us that we can. Your mother and I will be your very willing students. We will be responsive to you.*

**Here's what to do to keep your children away from the wrong crowd.**

I couldn't figure out how teenagers could be on drugs for three or four years before their parents found out. After much thought and observation, however, I discovered that the segmentation of families explained this phenomenon.

Central air conditioning and heating have enabled adolescents to keep their bedroom doors closed whenever they want. Private phones allow them to be involved with kids their parents know nothing about. Private stereos and TV's are programming kids against their family's values. The sheep and the shepherds have begun to live on different hillsides.

By the time the parents find out about impending dangers, it's nearly too late. Their kids are already deeply involved with the wrong crowd, and their appetites are already whetted for unhealthy sources of gratification. But you can take steps to prevent this from happening in your family.

*1. Bring the whole family back into the living room or family room again.* The main antidote for the "wrong crowd" problem is being a family rather than a segmented household in which everyone has his or her own stereo, phone, and individual activities. Begin to gather in the living room again! Be a family and communicate. Enjoy family activities together.

*2. Have a lot of fun together.* Boats, lake cabins, snow skiing vacations, camping expeditions, and the like are much less expensive than counseling fees and rehabilitation programs. And being together in happy settings can create a wonderful atmosphere for children to mature.

Make a family out of your family. Stay together. Help your children have fun. Have fun yourself. Involve their friends in your family.

Don't gripe at your children in front of their friends. Do your best to make it fun to be in your family. You only pass this way once; you've got to grab all the family time you can.

*3. Enjoy a family-style family.* The concept is stated something like this:

*Although we each have our own friends and interests, we are a family, and we revolve around familyhood. We are not fragmented into different orbits, each revolving around things excluding the other family members. Being a family together is most important to us.*

Some parents make the mistake of revolving the whole family around the children. The kids and their activities are central and they are always treated like guests in the home.

This mistake becomes apparent when I ask the teenagers at our Success Classes for Teenagers about their parents' needs. They respond by listing such things as not being too strict on their kids, being understanding, being fair, not playing favorites, not getting onto their kids in front of their friends, and so forth.

What's wrong with this list? It's not concerned with the parents' needs; it describes the kids' needs. Many teenagers have been raised to see things only from their own points of view.

I've been amused that adult leaders who help kids make that kind of list don't recognize what's wrong with it, either. They just help the kids list how parents should better serve their needs.

Structuring a family to revolve around the kids is counterproductive because self-centered kids are produced. They are going to expect more and more service.

On the other hand, some parents revolve their families around themselves. The parents' desires and wishes are most important. Kids are left with baby-sitters weekend after weekend while their parents enjoy recreational pursuits with their adult friends.

Worse yet, kids are left to take care of themselves without supervision, which sets them up for big trouble. Children, by nature, are explorers. If they are left unsupervised, they will venture into forbidden territory apart from the guidance of their parental shepherds. It's almost certain to happen.

Families should revolve around the whole family. Kids are persons and are as important as parents, and vice versa. Each family member should be considered.

Each parent should help the children become aware of the other parent's needs and help him or her with those needs. Cooperation at the price of inconvenience must be taught.

### Here's what to do when your children are already involved with the wrong crowd.

1. Establish the following understanding with your teenagers:

*If you are involved with a friend, our whole family is involved with that friend. We have a family-style family. Therefore, we can have something to say about who your friends are.*

2. Require a complete and clean break with the wrong crowd. Adopt this slogan:

*If you make bad music with someone, you don't get to band with him or her anymore.*

I basically believe in the "cold turkey" approach, the complete removal of contact with the wrong crowd.

Breaking friendships is like open-heart surgery—it is difficult to perform and healing takes time. Some parents invite other parents to their home and display the evidence to them, explaining why they are saying that the kids can't run around together anymore. This is ideal when all parents involved can put on a united front.

Some parents change school schedules to get their kids out of the same lunch period with members of the wrong crowd, even when it means dropping from an upper-level to a lower-level class.

Some parents get job transfers and move out of the area, or send their children to live with relatives, or put them in private schools or in wilderness programs (in superstubborn cases when nothing has helped and parents sense that they are in danger of losing their child to a lethal consequence of wrongdoing).

And some parents take their young people out of one college and put them in another to get them away from the wrong crowd.

God knows how lethal the wrong crowd can be. Review the Old Testament and observe how God struggled to keep His people away from the wrong crowd. And notice what happened when they got with the wrong crowd. God knew that the wrong crowd was family enemy #1.

Two elements must change before a child will begin to improve: (1) the rebellious attitude and (2) the crowd that feeds it. A good place to start is to cut off the support group feeding the rebellious attitude.

You must interrupt this formula:

Erroneous attitudes and actions + the crowd that feeds it = continued degeneration.

If and when you interrupt it, you'll need to remind the child of the slogan: *If you make bad music with someone, you don't get to band with him or her anymore.*

3. Try to get the cooperation of the other parents. *If* all sets of parents involved are united, and *if* the kids have just begun to do wrong, *then* something great can happen. You can form your own peer group of parents and work together to help your children stay with the right things and stay away from the wrong things. You can use this book to develop consistency among the parents.

This cooperative effort can mean that the children involved will be holding to the same basic family rules and their parents will be monitoring their progress. While this closer supervision is happening, the families can provide wholesome, supervised activities for the young people where it is *in style* to do right and *out of style* to do wrong. This level of cooperation can most easily be achieved when the families involved are within the same church denomination.

*Note:* Some parents, whose children have gotten in trouble with "best friends," believe the kids can get counseling together and change together without the kind of support system described here. If it works, it will be an exception to what I've seen.

Perhaps there's a slim chance if the offending teenagers' attitudes are that they each are very regretful of their bad behavior and have sincerely committed to doing better, and if there's a way to monitor their attitudes and intentions to be sure that they don't change back to the old ways. Still, I doubt that it will succeed.

But if cooperation among parents can't happen or is unwise, my best advice almost without exception is to require a complete break with the wrong crowd.

4. Don't surrender to the in*timid*ation that goes this way:

*If we tell him he can't run around with so-and-so, then he will rebel and do it for sure. If we don't say anything, maybe he will quit on his own.*

You must do what is right and not compromise with what is wrong. Remember, those of us in our counseling agency have never seen anyone change who has kept his or her active contacts with the wrong crowd. Don't forget how deadly the consequences of today's wrongs can be. And remember the question raised earlier: Do you want to take your stand and have a crisis at this trench, or do you want to wait until the entanglements become more entrenched?

5. You absolutely have to be true to your own principles. As you work with these problems, you have to be true to your own principles because, after it's all over and destinies are plotted, you must still respect yourself in order to go on with your own life.

Besides, *your kids desperately need you to stay true to your moral principles.* Compromising confuses your kids. So long as you stay true, your kids will know where to return to; they will have roots.

But if you go soft on the principles you have held to all these years, they'll think that nothing is sacred anymore. They'll think, *Well! Mother and Dad really didn't believe what they taught all those years!* Then they'll mourn the loss without knowing why they've become depressed, and they'll feel as if they've lost a best friend.

If you are fair and reasonable Christian parents, your kids don't actually want you to compromise your moral and spiritual values—no matter how much pressure they put on you to do so. That's what their homing instincts are tuned to. They don't want their *roots* to rot! No root rot, please!

Reject the wrong, but never reject your children. Always be there for them. You won't keep them up while they are going down, but you will certainly help them up when they make a convincing commitment to going back up.

6. Maintain a happy and positive family atmosphere, as much as possible, providing a lot of fun opportunities so that giving up the wrong crowd is not surrendering to loneliness and boredom. A teenager who is faced with the choice of partying or hanging in with loneliness and boredom week after week will almost always drift back into partying with old friends.

7. Always give your teenagers opportunities to meet new people their age. Campus Life, youth camps, Christian rock concerts, rallies where several church groups come together, and the like are fertile ground for growing new relationships. Teenagers can more easily give up the wrong crowd if they find others from the right crowd that they like better.

"Nature abhors a vacuum," scientists say. You need to apply their discovery to teenagers. Kids can't/won't live in a vacuum that's void of friendships. They're not going to give up the wrong crowd and stay free of it very long unless they are able to fill the vacuum with the right crowd.

Counselors at our agency often pray that God will put the right individual in a young person's pathway. That individual can do more for a kid than counseling and can do it more rapidly. I'm amazed at this, actually. Sometimes in counseling we're doing everything we can to motivate a young person to change from a negative orientation to a positive one without much success. Then he or she meets someone from the right crowd and comes in next time casually saying, "I'm not into that stuff anymore."

We let out a deep sigh of relief and thank God for the witness of the positive peer group. Of course, the counseling then reinforces the wisdom of the child's new orientation. And I enjoy watching parents beam as they see the child beginning to agree with his or her upbringing.

CHAPTER **9**

# PERSEVERING IN YOUR LOVE

**Tower of Conviction 12: We will strive for cooperation, not "happiness."**

This conviction is important for at least three reasons. First, happiness is slippery. Once you find it, it's hard to hold onto it.

Second, happiness is usually an unrealistic goal. It's very hard to get everyone in the family to be happy at the same time. I'm sure you've had the experience of posing for a family portrait and trying to get everyone to look pleasant all at once. Someone usually isn't with the rest or at their best. If the goal is for everyone to stay happy, you are going to be disappointed and frustrated most of the time and feel that failure prevails.

Third, since constant happiness is not essential to successful familyhood, I would rather put the emphasis on what is essential—and that is cooperation. Cooperation is an achievable goal. In fact, if your children don't learn to cooperate in your home (even when they'd rather not), they haven't learned how to be successful in the real world. By requiring cooperation, you are being consistent with how your children will have to become in order to be successful in the real world. That's wonderful of you to do that for your children!

**_Achieving cooperation, not happiness, is your goal._**

Relax as cooperation is restored in your home, and be absolutely sure to offer your compliments and show your appreciation to individuals who are deserving.

Teenagers are supposed to flex their muscles of independence. It is quite normal for them to go through a stage of not liking you and being dissatisfied with what you are providing. This is a part of the normal process of young people elbowing their way into adulthood. Understanding this should help you relax a little.

Teenagers are people in transition . . .

from childhood to adulthood,
    from dependency to independency,
        from merely receiving to producing, too.

If they never got restless with being in the nest, they would never flex their muscles and build their own nests. They would be victims of retarded maturity, and you wouldn't want that.

Your kids don't have to like you or enjoy you at the moment, and they don't have to be "happy." They just have to cooperate.

## Tower of Conviction 13: We will not give up on our child.

Erecting this tower means you will hold to your stand that you will not keep your children up while they are going down, but you will stay determined to swing full force behind them if they teach you that they sincerely want to change from destructing to constructing, from degenerating to regenerating. You will always be there to help them go up. You will continue to courteously and compassionately invite them to go up.

In spite of how obnoxious they have been, you are the only ones who really care about them. And the big picture is *eternity*. You will definitely keep on trying to get your children in position to make heaven their home.

### Some of the worst-behaving young people have changed for the better.

And your young people can, too! Rejoice with me over some successes . . .

I called an industrial complex this week because I needed a favor. The male voice answering the phone said, "You can't guess who you're talking to." I couldn't. When he identified himself, I nearly shouted out loud! This man had been a passively but stubbornly defiant teenager I had worked with years before who would listen to me courteously and just keep on doing the same wrongs.

Now he has a good position with one of the nation's largest chemical complexes, and his supervisor told me that he is the best he has ever seen at his job at his age. And best of all, he has become a Christian.

Two nights ago my older son (now seventeen) and I stopped by a grocery store to get some milk and ice cream. In the parking lot, a woman in her late twenties came up to me and hugged me. Her hug was such a joy because of the healing she had experienced. When I first met her, she had been riding with a motorcycle gang and had gotten into all the wrong things they were getting into. I had helped her convert to a Christian lifestyle and to rebuild a measure of self-respect. That was ten years ago.

A fellow in his mid-twenties, who had served two terms in prison and whom I had met years ago in the county jail, came by my office last month. Today, he is working with his church's ministry to parolees, helping them to reenter the free world. He's been a consistent Christian for more than five years.

And don't forget the apostle Paul. He changed from commanding the murder of Christians to becoming the world's most celebrated e*vangel*ist. In addition, he wrote a considerable portion of the New Testament. You can read about the impact of his total change in Titus 3:3–8.

Think back. Tower of Conviction 3 states: Our child can change. Tower of Conviction 13 reinforces that with: We will not give up on our child.

This month I attended a countywide rally honoring the sanctity of life. I noticed a lovely woman in her early twenties who had turned her back on God and good during her high-school years. She ran around with the wrong crowd; she cursed her parents; her dad caught her in bed with a guy in her bedroom; she was a shoplifter and a compulsive liar.

Now she's married, has a child, and is leading the way spiritually within her family. She has truly discovered the sanctity of life.

This week I saw the mother of one of the "worst" teenagers I have ever met. He made it a "bad year" for many a teacher. He could have hung his nameplate on the principal's office door because he was there almost as much as the principal.

He was a regular at juvenile detention. Counselors began to feel that their time would be better invested with someone else. Actually, he had become an irritant to them, reminding them that their counseling didn't always help.

Rejoice everyone! Today he and his wife and daughter are a model Christian family and are active in their church. He is a decent, legal, cooperative, and productive American citizen.

*Your rebellious one may be the one you're closest to in his or her adult life.*

Parents and children who are suffering through terrible times of teenage rebellion have the potential of being the closest families of all. I've seen it happen many a time . . .

- because love is so thoroughly proven by parents.
- because adult children have learned through the road of hard knocks that their parents' values are right.
- because they have finally learned that their "friends" (for whom they traded their families) are afflicted with raw selfishness underneath their enticing wrappers.
- because adult children are driven back to their parents through their conscience, their realization of responsibility before God, their need to make things right, their appreciation for what their parents have done for them, and their need to harmonize their lives with their roots and be family again.

### Tower of Conviction 14: We will help our child have opportunities for spiritual conversion (a change of mind-set).

#### What is the real problem?

Think for a moment. What is your child doing? Perhaps he is lying to you. Or she is using God's name in vain or stealing. Maybe he is dishonoring you. Or perhaps she is sexually active. These are all sins against God. Your child is breaking the Ten Commandments! If he or she gets right with God, he or she will be more obedient toward you. So, in most cases, the problem is a spiritual one.

#### A mystery is solved.

That's one of the big reasons for failure. Many parents and counselors are trying to heal a spiritual problem as if it is something else. That's like trying to heal a broken bone by giving medication for pain relief. It won't work.

Many counselors diagnose sinful behavior as a mental problem. But it's a spiritual problem that can symptomize itself mentally and/or socially. The root cause of the problem is an improper mind-set, which is a spiritual problem.

Defiant and rebellious teenagers who show symptoms of sinful attitudes and behaviors need to *convert*. They need to change their mind-sets . . .

- from pursuing evil to pursuing good.
- from having everything in common with the wrong crowd to having nothing at all in common with the wrong crowd.
- from being self-indulgent to becoming others-minded.
- from being unmotivated to caring about their contribution to God and humankind.

And I've described much of what is meant by Christian *conversion*. I know of no other way for truly converting a mind-set than through *conversion*.

### Personal experience teaches this truth.

When I was having problems as a teenager, my family tried everything in the way of discipline. But none of it changed me. I changed when I had a very calm religious experience in an indoor camp meeting in the downtown Music Hall in Houston, Texas. I became loyal to Christ, and I forsook my wrong behaviors without further discipline from my parents. They were so-o-o relieved!

### Christ is the Head of the search and rescue team for saving wayward teenagers.

*To be saved* means to stop the downward spiral into oblivion by taking hold of Jesus Christ and hanging on for dear life. *To be born again* means to escape the slavery of temporary thrills (perishable) and embrace the freedom of eternal values (imperishable), again through Christ.

Uncivilized behavior changes when the pain to be endured isn't worth the pleasure received *or* when teenagers make a *commitment to Christ* and, thereby, have a change of mind-set (if the uncivilized behavior isn't actually caused by physical problems or mental illness).

God changes the heart, the mind-set, and that is precisely what these teens need. God helps individuals heal from the wounds of the past so that they can let go of excuses for doing wrong in the present, and that, also, is precisely what rebellious teens need.

Jesus said that He is the only way for *Salvag*ing people (*Salvat*ion). Since that is true, you are going to have to include Him in any attempt to rescue your children.

John the Baptist introduced Jesus by preaching, "Repent, for the kingdom of heaven [the kingdom of wellness] is at hand." In those words are the prescription for changing the mind-set and the offer to exchange the sinking party boat for God's life preserver: the Savior Himself.

### God is trying to preserve the lives of kids.

Let me illustrate what I mean. I was in juvenile jail one day speaking with seventeen detainees. I asked them to help me list all the things a kid could be put in jail for. They gave me a long list:

being truant
attacking a teacher
assaulting a parent
stealing
breaking and entering
committing rape
using an automobile without permission
using drugs
getting caught with drug paraphernalia
being a minor in possession of alcohol
driving while intoxicated
being intoxicated in public
shoplifting
writing hot checks
abusing credit card privileges

They seemed to enjoy being streetwise in front of one another.

With this long list of crimes on the chalkboard before them, I asked, "Which one of these does God want you to do?"

Silence. A very long silence. A boy finally muttered reluctantly, "None of 'em."

I replied with awe, "You mean you have to disobey God to get in jail!"

Then I asked, "What would happen if you gave your life to God and began to live like He wants you to?" No answer. I helped them out, "You would be free! Free of all this!"

Mary Magdalene of the New Testament is a good example of a sudden change in mind-set. She had been overcome and dominated by evil. But Jesus touched her life and changed her mind-set so completely that she was one of the last ones at His crucifixion, and she was the first one at the empty tomb to see the resurrected Christ.

### Synchronizing with Christ protects individuals from making grave mistakes.

When I was a chaplain in adult jail, a man came up to the bars and suddenly challenged me: "If you can prove there's a God, I'll accept Christ right here and now."

Always before I would have shrunk back from this challenge. But at the very moment he accosted me, I was inspired with an answer. I replied, "I can prove to you there is a God if you will help me." He agreed, being amused.

"Think back over your life," I said. "When you obeyed God, how was it? Were you more honest? More understanding? More responsible? A better son to your parents? A better husband to your wife? A better father to your children?"

He said, "Yep."

I asked, "When you ignored God, did you remain that way?"

He backed away from the bars of the cell, stretched out his arms, and exclaimed, "I'm here, ain't I!"

With one hand grasping the bars, I explained, "God loves you, and He is trying to protect you from all this. But He can't unless you give your life to Him and begin to synchronize your choices with what He wants for you."

*Present your children with opportunities to change their mind-sets spiritually.*

Christian *repentance* means three things: (1) breaking through denial and admitting to having been doing wrong; (2) asking for forgiveness for the wrongs and making restitution (restitution should be made when it will heal); and (3) turning away from the wrongs and becoming loyal to Christ instead. Sounds exactly like what misbehaving teenagers need to do, doesn't it?

What happens through Christian conversion is awesome. The theological terms are *regeneration, justification,* and *adoption.*

Your children will be changed from degenerating to regenerating through the new birth (see 2 Cor. 5:17; Rom. 6).

Their guilt will be resolved through being justified before God through Christ (see Rom. 5:1).

And they will be adopted out of the wrong crowd into the right crowd, God's family to be specific (see Eph. 2:19).

Help your children have opportunities for Christian conversion. This is best accomplished as a family since you certainly don't want your children to get the idea that you are doing this as a defensive maneuver, a manipulation to win your side of the argument. Attend church together, take in Christian concerts, participate in the summer camps, and help your church youth group to be attractive—interesting and exciting.

But if a child isn't open to hearing the Christian message, please don't bruise the fruit before it ripens by harassing your child about Christ. If you nag at a teenager about Christ or always quote the Bible to prove how "bad" he or she is, then Christ and the Bible may subconsciously become a source of irritation. The effect of nagging is this: To become committed to Christ, the child would have to fall in love with a source of irritation, give in, and let you win.

If you haven't been attending church, you can begin now by saying to your children . . .

*We've been putting pressure on you to do better, and now we have discovered a place where we need to do better ourselves. We haven't been attending church. We are going to begin to look for a church home for our family this Sunday.*

Expect a wayward child to be resistant to becoming a committed Christian because he or she will have to admit to doing wrong, give up old friends, be seen as a "loser" by those friends, and discipline sinful appetites that are now screaming to be satisfied. Please be patient.

Maybe you are not the one who should talk to your child about spiritual needs. Perhaps your pastor, a youth leader, a Sunday school teacher, a Christian counselor, a neighbor, or a relative would have a greater influence right now. Pray that God will put the right witness in your child's pathway.

### Tower of Conviction 15: We will continue to or begin to set good examples of self-control before our children.

***Are you out of control?***

Children learn much of what they know by being with you. If you are out of control, they almost always will absorb that tendency from you. I will mention only three areas where some parents have serious control problems.

First, they are dominated by abuses. Parents set poor examples of self-control when they drink excessively, smoke pot, do drugs, have affairs, throw tantrums, and the like. Such parents have actually programmed their children to live erratic lives.

If you see yourself here, you urgently need to begin to set good examples of self-control for your children. Values are caught, more easily than taught. Say something like . . .

> *You know that I have done wrong. You've watched me. I want to apologize for the pain I've caused you and the family. And now I am committing myself to do better, and I'd like us to do better together.*

Don't throw in the towel if your children reject your proposal to reform together on the buddy plan. You are obligated before God and humankind to become more responsible. But be encouraged as you improve; your children's roots have stopped decaying and have begun healing, and the children will be positively affected over a period of time. *I promise.*

Second, parents are out of control when they are abusive in their actions and reactions toward their children.

- Don't go off on verbal abuse tangents.
- Don't bully your children physically.
- Don't unload on the child's brothers and sisters about how lousy the "black sheep" is doing.
- Don't gossip about a child to the neighbors.
- Don't say "no" for no reason.
- Don't ridicule a child in front of friends.
- Don't tell a child that he or she is just like the most contemptible relative you have.

*Don't offend your child's personhood!* Insulting a child by calling him or her vulgar names or physically abusing a child destroys self-image and injures personhood. Such attacks are clearly out of order according to Jesus the Christ who preached, "Whoever says to his brother, 'Raca!' shall be in danger of the council. But whoever says, 'You fool!' shall be in danger of hell fire" (Matt. 5:22).

Brutally insulting a child has at least three horrible consequences. *Insults lower self-image.* A child can feel, "I am worse than a zero! My father (or mother) judges me to be a total failure! I can't ever please anyone!"

Your child has to have a good self-image to change for the better; don't cause it to become *the missing link*. Your child's good self-image is essential for believing that he or she can succeed in positive ways.

*Insults can turn your child away from trying to please you* and turn toward people who can be pleased more easily. That usually means involvement with the wrong crowd. Don't forget: Whoever values the child the most (and shows this valuing) usually gets the child.

Another awful consequence is that *the other children in the family may resent you,* too. If you bully a misbehaving child, your other children may give you problems as well. They may resent your bullying so much that they may become rebellious because of it. As I indicated earlier, I believe the drive for being treated justly ranks just above the intensity of the sex drive in young people.

While we're on this subject, you must realize that if you are being abusive to your children, it's possible that you are also indirectly being abusive to your grandchildren and great-grandchildren. Those who were abused as children usually pass the abuse along to their own youngsters (in spite of the vow they would never do that).

Instead, be an example of self-control and make the positive side of life attractive to your children by the way you model it before them.

Third, some parents have serious control problems in that they are mean "Christians" toward their children. The children of mean "Christians" are very hard to help because mean "Christians" tend to turn their children against being good by making good look unattractive.

Mean "good" people disappoint kids so thoroughly that they turn away from the positive side of life. They may consciously or subconsciously think: *If being a Christian is being like my rude and hateful parents, I am going to go the other way as far as I can go.* They seem to become mentally allergic to Christian guidance (unless other Christians in their environment have shown them a more accurate, tender, and graceful side of the faith).

Such parents do extra damage when they quote the Bible to justify their rudeness and relentless overreactions. Kids can grow up feeling, "I don't want to have anything to do with the Bible. That's the book that got me all those hassles."

Instead, show Christ to your kids in the way you live in front of them. Harmonize your attitudes and actions with Christ by preexamining them with the question "Will this heal?"

Incidentally, one of the most damaging situations I've dealt with was a case in which an abusive, alcoholic father converted to a mean "Christian" father. He went from being abusive to his child in the name of alcoholism to being abusive to him in the name of Christ. His son's emotions went sprong! I gave this young man an extra portion of my support and friendship, and I involved him in our family's activities to give him a fresh new view of Christian family life.

The following is a complete list of the towering convictions that fair and reasonable Christian parents need to hold to as they seek to help their misbehaving children.

# The fifteen towers of conviction for parents

*-Relief for Hurting Parents* © 1989 R. A. "Buddy" Scott • Allon Publishing

We are imagining that our home is a family fortress. Along the walls of this fortress, we are building towers of conviction to protect our children. They represent the basic beliefs we, as parents, are seeking to adopt for nurturing our children (see the fifteenth conviction). With them, we are getting ourselves in position for helping our children. Our convictions are...

1. We are breaking through denial and admitting that our child is, in fact, ignoring our guidance on purpose.

2. Our child does wrong because of his or her choices, not because of mental illness or physical problems. (Don't neglect to confirm this conviction with a thorough physical from a doctor.)

3. Our child can change, and it's our responsibility as parents to give him or her a decent opportunity to improve.

4. We have the right and are responsible before God to require our child to live as an American citizen in our home—to live a decent, legal, cooperative, and productive life.

5. We must raise our child consistent with how he or she will have to become to be successful in the real world. These catchy concepts will help us be consistent (applied matter-of-factly, without a hateful attitude):

   (a) If you are rude to the suppliers, you shouldn't expect new supplies.

   (b) If you don't do your part in the family, you don't get family privileges.

   (c) If you mess it up, you'll clean it up.

   (d) If you abuse it, you'll lose it.

   (e) If you waste it, you'll replace it.

   (f) If you want more than necessary, you'll pay the extra.

6. We refuse to be conned by our child.

7. We will cause our child's tools of in*timid*ation and manipulation to become useless.

8. We will be sure the discipline we choose to use is a natural consequence of the offense.

9. We are *responders*, and our child is the *teacher*. We will *respond* fairly to what our child *teaches* us.

10. We will allow our child to experience the pain of his or her own wrong choices.

11. We will see the wrong crowd as family enemy #1.

12. We will strive for cooperation, not "happiness."

13. We will not give up on our child.

14. We will help our child have opportunities for spiritual conversion (a change of mind-set).

15. We will continue to or begin to set good examples of self-control before our children by living in harmony with the seven commandments for developing a proper posture (role model) as parents. The first commandment is: *"Thou shalt monitor your attitudes and actions toward your children with the Good Shepherd by always asking, 'Will this heal?'"* (See chapter 2 for other commandments.)

CHAPTER **10**

# DECIDING HOW TO DISCIPLINE YOUR CHILD

Y ou've reconsidered your parental posture and you've taken on some new
convictions, but how do you actually apply all this to misbehavior? This
chapter provides you with a form, a tool, to use to develop these new patterns
of thinking and reacting. Again, I request that you wait to use this tool until
you have read and understood the remainder of this book.

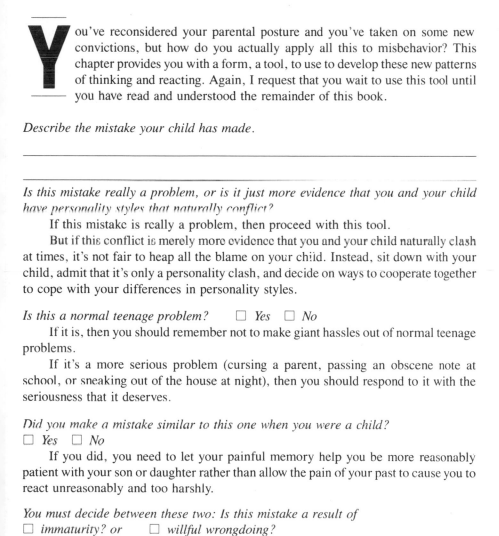

*Describe the mistake your child has made.*

_____

_____

*Is this mistake really a problem, or is it just more evidence that you and your child
have personality styles that naturally conflict?*

If this mistake is really a problem, then proceed with this tool.

But if this conflict is merely more evidence that you and your child naturally clash
at times, it's not fair to heap all the blame on your child. Instead, sit down with your
child, admit that it's only a personality clash, and decide on ways to cooperate together
to cope with your differences in personality styles.

*Is this a normal teenage problem?* ☐ *Yes* ☐ *No*

If it is, then you should remember not to make giant hassles out of normal teenage
problems.

If it's a more serious problem (cursing a parent, passing an obscene note at
school, or sneaking out of the house at night), then you should respond to it with the
seriousness that it deserves.

*Did you make a mistake similar to this one when you were a child?*
☐ *Yes* ☐ *No*

If you did, you need to let your painful memory help you be more reasonably
patient with your son or daughter rather than allow the pain of your past to cause you to
react unreasonably and too harshly.

*You must decide between these two: Is this mistake a result of*
☐ *immaturity? or* ☐ *willful wrongdoing?*

Your decision here will decide how you will handle your child's mistake. If it was immaturity, then you will gently teach and guide.

If it was willful wrongdoing, you will continue using this tool for deciding how you will respond with discipline.

### Follow these steps to decide to respond with discipline to your child's willful wrongdoing . . .

1. If at all possible, adopt a united front with your spouse. Use this form for discussing the offense and deciding how to discipline together.

2. Side up with the Good Shepherd, the Good Supervisor of parents, through prayer. Prayer is your opportunity to tune your mind and heart to the mind and heart of Christ before you begin making your decisions. This companionship will help you give your child a decent opportunity and a re*assur*ing and supportive atmosphere for improving.

3. Choose a posture. Place a check mark beside the posture you choose to have. Place an X beside the postures you choose not to have.
   - ☐ Cowpunching parent
   - ☐ Raging parent
   - ☐ Intoxicated parent
   - ☐ Vengeful parent
   - ☐ Shepherding parent
   - ☐ Gossiping parent
   - ☐ Attacking parent
   - ☐ Punishing parent

   ☐ _____

4. Choose an attitude. Your attitude *is* a matter of choice. Place a check mark beside the mind-set you choose to have. Place an X beside the mind-sets you choose not to have.
   - ☐ A mind-set to make him or her feel bad
   - ☐ A mind-set to cut him or her down to size
   - ☐ A mind-set to discipline, heal, forgive, and reconcile
   - ☐ A mind-set to get back at him or her
   - ☐ A mind-set to convince him or her of what a despicable person he or she has become

   ☐ _____

5. Describe how the child's offense is unhealthy to himself or herself, to the family, or to the community:

   _____

   _____

6. What did the misbehavior or unkind attitude *teach* you about your child?

_____

_____

7. What natural consequences should follow?

_____

_____

8. Based on the natural consequences and what your child has taught you about himself or herself (the sixth and seventh steps above), decide how you will respond:

_____

Be careful to decide on a realistic response so that you won't have to back down later and seem inconsistent. Also, kindly allow your child to experience the pain of his or her own wrong choices without its looking like you arranged the pain. If a child thinks the pain is coming from you instead of from the wrong, he will transfer the anger from what he has done to himself to what *you* are doing to him, and he will be so preoccupied with anger toward you that he will miss the lesson the pain has to teach. For example, if your son stole a bike from a neighbor, it would be better for the neighbor to get the police involved on his own (a natural consequence) than for you to openly suggest that the police be called (an engineered consequence). But some kids who do wrong are so far into denial that they won't take the blame for anything. Just do your best.

9. Check your response with the question "Will this heal?" Change it if it doesn't pass this vital test.

10. Does this response issue a negative challenge? If you're thinking of saying, "Do it again and see if I don't kick your rear out of the house!" you're about to issue a negative challenge. Negative challenges won't pass the test of "Will this heal?"

11. Meditate on these questions: How can I present my response to my child without projecting defensiveness and making it easier for him or her to reflect defensiveness? How can I project a win-win atmosphere?

_____

_____

12. Courteously and compassionately, but with conviction, present your response to your child using an outline similar to this one:

A. Say something like, *As we begin our talk, we want you to know that we love you, and we are in touch with your good qualities. We do not see you as a mistake just because you have made a miss-take. We believe that you have the potential to get things together better, and we think you'll be just fine in the near future.*

B.  Say, *We want to tell you how we understand what has happened. . . .*
    After you finish your explanation, ask, *Do you have anything to say that will help us understand more clearly?*
    Then listen. Take time to hear. Teenagers need to be heard. If you don't take time to hear them, they won't feel that they were given a fair hearing, and they will be more resistant to discipline. If no new information is introduced that helps you understand that the offense wasn't as you first assumed, then proceed.

C.  Say something like, *But since you have chosen to teach us* _____

    _____

    *You have chosen for us to respond by*

    _____

D.  Say, *Here's how you can teach us to trust you again in that area:*

    _____

E.  Say, *Here are the positive rewards for succeeding in reteaching trust:*

    _____

F.  Be assuring, *We will be by your side helping you succeed because we love you and value you.*

G.  Listen. Always remain available to hear and to talk.

H.  Be supportive while your child is going through the uncomfortable consequences. Choose the mood that will give your child a *decent atmosphere* in which to do better. Place a check mark beside the mood you choose to have. Place an X beside the moods you choose not to have.

    ☐ Parent who keeps reminding the child of the misbehavior: "You could be going with them if you hadn't blown it."

    ☐ Parent who finds joy in another person's suffering: "Isn't grounding fun? You seem to be having such a good time! We ought to do this more often!"

    ☐ Parent who twists the knife: "With every dish you wash, remember what a disgusting little creep you've been."

    ☐ Parent who projects failure: "You had better get used to this 'cause I know you, and you're just gonna mess up again! You always do!"

    ☐ Parent who is supportive of the child during discipline: "This will be over soon, and everything will be all right again. I know we can make it through this."

    ☐ Parent who takes unfair punches: "Sure you [another child] can use the car. Your brother's had his wings clipped, and he won't be needing it."

    ☐ Parent who hits someone who is already down: "I can't find my watch! Did you steal that, too?"

    ☐ Parent who harasses: "Get in there and cook supper! You need the practice. At the rate you're going, you'll have your own family to cook for by the time you graduate from high school. . . . Graduate? Did I say graduate? Ha! That's a laugh!''

☐ Parent who broadcasts humiliation: "Yes, Mom, your grandson's up to his old capers. He never learns. This time he skipped school and got drunk."

13. Carry through consistently. Be consistent, and your son or daughter will learn what he or she can depend on.

14. Encourage your child while he or she is on the frustrating journey back to good standing. Be complimentary and affirming of your child at each and every opportunity.

15. As a family-style family, plan some family fun while your child is living with the uncomfortable natural consequences of his or her mistake.

16. Use the intensive care instruments in the shepherd's tower to monitor your son's or daughter's emotional, social, and spiritual health during this stress (and afterward). I'll give you these instruments and show you how to use them in later chapters.

17. Find emotional support for the stand you have taken with your child. Taking a firm stand can be especially difficult for easygoing parents who find it hard to watch their child suffer inconveniences. *Relief for Hurting Parents*, and the people who read it and agree with it, can give you that support. At the other extreme, parents who are very strict may need to control themselves from being harsher than is constructive. You'll need support to reach a more balanced position. Again, this book, and the people who read it and agree with it, can give you that support. Support groups for parents are discussed in chapter 24.

# ──── PART III ────
# Towers of Strength

To maintain your towering convictions and your good posture, your family fortress is going to need great strength. Therefore, the next seven chapters will help you erect towers of strength. One will stand at each corner of your fortress walls, two at the front gate and one within the courtyard. These towers are tall and will stand above your towers of conviction. They will keep you strong so that you can hang in there with your convictions and be consistent in doing so. Remember, *consistency* is one of the secrets of winning with your children.

Your objective is to build your towers of strength as strong as possible so that you can gain maximum strength for energizing your convictions. As you read through this portion of the book, you will find that you are very strong in some areas but you need to strengthen other areas.

Strengthening your weak towers is a way to make progress, no matter what else is going on around you. Be especially sure to use the time between crises to strengthen your weak towers. You may find a tower that you can't seem to erect very well; if that is the case, then your opportunity is to build your other towers stronger to compensate for the weakness. ■

CHAPTER **11**

# DIVINE COMPANIONSHIP

### Tower of Strength 1—the Creator's tower:
### Our child is God's child, too.

Christian or not, whether you intended to or not, when you had your child, you joined with God in creation. *You created with the Creator!* Your child has three parents—a mother, a father, and a heavenly Father (by creation, if not by redemption). The three of you, together, created the precious package that was delivered into your arms on the day of your child's birth.

The problems you are now having with this child are God's problems as well. He's been in on this from the very beginning. You don't have to face these problems alone. God cares even more than you do, and He shares the burden with you of turning your child away from making self-destructive choices. All His resources are your resources for helping your child and for meeting your own needs.

Let's consider several reasons why you need the Christian touch.

### If your child has a problem on the same level of seriousness as a terminal illness, then you will need divine help.

Kids who have thrown their morals to the wind, who have begun to walk over their parents unmercifully, and who have become lawless are in grave danger: They are left unprotected by the supervision of their parents, the laws of their land, and the guidance system of their God. Their dangers could be of terminal significance.

Such dangers could include being maimed or killed in a car wreck by an intoxicated driver, becoming mentally ill due to bad drugs or getting knocked off by a nervous drug dealer, being used and abused while passed out, getting a girl pregnant or a girl becoming pregnant, living with the nagging memory of an abortion, contracting a deadly disease, enduring the risks of street life, or simply losing the desire to amount to anything.

I see this last danger happening more than the rest. As school dropouts who feel too far behind to try, young people lock themselves into labor pools—jobs that look different from slavery but actually aren't that much different.

Everyone needs God on his or her side when battling against a potentially terminal problem.

### Degenerative rebellion coupled with the wrong crowd can be as serious a problem as alcoholism.

Actually, degenerative rebellion is similar to alcoholism in the way it expresses itself and in its outcome. I'm not calling your child an alcoholic; I'm only saying that rebellion, when it is unrelenting and deeply rooted in the wrong crowd, is similar to addiction in its level of seriousness and in what is needed to break free of it.

□ *Unrelenting rebellion has a lot in common with alcoholism.*

More specifically, notice how they compare with each other . . .

Your child goes off with the wrong crowd like many alcoholics go off to drink.

You stay home and worry like the spouse of an alcoholic.

The teenager ignores the family to enjoy being with the wrong crowd, as do some alcoholics.

The teenager will go against family members and trade them off for the wrong crowd like the alcoholic will for a bottle.

There are hangovers in both cases: The alcoholic hangs over from the residual effect of the drug and second thoughts; the teenager hangs over from alcohol, drugs, guilt, or bad experiences with peers. (That's when he or she is most frustrated and most easily provoked. Proceed with caution.)

The alcoholic lies to get to drink, and the teenager lies to get to be with the wrong crowd.

The alcoholic sometimes sneaks around, and a wayward teenager does, too.

The alcoholic says that he or she doesn't have a problem and if everybody would just mind his own business, everything would be okay; that sounds like the comment of a rebellious teenager.

The idea that counseling is needed makes most alcoholics mad, and most rebellious teenagers respond the same way.

The alcoholic sometimes promises that things are going to get better, and a teenager makes empty promises as well. The alcoholic pumps up hope and pops it with another ruthless disappointment; a misbehaving teenager does the same thing.

I could go on, but do you see what I mean?

The purpose of this comparison is to illustrate both the seriousness and the nature of the problem that you are dealing with. You must realize that you need the resources of God to help you and your child.

The giant difference between the two is that unrelenting rebellion has no actual physical addiction like alcohol or certain drugs do. Chemically addicted bodies crave alcohol or drugs, but rebellious teenagers do not have a physical addiction to rebellion. They will not have to go to a meeting like Alcoholics Anonymous every week for the rest of their lives just to stay free of rebellion like many alcoholics choose to do just to stay free of alcohol (unless the teenagers have become chemically addicted to something while they were with the wrong crowd).

But they may have become mentally dependent on the wrong crowd. They may suffer withdrawals due to their loneliness for the comradeship they developed with their "friends" in that crowd (they become very close because they are harboring secret sins and secret plans together), and they may also miss the pleasures they enjoyed together.

Sometimes I wonder, though, which is stronger: physical addiction or mental dependency? At times in my counseling with teenagers involved in underage drinking or moderate drug abuse, I believed them to be more "addicted" to the wrong crowd than to the chemicals they were using.

Things get super complicated and perplexing when teenagers actually are physically addicted to drugs or alcohol. Such teenagers have compound, complex problems: They are physically addicted to chemicals and mentally and socially dependent on the wrong crowd. Their root problem may have gradually shifted from rebellion to chemical addiction; however, the symptoms will often continue to be read as merely indicative of rebellion.

☐ *The only rehabilitation efforts that are being successful with the chemically addicted have a religious base.*

I remember going to a major convention on alcohol and drug rehabilitation, and I was from a county that at that time had no recovery units for chemical abusers. I felt somewhat inferior.

Program directors of large hospitals were in attendance. One of them asked me, "What do you have for alcoholics in your county?"

I answered sheepishly, "All we have is AA."

Picking up on my hesitant manner, he became animated and said, "All you have is AA! That's all we use in our giant hospitals!"

It's true. Some medications are useful in detoxification, but the actual healing comes through the religious principles infused within the twelve steps of Alcoholics Anonymous.

If you examine the twelve steps closely, you will find that they are the steps of Christian conversion laid out in a process. At the beginning, individuals admit that they can't handle life on their own and they need a Higher Power, then there are the moral inventory, repentance, restitution, growth, prayer and, at the end, there is the twelfth-step call to help other alcoholics (witnessing).

Think about rehabilitation and salvation. Rehabilitation involves rehabilitating a debilitated person. Salvation involves *salva*ging a person who is perishing. These terms are actually synonyms if rehabilitation is taken far enough to include eternal wellness.

### You need the resources of God to cleanse the wounds inflicted on your marriage.

You and your spouse need to clean your wounds caused by the distresses of dealing with your troubled child. If you don't, they will get infected, and your marriage will begin to deteriorate. One or both of you may gradually begin to fall out of love, grudge by grudge.

Nearly all marriages become battered in the battlefield of having severe problems with children. Those that fail usually fail because of the grudges that have built up. They pile up within the family fortress, sour, and foul the oneness of marriage, causing emotional withdrawal and separation.

Removing the grudge garbage from the family fortress is everyone's chore. You'll lose family members if you allow your house to become a warehouse for garbage and begin to stockpile grudges. If someone else won't take out the garbage, then you're still responsible to deal with your own.

For the marriage to survive in its best form, each marriage partner must continually clean out the grudge pile and call off the grudge parades. Communication lines can be reestablished when one gently takes the initiative to introduce forgiveness into the conversation:

> *I love you. I respect you. And I want you to forgive me where you feel I've done you wrong. And I do forgive you where you've hurt my feelings. Our marriage is more important to both of us than harboring resentments. Let's refuse to let evil come between us and pry us apart. Let's talk. . . .*

A few weeks ago, a husband told me about how he approached his wife when she became hurt, angry, and emotionally removed from him. He said, "Sweetheart, I don't know why you're upset, but I do know that I love you so much that I'll want to make it better if you'll tell me what it is."

Tower of Conviction 15 was about self-control: We will continue to or begin to set good examples of self-control before our children. If grudges aren't controlled and are allowed to pile up, they will finally get so high and overshadowing that they can appear to be sufficient evidence that the marriage can't work and "proof" that you "deserve" a divorce. So one spouse says (or both say), "I've had it! I'm getting out of this mess! Look at this pile of garbage (list of grudges)! I'd be crazy to keep putting up with this!"

Rotting grudge piles between spouses are the greatest reason for divorce in America today. God has the only way of cleaning out grudge piles. And that is *forgiveness!*

Jesus died to forgive sins and clear out grudges, and He offers to share His forgiving nature with us. Jesus taught us to pray, "Forgive us our trespasses, as we forgive those who trespass against us." God forgives us *as* we forgive others—a vital process for maintaining health and well-being.

Christ relieves you of harbored bitterness as you make yourself a part of His symphony of forgiveness through the Lord's Prayer. He will help you clean out your evidence (your grudge pile) that you jolly-well have plenty of reasons (grudges) to stay mad.

And by means of the resources of God, you will have saved your marriage. You will have invited the Great Physician to make a house call at your family fortress. He comes to clean wounds, to remove guilt, and to reestablish communication and unity—to help you and yours take out the garbage from your lives and from your home. Now you can heal, but don't forget to allow yourselves some time to heal.

### You must have the spiritual maturity necessary for completely forgiving your child.

Just as forgiveness clears away the pile of grudges that may have built up between you and your spouse, it is also vital to remove the pile of grudges that may have built up between you and your child. A pile of grudges festering between the two of you means that you will become alienated from each other.

Deep-cleansing forgiveness removes the grudges and reopens your arms and your heart to your child, and it is essential to the rescue, recovery, and reconciliation process for which you are hoping and praying. With your pile of grudges gone, you are halfway there. When your child removes his or hers, the barriers will be gone, and you can host a family reunion.

But someone might ask, "How do you forgive someone when you don't feel like it and when he or she hasn't even apologized?" I'd like to answer that question with a story . . .

Let's imagine that your child rebelled against you, left home, and journeyed to a distant city beside the sea to get away from you and continue living his defiant lifestyle. You get your yacht and tie a huge barge to the back of it with a very strong rope. Then you take all your grudges out of your heart—the ones you've been stockpiling and warehousing—and pile them on your barge.

And off you motor in your yacht dragging your garbage barge. You're headed toward your child's seaside city to tell him off, to show your garbage collection to him, and to make him realize what an ungrateful little wretch he has been.

The longer you pull your garbage barge, the more it begins to stink. You notice that it has begun to affect you inside as you catch yourself secretly rehearsing how you will tell him off. You notice that your whole family is suffering from the anger and resentments you have piled up. You've even begun to notice physical symptoms of the unsanitary burdens.

You set your brow and scream, "But I don't feel like cutting my barge loose! Look at that pile of garbage! I deserve to be mad! I'm going to pull this barge up to my kid and throw him in his own garbage! He's going to know how badly he's hurt me!"

The pull is long and hard. You have time to think. There's a bad storm brewing. The diesels groan. You're running low on fuel. Your frustration factor is at an all-time high. The stench is getting worse. Your family is hurting. Suddenly, the truth dawns: "I had better get rid of this garbage, or it's going to get rid of us!"

You ask yourself, "What do I really want, anyway? Do I want to prove how 'bad' my son is, or do I want him rescued and safe?"

You answer your own question: "I want him back." Then you wonder: "Well, what good is this garbage barge?" And it hits you: "Will this thing heal? Jesus wouldn't be pulling a garbage barge behind Him to show someone how contemptible he is. The Bible says that He came to us not to condemn us but to redeem us."

You come to a conclusion: "This grudge parade is sinful, and no matter how much I want my son to feel the pain that he's caused me, I must exert self-control and go by what's right before God and humankind."

You remember a principle you've been trying to live by: Thou shalt discipline rather than punish. (Be a shepherd, not a cow puncher.) You're amazed at what anger can do. You decide to abort your spiteful mission.

You walk to the back of your yacht with knife in hand. You stare at the garbage on your barge. You're still hurt, and you don't feel like letting go of your grudges. But Christians don't go by feelings; they go by wisdom. Putting wisdom over feelings, you reach down and cut yourself free. The barge drifts to a stop, and you leave it behind. It vanishes in the golden triangle of God's mercy, grace, and forgiveness. You're no longer a garbage collector.

Your yacht looks attractive, without the garbage barge, as you motor into port. The barge is out of sight but not out of mind. You remember it, but you know you've cut it loose. You're tempted to miss it, but you remind yourself: "I chose to abandon it, it's gone, and I am free of the consequences of hauling garbage."

You finally understand that to forgive and forget literally means to forgive and forsake. You won't forget the barge, but neither will you let it become a drag to you again.

You see your son and you simply say . . .

*We came to seek and to save that which we've lost. We are here to tell you that we love you, and that we want to help you rise again. We'd love to help you up. We're not assisting you now because we can't bring ourselves to help you hurt yourself. But we are praying that we will get to help you rise again. We just want you to know that our arms are still open to you.*

You return to your yacht for a peaceful cruise home. For the first time you notice the beauty of the light blue skies, the fluffy white clouds, the deep blue water, and the air's clean smell because you feel so much better. You know you've done what's right, you know you've done your best, you know you've tuned your life to God's symphony of forgiveness, and you are now flowing within the promises of God. You decide to rename your yacht. You'll have *Easter* painted on its bow in memory of your resurrection from your grudges.

Parents, please cut loose your garbage barge and return to the land of the living. Pray the Lord's Prayer and share in the forgiving nature of Christ. God is near you; you are building the Creator's tower.

There are other people you need to forgive or else grudges will form an imposing barrier between you and them.

Your other children may have cut you deeply, saying something like: "You're so unfair! No wonder Sissy can't stand you!"

And perhaps someone in the PTA said: "I'm so sorry to hear about how much trouble you're having with your daughter. Of course, I can't understand what you're going through since we haven't had any trouble with our four."

Or maybe your sister-in-law said something like this: "Have you thought of taking a course in parenting?"

Or perhaps one of your parents or your spouse's parents made a passing remark: "I knew all along that you were going to have trouble with that one. I just never would come out and say anything."

Parents, for *good*ness sakes, keep on removing the garbage and refusing the refuse.

### You may need to be forgiven.

You need guilt relief if you are like most hurting parents. You may be guilt-ridden by what you have done wrong in relation to your children and by what you could have done but failed to do. You may be guilt-ridden by how you've treated your spouse or your other children during these bad times. You may be guilt-ridden because you are harboring secret sins and your child's wrongdoing reminds you that you are a guilty disciplinarian.

Through your asking God for His forgiveness, Jesus relieves you of your guilt. "What if I've asked forgiveness but still feel guilty?" you might ask. Then you need to rename those uncomfortable feelings. Rename them regret because that's all they are. Those residual bad feelings are feelings of regret, and they will always be there because you will always feel bad that you did something wrong.

Understand that your ill feelings could get worse as you become a stronger Christian. The better you get as a person, the worse your past mistakes will look, and you will become even more ashamed of your sin. The whiter your life becomes, the uglier the stain of the past looks in relation to it. The awful feelings you feel *can't be real guilt* if God has forgiven you because you are no longer guilty; you are forgiven.

So being forgiven turns your guilt into mere regret and relieves you of the painful awkwardness of being out of sync with your Creator. (Plus, as one pastor preached, "Jesus forgives you to give you your self-respect back," and that's a big plus!)

God's symphony of forgiveness provides for double relief: Receive forgiveness and be forgiving. By being forgiven, you are relieved of guilt. By being forgiving, you are relieved of grudges.

### You need to have your tanks of love refilled.

We don't normally think of love as something that can be used up, but I think there is a sense in which it can. You can feel drained.

In times like these, you need in-flight refueling, and God is the supernatural resource for love. You have to be well-supplied with His love to keep on loving someone who is acting unlovable.

When you feel drained, you need to find a quiet place and get alone with God and take on more of His love. Or you need to have a talk with one of His inspiring Christians and transfer some of that person's love to you. Or you need to attend one of His awe-inspiring spiritual events.

**You need the support of your church when you are going through great trials and tribulations.**

Church members who are understanding can support you with friendship, love, prayers, phone calls, and visits. They can provide companionship for doing the difficult things, such as attending a court hearing. They can provide inspiration for hanging in there when battle fatigue sets in. And your church may have an opportunity to minister to your teenager.

Churches need to wake up to their mission to the hard-to-love teenagers,

> to those who need *salvaging* the most,
>> to those who need rehabilitation,
>>> to those who need to be born again,
>>>> to those who need to be *resurrected!*

Rehabilitation and salvation are almost the same, except that salvation is eternal. Why have so many of our churches backed away and left the task of rescuing the perishing to secular groups? Jesus loved the "unlovable," and He still does. Do your church members?

Perhaps a blessing that will come out of your trauma is that your needs will reawaken your church to its commission to seek the lost and rescue the perishing. Neglecting the lost because it's tough to work with them leaves them lost; the perishing are rarely redeemed unless someone is reaching for them.

**You must come up with some new reasons to keep life worthwhile and some ways to keep the bully named depression and his partner despondency shoved away.**

If yours hasn't been a religious family, your whole reason for living has most probably been to succeed in your career, to provide a nice nest, and to raise quality kids. If the kids fall out from under you, you can think, *I've given my whole life to raising a family. . . . I've turned over every paycheck (keeping almost nothing for myself). . . . I've sacrificed the things I wanted to do. . . . I've washed countless dishes and laundered countless clothes . . . and made trips without number . . . and none of it has counted! What I gave my whole measure of youth to is slipping through my fingers! What's life all about anyway?*

Choose one: Better *or* bitter?

Once an abused parent asked, "Do you believe I will ever smile again?"

I enthusiastically responded, "Yes, I'm sure you will. You will be happy again if you will make a commitment to get better instead of bitter."

She didn't see how it could happen, but in time it did.

Your problems are calling upon you to choose between the high road and the low road, to take the better route or the bitter route.

You can choose bitterness by focusing on how awful your life has become, by parading reruns of your grudges through your mind. But with God's help, you can choose the better route and have a promising future to look forward to.

☐ *Choosing to get better synchronizes you with God's favorite creative act.*

To choose better, you need to put yourself into a reassessment process. You may think that's asking too much of you right now, but try to be thankful that you are being called upon to take a good look at everything in your life. It's a sad truth, but it seems that only the traumas of life shake us loose from our comfortable positions and give us opportunities to grow. Don't waste your suffering. Grow!

Growth is often a wonderful by-product of suffering. I would not be as understanding today if my life hadn't been shattered in the yesterdays. Even my sins and mistakes have made me more understanding and empathetic. James has something positive to say on this subject:

> My brethren, count it all joy when you fall into various trials, knowing that the testing of your faith produces patience. But let patience have its perfect work, that you may be perfect and complete, lacking nothing. If any of you lacks wisdom, let him ask of God, who gives to all liberally and without reproach, and it will be given to him. (James 1:2-5)

Choosing to get better rather than bitter synchronizes you with God's favorite creative act, which is bringing good out of bad. *He loves to make Easter happen again and again!*

The same applies to your teenager. If he or she will become loyal to Christ, the Resurrector, He will bring *Easter* to your child's life and create good out of the bad. Jesus is *the Transformer!*

If your family hasn't been religious, the greatest benefit that could blossom out of your earthly suffering is to become a Christian family. God wants you, His prodigal family, in the same way that you want your prodigal son or daughter.

*To choose better instead of bitter, reexamine your present priorities!*

- What is truly important?
- What can you give your life to that will be lasting?
- What is of eternal significance?

Fortunately for you, a king went through the similar mental anguish, and he wrote a book about it. You can read about his struggle and his conclusions in the biblical book of Ecclesiastes.

Also, I would suggest you meet with a minister and open up to him. Say, "I have been going through thus and so, and I would like you to help me reexamine my priorities." Ministers are great at helping in that way.

*Get in touch with life after life.* Almost nothing earthly—limited to this time and space—can keep life worth living. You have to break the mortal barrier to come up with sufficient worthwhileness—life above and beyond this disappointing world— immortality.

*Develop new interests.* You need to do this although you are not in the mood, and you may have to make yourself get started. Good feelings will come later, I promise.

Begin your journey with God. (Now is a good time to put Christ at the center of your family.)

Become active in church.

In addition . . .

- take that college course you always wanted to take.
- buy the computer equipment you've been wanting.
- go on the cross-country ski trek you've been dreaming of.
- volunteer to work in a service organization.
- destine to enjoy life in spite of your troubling and troubled child.

For the sake of your mental health, you need to find some fulfillment for yourself other than child rearing. A by-product will be that your "problem" child will have less control over making you miserable. As you become happier, you will be able to deal with your teenager with fewer feelings of desperation.

One effective posture parents assume is to kindly and sincerely speak to the child this way . . .

*Our family is returning to being happy again. We love you, and if necessary, we'll pause awhile to talk to police or juvenile probation officers. But afterward, we will continue to enjoy our interests.*

These parents have matter-of-factly, but without projecting rejection, said to the misbehaving teenager . . .

*We don't want you to mess up your life, and because we love you, we'll always be willing to help you stop doing that. But we aren't going to be miserable with you. Life is too good for that; there is too much to enjoy to destroy ourselves hating the way things are.*

Earlier, I mentioned being careful not to impose superguilt on a teenager. Superguilt (i.e., deep-seated ill feelings over nearly destroying parents in one way or another) can lock a child into staying on the run to avoid having to face the damage he or she has done. So, *you had better get better!* If you don't—if you go under with bitterness and become invalid—you are in danger of imposing superguilt on your teenager.

☐ *You may want to seek personal counseling.*

It's very hard to go against your emotional tide, and you may need some help with it. Feel free to reach for that help.

There's no need to feel badly because you haven't been handling the situation well enough on your own. People are supposed to help one another along in life. *We are community. Counseling is communing.* No counselor will feel like you're a weak person for wanting to get better rather than bitter. He or she will only want to help.

*God will resurrect good out of your bad by using you
to help other hurting parents.*

No one can understand hurting parents like those who have been through it. In the field of psychology, it's a known fact that no one can help like someone who's been there.

Abused parents who have the courage to make it in spite of their problems can one day be the saving factor for other parents beginning to go through the same thing. God will be able to use you in wonderful new ways, giving you opportunities of ministry that you weren't sensitive enough to do prior to your family problems. Wade on through! Someone is going to need you!

*Suffering, when combined with a Christian commitment,
can help you become wiser.*

Having suffered as you have as abused parents, the secrets of life can open up for you as never before, provided you let these pressures press you toward God. The Bible, for example, will have messages for you that you would have missed had you not experienced your problems. You'll find new freshness throughout the Bible; read, enjoy, flex, and get stronger.

But for *good*ness sake *don't read the Bible to harass yourself with condemnation.* That's an awful thing to do to yourself. Jesus said, "For God did not send His Son into the world to condemn the world, but that the world through Him might be saved. He who believes in Him *is not condemned*" (John 3:17–18, emphasis added).

Instead of going on guilt trips as you read, look for encouragement and direction. Suffering can make the Bible speak to you as it never has before. For example, you'll see the story of the prodigal son in a fresh, new way (I'll review that story in chapter 18.)

☐ *Reconsider a couple of biblical stories.*

How about the story of Samson? When Delilah cut his hair, she sheared away his strength. When your child got into the wrong crowd, they "peered" away her strength (family loyalty, a peaceful conscience, unearthed appetites, and positive friendships). As my friend and fellow youth counselor Dave Talbott observed: Samson got it through "shear" pressure, and kids get it through peer pressure.

The story of Adam and Eve in the Garden of Eden will also take on new dimensions for you now. Consider this: Everyone has a tree like the forbidden one in the Garden of Eden.

Adam and Eve had the whole world to enjoy, but the fruit of one tree was guaranteed to be destructive to them. I believe each of us is in a similar situation. Although we have the whole world to enjoy, we have a tendency toward a lethal sin that could deceptively drag us to our deaths if we choose to partake of it. Each of us has a poison tree in the garden. I know this is true from listening to people's secrets and from knowing my own.

It's helpful and sobering to imagine a tree with our particular potential killer growing on it and God saying to us what He said to Adam: "Of the tree . . . you shall not eat, for in the day that you eat of it you shall surely die" (Gen. 2:17).

Your teenager's lethal tendency could be the wrong crowd, drugs, alcohol, sexual obsessions, kleptomania, lack of motivation, gossip, or several other possibilities. Help him understand about the poison tree in the garden of his world.

The *lethal tendency* is sometimes easy to identify. The teenager who drinks a few times and becomes a compulsive drinker has found his or her lethal tendency. The kid who lies for no reason has found his or hers. The young person who is so rebellious that he or she trades everything for a drug-dealing dropout has found his or hers. And there can be more than one lethal tendency.

☐ *To die is to digress.*

Help your teenager to see *die* as "digress." The Hebrew usage of the word *die* in Genesis means "dying, you shall die." It's a process of dying that is set in motion but *can be interrupted*.

The New Testament counterpart to God's warning to Adam and Eve is for you and me and our children. It is James 1:15: "Then, when desire has conceived, it gives birth to sin; and sin, when it is full-grown, brings forth death." Don't let sin get full-grown! Interrupt it! *You must short-circuit sin!*

☐ *Nothing is sacred to the pleasure chaser.*

Adam and Eve didn't set out to hurt God; they set out to *enjoy*. But God got hurt in the process.

The same holds true for parents. Rebellious teenagers aren't usually out to hurt you; they are out to *enjoy*. You get hurt in the process. They don't want to hurt you; they're hoping you won't even find out!

Try not to take it so personally. Nothing is sacred to persons chasing pleasure. They will violate anything and everything to get to their pleasure goal. They will use and abuse your car, your credit cards, your home, or an empty Sunday school room; and they will steal from their grandparents as means for doing wrong. They have tunnel vision; they only see what they are going after.

Realize, though, the talents they use to get them to their negative goal are precisely the same talents they need for getting them to a positive goal. They *can* resurrect if they change goals, if they change the focal point of their lives. Since this is true, they are not mentally ill, and you are right in requiring them to be responsible for their own behavior.

☐ *Understand temptation's method.*

Adam and Eve were deceived, and the consequences were played down: This is always temptation's method. You have been wondering why your children won't hear you. They won't because they are deceived. Desires for illicit pleasures are seeking satisfaction while consequences are lying low—until the children are "hooked."

Thus . . .

Glittering pleasure *minus* seeing the consequences = DECEPTION AND DENIAL

You have been trying to counter temptation's method by reversing its method. You have been emphasizing the consequences and playing down the pleasure. That is the right way if you are doing it courteously (so that your kids can hear you). Your children need to hear the other side of the story.

Thus . . .

Focusing on the consequences *minus* the glitter = CORRECT EXPOSURE

Good news. Things are getting a little clearer. In the mid-eighties, we entered a new era in America and the world. In this new era, the consequences of wrongs have been brought out in the open and are now visible. In the sixties and seventies and early eighties, the consequences of doing drugs, drinking, having illicit sex, and the like were not obvious at all, mostly hidden, in fact. Parents found it nearly impossible to get their kids to understand that there are terrible consequences to those kinds of mis-behaviors. But now, there are sports heroes dying of drugs, and there is abundant publicity against drug and alcohol abuse. Now, there is widespread information about herpes and AIDS. This is the new era of unveiled consequences. *Thank God that we are leaving the modern Dark Ages!* People can actually become aware of the dangers *before* they get into trouble.

☐ *Wrongdoers try to dodge guilt.*

Your teenagers may be saying, "Yeah, but *you* did such and such." Adam and Eve were ashamed; they were naked and tried to hide. Wrongdoers don't want to be seen as guilty as they are. I noticed this in jail; to keep from appearing in a bad light, inmates would say, "But I was drunk or stoned." They blamed chemicals for their wrongdoing.

Adam blamed Eve and came close to blaming God by saying it was the woman God gave him who handed him the fruit. Eve blamed the serpent. Blame. Blame. Blame.

If your kids are lying and sneaking around behind your back, they are likely doing so because they don't want to be "naked" before you. That's also one of the reasons why they scream at you: They are trying to dodge emotional, social, and spiritual nudity.

Furthermore, this explains why you hurt so terribly as people in your community find out about your problems; you don't want to be "naked" before anyone, either. I've comforted parents as they've grieved over an indictment of their son or daughter appearing in the newspaper.

☐ *Parents should follow God's example.*

God was hurt and upset, and He disciplined Adam and Eve *consistently* with His promise to them; yet, He never stopped loving them. All parents should follow God's example.

This is consistent with the real world. You are right if you discipline your teenagers (if your discipline is in harmony with the question "Will this heal?"). You are wrong if you are not *consistently* disciplining your teenagers.

**God's way is a system that is as reliable as His integrity.**

If you are fair and reasonable Christian parents, you are flowing with God's system, and God will bless your parenting. If your teenagers are bucking God's system, they are sentencing themselves to living apart from His blessings, by default.

Throughout my nearly twenty years of visiting with people about their problems and more than ten years of specializing in teenage problems, I've discovered how perfectly dependable and consistent God is. The precision of God's system has become more and more apparent to me: Flowing with His promises brings safety, growth, success, serenity, and security; bucking them allows deterioration. There are no exceptions.

In 1978, I was teaching a Bible study to inmates in Retrieve Prison in Brazoria County, Texas. One of my favorite people in the group was a huge black man, a seven-time loser as he referred to himself. He towered above me, and when I would shake his hand, his hand would dwarf mine.

But this giant was tenderhearted. Talking to him, I could sense his companionship with God; I could feel his love for me as his personal friend.

One Wednesday evening, I mentioned a theme I was trying to develop for my newspaper column. I said, "Flowing with God's promises brings peace. Bucking them by ignoring them strikes turmoil."

My friend lingered after everyone else left. He wanted to tell me his thoughts on my theme. He said that we reap what we sow: "The seed grabs hold, grows up, and becomes a mammoth tree loaded with fruit containing seeds like those sown. A sin can grow into a tree of sinning. One sin calls for another until the briars and vines entangle the offender completely.

"It's the law of cause and effect," he said. "When the cause is wrongly initiated, the effect can be nothing but wrong.

"A bad means," he explained, "always brings a bad end." He quoted the Bible promise in Numbers 32:23: "*Be sure* your sin will find you out" (emphasis added).

He quoted another Scripture:

Do not be deceived, God is not mocked; for whatever a man sows, that he will also reap. For he who sows to his flesh will of the flesh reap corruption, but he who sows to the Spirit will of the Spirit reap everlasting life. . . . Therefore, as we have opportunity, let us do good to all. (Gal. 6:7–8, 10)

He gave me a parting Scripture as he walked me to the steel door that was about to close between us. He quoted Psalm 85:10: "Mercy and truth have met together; righteousness and peace have kissed each other." In other words, flowing with the promises of God is lovingly involved with inner tranquillity. My column was easy to write after I had spoken with this man of God in prison.

Now think of what all this means to you: *If you remain attractive* as Christian parents before your children *by flowing* with the promises of God and *by monitoring* your every attitude, action, and reaction with "Will this heal?" then you are on the what-is-guaranteed-by-God-to-turn-out-right side of life. Your teenagers, ignoring these promises, are on the what-is-declared-by-God-not-to-turn-out-right side of life.

This means that *if you will hold steady in your position,* without turning your children off by making rude comments and exhibiting hostile attitudes, your children will eventually see what turns out right. They will much more likely be reattracted to you and your moral and spiritual values and will more likely return home to their roots.

The moral of this story is this: Don't try to win your children by acting like the devil. Seek to win them by remaining attractive and approachable, like Christ.

If you are flowing with the promises of God, your very lives will *pull* your children in your direction, and the pain and agony that are sure to happen to your children from bucking the promises of God will *shove* them in your direction. If you've erected no insurmountable barriers (returned evil for evil, returned *rejection* for *rejection* or returned *rejection* for *ejection*), then the pressures will be in favor of your children returning to you. You *pull* and the natural *repuls*iveness of soured sin will *shove*. And tremendous pressure will be on your children to turn away from sin and return to God!

Keep pulling and let sin shove for as long as you have to. Don't allow any insurmountable barriers to get in the way of reconciliation, and you'll be doing your best to save your children.

Your primary responsibility in seeking to rescue your children is to hold steady in your attractive position as fair and reasonable Christian parents—and be patient.

Why does there have to be a religious touch? Because of the magnitude of your problems and the kinds of solutions you need. Even if your family hasn't been a religious one, you can see the necessity for your family deciding to become a Christian one and building this great tower of strength: Our child is God's child, too.

# CHAPTER 12

# CONSCIENCE

**Tower of Strength 2—the chaperone's tower:**
**Our child has a *guard*ian conscience.**

A s a speaker for girls' camps, I have learned the power of homesickness. Invariably, a few girls are so homesick that they simply can't stand it and end up going home.

It's amazing! Their friends are there. The pool is issuing its sparkling invitation. Docked sailboats are waiting to bow before the wind. Aerobics, nature hikes, softball, volleyball, and table tennis are on the program. But they are not enough.

A few girls will still be chanting through many tears, "I just wanna go home." Eventually almost all the girls would be chanting the same chant if we stayed too long.

A family spoke to me about the homesickness of the husband and father. He was a well-educated person with an impressive position in a progressive company. His wife was working in a job she liked very much. His children loved their high school and wanted with all their hearts to stay there and graduate with their friends. But he wanted to go home to where he had always lived.

It wasn't that this gentleman was self-centered and inconsiderate of his family. He just had a burning desire to return home, a desire that stubbornly refused to be quenched. The pull of home can be that strong!

You've likely felt the burning desire: There's no place like home. This sets the stage for me to say something that will encourage those of you who are grieving over the misbehavior of your children. Your children—having turned their backs on their Christian upbringing—*are away from home emotionally, socially, and spiritually* (even if they are still living at home), and they will not feel at ease inside until they *come back home*.

Compare the feeling to the worst that you've felt when you've been away from home physically. That same kind of cry for roots is gnawing inside your children. Pray that God will use "homesickness" to minister to them.

### What are the components of the teenager's conscience?

The teenager's conscience is made up of the following:
1. The inborn awareness of right and wrong.
2. What society has programmed into the teen as to what is right and wrong.

3. What you have taught with your words and by your example.
4. What the teen has learned about individual responsibility to God.
If the teenager ignores all these elements to do wrong, he or she is *away from home*, and his or her *guardian* conscience will be slowly kindling a burning desire to return home.

### Do kids listen to their consciences?

Maybe some parents are thinking, *We don't think our teenagers ever listen to their consciences*. Perhaps not right now because they are so excited about the new thrills and frills of what they are doing. But, believe me, your good influence is there and, like "Old Faithful," will be boiling up from time to time spewing red-hot messages of contradiction at the wrongs your teenagers are doing.

To assure you of this, let me share some stories that illustrate the extremes of misbehavior—perhaps far beyond where your teenagers are. But if these individuals have consciences, then surely your teenagers do, too.

☐ *Even most criminals have active consciences.*

For five years, I served as chaplain of the county jail. I had complete access to the cells and visited each one each week. Between three thousand and five thousand men and women were booked in each year, and I had opportunities to speak with many hardened criminals.

I spoke with a man who had earned $250,000 by killing for hire, and I asked him, "Do you feel guilty about the people you have killed?"

He replied defensively: "No! I just killed creeps! I ain't killed nobody that's any good! . . . Anybody that's so bad that somebody else'll pay $20,000 to get him knocked off oughta be knocked off! Society should be givin' me a trophy for gettin' rid of creeps instead of locking me up. . . . I get rid of people the justice system can't even do anything about!"

Sounds as if he has no conscience, doesn't it? If he doesn't, why is he so defensive? Why does he have a system of rationalization set up to defend himself against the voice of his conscience?

I had a good reputation with the inmates for maintaining their confidence. They would talk to me as they would talk to no one else. On several occasions an inmate told me about his guilt and later entered a plea of not guilty in court. I never met an inmate who didn't have a conscience (unless he was mentally distraught or was under the influence of alcohol or other drugs).

A fellow who was in jail for operating a sizable illegal drug manufacturing lab told me privately: "It's simple, Chaplain. I knew I was doing wrong, and I knew what the risk was. But I decided to take the risk to try to get the big bucks. I got caught, and now I'm in jail." Notice how conscience was at work.

I ate a couple of lunches with the last living member of the Bonnie and Clyde gang, Floyd Hamilton. It might seem that no one in that gang had any conscience at all, but Floyd's conscience prodded him to God. He became a Christian, and he began to work in prison ministries after his release. He is one of the most conscientious men I've met.

The question you may be asking about these criminal offenders is: "If the conscience is still there, how can they keep doing wrong?" Because the conscience can be temporarily sedated by rampaging appetites and emotions (like the lust for money and power, sexual lust, or anger), by chemical means (alcohol or other drugs), by rationalizations, by peer pressure, and the like. I'll agree that in some cases the conscience, as rationality can be, has been damaged beyond repair, but this is generally not the case.

Be assured; your teenager has a *guard*ian conscience.

### The Bible makes reassuring promises.

The Bible promises two things that are greatly in your favor as you seek to help your children.

First, a child cannot leave his or her conscience behind: "Train up a child in the way he should go, and when he is old he will not depart from it" (Prov. 22:6). This Scripture has been frequently misinterpreted. People have interpreted it to mean that it is impossible for children to stay rebellious and continue to do wrong if they've been raised right.

That's not correct. The Hebrew word interpreted "depart" here has an alternate meaning of "leave behind." I think a more accurate interpretation would be this: If you raise a child in the way he should go, he will never be able to so sear his conscience that he can leave your teaching behind.

The fact is, if you have taught your children to do right, you have given them the gift of a built-in, *guard*ian chaperone that will go along with them wherever they go. Trust that the chaperone is in place and cannot be rejected. You are always with your children.

Second, the Bible declares that wrong always turns out wrong. Or as I often say, "You can't get happy by getting guilty." The New Testament warns, "Do not be deceived, God is not mocked; for whatever a man sows, that he will also reap" (Gal. 6:7).

It is impossible for teenagers to find lasting enjoyment in wrongdoing. The wrongs remind them that they are wrong in doing wrong—a consequence that has to be terribly uncomfortable. The wrongs are reminders that they are away from home mentally, spiritually, and socially.

How can you help prevent your children from temporarily turning down the volume of "the still small voice" of the conscience? And how can you help them turn up the volume instead?

### How do criminals turn down the volume of the "still small voice"?

Nearly 80 percent of all inmates return to lockup within eight years after release. Why? What affects the conscience so that they find it easy to commit other crimes? There are several reasons.

☐ *Repeat offenders lose their support system in the positive side of life.*

Fathers have gotten tired of trying to help them, and offenders have hurt their mothers so badly that they don't feel comfortable facing them anymore. Straight people find them offensive and avoid contact with them. Almost nobody will hire them.

Offending teenagers also lose their support system in the positive side of life. Parents may make acidic comments like . . .

- "I wish you had never been born!"
- "I don't care what happens to you!"
- "God wanted to punish me so He sent you along!"
- "If it wasn't for you, we wouldn't be getting a divorce!"
- "You're the reason I drink too much!"

Teachers finally tire of disruptive teenagers, their unwillingness to try, and their con jobs, and they turn to those students who are trying to make something of themselves. Achieving students think of "problem" students as gross and tell them as much with their scornful attitudes toward them; and the "problem" students return the pain. A great gulf of alienation results, and these young people lose their support systems in the positive side of life.

□ *Offenders lose respect for persons they grew up respecting.*

No matter what they have done, offenders believe they should be treated fairly. I think it goes this way in their minds: *If I'm so wrong, then the straights who arrest me and jail me had better be flawless if they're so great.* Instead, perhaps an arresting officer shoved them, a minister wouldn't pick up their check and bail them out of jail, a lawyer wanted to plea-bargain them out when they felt that they could win the case, and they got more time than other guys who did lesser crimes. They look around in prison and notice that mostly low-income people are there. It all looks so unjust that they conclude, *Why should I do right? Even the respectable people aren't respectable!*

Kids are also vulnerable to these feelings because they are just beginning to discover that the world is not fair. They still feel that parents and teachers are supposed to always be fair. They *know* it's not right to prefer one child over another, to require more work of one child than another, to be hard on one and soft on the other, and such injustices are almost guaranteed to cause them to swirl into a hurricane of rebellion.

Also, the parents may be doing something that a teenager feels is more wrong than what he or she is doing:

> invading privacy
> being prejudiced
> abusing alcohol while objecting to the teen's drinking
> living with someone out of wedlock while hauling the teen
>   to counselors for being sexually active

□ *Offenders have lost their self-respect.*

Offenders have almost no personal pride because there is so little to be proud of about themselves. They go deeper and deeper into despair. One day in the county jail I noticed five inmates who had BORN TO LOSE tattooed on themselves.

Teenagers desperately struggle with self-worth, and anything you do to destroy their self-worth turns down the volume on the "still small voice." Be as kind and considerate of your children as you are of your coworkers, neighbors, church members, or service club members. Show respect.

Watch yourself. How do you talk to your teenagers? Would you call a neighbor a bungling idiot if he accidentally dropped the remote control to your TV? No. You'd likely say, "No problem; it's still under warranty." Then why be verbally brutal when your child makes the same mistake?

And don't tell all the grandparents and aunts and uncles what "awful" things your teenagers have done. (Again, teenagers feel that this kind of gossip is worse than anything they might have done.)

If there's no one left who respects a teenager, *there's no respect left to maintain*. Thus, a primary inhibition is lost, and she'll more readily give up on trying to do well. Or he'll more likely begin to act like the renegade that "everybody" has decided that he is.

When I was a child, my family respected me. If I did wrong, I knew I was living below their respect and my *guard*ian conscience put me in the torture chamber. I became so homesick emotionally, socially, and spiritually that I couldn't stand it. I returned home.

☐ *The offenders' tremendous losses cause them to despair of success.*

They give up on the American dream and are often bitter because they don't have it. They continually think of themselves as losers.

Many teenagers do, too. They get so far behind in school that they despair of ever catching up. They see their old friends graduating from high school and leaving them behind. They realize everyone has begun to expect the worst from them.

☐ *Offenders return to jail because they don't give up the wrong crowd.*

The wrong crowd becomes very valuable to offenders because it provides them with what they have lost. They have lost respect, admiration, trust, best friends, and places to stay. Together, they can form a mutual admiration society and recapture a measure of these losses.

They have developed a lot in common. They have been mistreated, they don't like the police, this one or that one has disappointed them, and they can exchange exciting stories about their daring escapades. Their support system is in the negative side of life.

Teenagers can also be captivated in the same sorts of ways by the wrong crowd. The wrong crowd has the power to temporarily squelch the "still small voice." Remember Tower of Conviction 11: We will see the wrong crowd as family enemy #1.

☐ *Addictive attractions cause problems.*

Alcohol or drug use, sexual activity, and the like produce success feelings artificially. They help "losers" momentarily escape their disappointing world—
their losses,
their disgraces,
their failures,
and their dismal futures.

To understand how attractive the addictions are, ask yourself: How many exhilarating emotional highs have I experienced in my whole lifetime? Ten or so maybe? Highs like getting your driver's license, getting your first car, graduating from high school, graduating from college, getting married, landing your first job, moving into a new home, and bringing your children home from the hospital. And how long did you have to wait between highs? Years sometimes?

Partying kids get *several* emotionally exhilarating highs *every weekend!* No wonder it's addictive! Partiers can experience the sense of well-being produced by alcohol, the rush produced by drugs, the thrill of having sex with someone new, and the freewheeling feeling of abandoning rules and responsibilities *every weekend*—and sometimes on weeknights, too, if they're "lucky."

These deceptive attractions are like cute baby gorillas that are so much fun at first, yet grow up to overwhelm and enslave their keepers.

The trick of the dark side is to turn attraction into addiction before the victim wakes up to the deception.

### How can you turn up the volume of the "still small voice" of a defiant teenager's conscience?

☐ *Bible study is the best way.*

You and I know that the Bible is the greatest tool for conscience building. But I cautiously include Bible study here because it may not have that effect right now.

Family Bible study can be counterproductive if the teenager gets the idea that you are using the Bible to win your side of the argument; he or she will resent it and be driven away.

I remember when I was a rebellious youth, a pastor's wife stopped her Sunday school lesson and prayed for me in front of the whole class. I hated her for that. I felt that she had used prayer as a weapon. Her capital punishment had embarrassed me to death, and I felt more rebellious than ever. I was quiet in her class after that, but I was sitting there resenting her, thinking, *If you're such a great Christian, how could you embarrass me in front of my friends like that?* I felt that she hadn't prayed for me, *she had prayed at me*. I saw her as a hypocrite.

Bible study can also be counterproductive if the quality of your lives doesn't support your Bible readings. Your children will see through you, and your hypocrisy will repel them.

Yet if you are able to present Bible study in a manner that is not resented by your rebellious teenager, it is the best of the best for turning up the volume on the "still small voice" of the conscience. I urge you to prayerfully deliberate on how you will be able to accomplish this.

If you have always had family Bible study, you may want to continue the chartered course even if the rebellious one resents it. He or she shouldn't be allowed the power to decide the destiny of the whole family's activities.

I would like to say something to parents who are reading this book for prevention: If you teach your children the moral and spiritual values of God and live by them, you have paired up your parenthood with God. If your children rebel against your values, they are rebelling against God as well. They are taking on both earth and heaven! Parents who haven't brought their children up with Christian guidance obviously don't have this powerful advantage.

One day your children will have their own opinions, and as far as they'll be concerned, their opinions will be better than yours. So, you had better nurture them with something higher than your opinions. You had better nurture them with God's wisdom so that they'll have something beyond mere opinion to strengthen them during that time.

☐ *Be sure your church is not boring to young people.*

Turning up the volume of the "still small voice" is exactly and precisely what your church is supposed to be doing for your children. But your church cannot accomplish its purpose unless your church is attractive to your children.

Missionaries say that hungry people can't hear the gospel until they've been fed. Bored kids, too, have a hard time hearing the gospel. *Make sure your church blends heaping helpings of fun and fellowship with their Christian education.*

☐ *Your own good example of self-control is essential.*

How have you reacted since you found out that your daughter is pregnant? Or that your son has been sexually active? Or that your teenager experimented with drugs? Or sneaked out at night? Or skipped school? Or broke into a house?

Teenagers seem to be able to cope with an outburst from parents when they first find out, but continued anger and relentless volleys of verbal brutality are intolerable. They feel that you should be able to handle situations more maturely once you've gotten beyond the initial shock.

A poor example of self-control discourages teenagers. There's the possibility that such a reaction will de*value* you to them, and they will have less of a desire to do well since you aren't as "together" as they thought.

If you haven't been setting a good example of self-control in front of your children across the years, begin to do so now. Your change will illustrate that they, too, can change. Change is possible!

Don't feel that your change is going to work wonders immediately. Your kids may even resent it at first. They may feel, "After you've made a mess of our childhoods, now you change! Too little, too late!"

Set a new example before them anyway. Time heals! They'll finally feel better toward you once you've stayed true to your commitments over a long period of time.

Don't be foolish in this, though. Don't try to get sympathy from them, don't expect praise, and don't tell them that their misbehavior is your only reason for changing.

Quietly change because it is right before God and humankind. This is the correct reason to change, and this is the only way for your change to have a positive effect on your children.

On the other hand, if you have done really well at living properly in front of your children—"always perfect" as they say—let your guard down and tell them some of the mistakes you made along life's way. Let them in on some of your struggles. (In talking about your life as a teenager, don't talk about the events or fads or whatever of your day; that makes your guidance seem out-of-date. Talk about relationships; relationship problems are similar in every generation.)

☐ *Share the burden of guiding your teenager.*

Relatives or close friends can have a powerfully good influence on teenagers and turn up the volume on the "still small voice." Many a time, I have encouraged a family to ask someone that a teenager respects to spend more time with him or her.

Kids have changed after they've been sparked with admiration for an adult outside their home. I advise you to be thorough in the things you try because you never know what will spark a young person's change.

A schoolteacher was a deciding factor in my own change. A minister helped me hold to my commitment to live a Christian life.

A family in our community is presently helping a girl maintain her break from the wrong crowd. They involve her in their lives—nothing big, just everyday things. They bake cookies together, grocery shop, and eat out. They are giving her life-preserving support, and this family is getting to have a wonderful ministry to another Christian family. The family being assisted in this case had the same problem as that of the apostle Paul and John Mark, two New Testament ministers who parted company over disagreements. They were all Christians, but the parents and the daughter didn't get along very well. Their styles didn't match.

I remember an eighth-grade boy who was being required to break away from his friends. A teenagers' Bible study found him, and the high schoolers took him in as if he was one of them. Their friendship made his change permanent. Their intense friendship and the Bible studies cranked up his "still small voice" to loud and clear levels.

Several years ago, a teenage girl told me, "I can't teach my parents to trust me and still go to the same school. I'm not strong enough to go against my friends." Her friends included one or two of the teachers who were partying with them. One of them had brought her home drunk a couple of times.

In response to her statement, we placed her in another public school, and the parents paid out-of-district tuition. The first person she met was a Christian guy who sang in a Christian singing group. He and his friends were the spark she needed. The right crowd instantly received her, affirmed her, exerted positive peer pressure on her, and kept her with them. She never turned back.

☐ *Stop trying to be better than your teenager.*

Another way to turn up the volume on the "still small voice" is to stop trying to be better than your teenager at everything. Beating your kids in basketball, knowing more about cars, laughing at their political views, or making fun of their driving leaves young people with no room to succeed with you (which they'll be desperately wanting to do as they compete for their own spot in adulthood). If they can't get any fulfillment with you, they'll turn to others for it.

☐ *Express faith in your teenager.*

Another way is to express faith in your teenager that he or she will ultimately do the right thing. Say . . .

> *Janna, I believe in you, and I believe with all my heart that you are going to be just fine. You'll search through it all and ultimately do the right things. It may take a while, but I feel things will be all right sometime in the future.*

☐ *Be respectful of your teenager.*

Treat all your children courteously on a day-to-day basis. Actively love them! Doing so will enable them to enjoy you more, and they will have more to get homesick for if they break fellowship with you.

What if you hid a tape recorder and recorded how you talk to your children? You might think, *That won't work. I'll be more careful if I am recording myself.* Good observation! Never mind the recorder; a recorder is already in place. The memories of your children are recording you—permanently.

☐ *Listen to your teenager.*

A teenage girl expressed her despondent feelings over the things that had gone wrong in her life. She showed little emotion as we talked about her various mistakes and disappointments, and they were big ones.

Then I asked, "Do your parents listen to you?" Her eyes instantly clouded with tears. Nothing was hurting her like her parents not hearing her. She was so-o-o lonesome to be *with* her parents.

Turn up the "still small voice" by listening to your children. Even if you disagree, be courteous enough to listen to them. They want you to hear their side. They can cope with your verdict better if they feel that they have been able to tell you their side of the story. If you refuse to allow them to, they're left feeling that you made your decision without all the facts.

Allow me to let you in on a trade secret. Much of my counseling consists of actually taking the parents' place in listening to children. Kids talk to me freely because I have earned their confidence, because there's no risk of getting punished, because they are lonesome to talk to an adult who will *listen* to them at length, because they believe I can help them.

Perhaps you could open up more conversational opportunities if you imagine that you are a coach or a tour leader for the journey of life, rather than a parent, and approach your children accordingly.

☐ *Ask a counselor to build your teenager's conscience.*

There have been times when I've told parents . . .

*Your teenager is so hostile right now that I am not even going to try to approach the problem head-on. If I were to, it would turn him off to me, and he would feel that I was ganging up against him with you. I would lose my opportunity to be heard by him.*

*Instead, I am going to use some conscience-building techniques with him so that he will have more within himself to contradict his rebellion. Please understand that this will take some time.*

*While I do this, you need to digest the material in this book so that you can become stronger parents at the same time.*

## How to turn up the volume of the "still small voice" In your teenager

The following summarizes ways you can turn up the volume on the "still small voice" of your teen's conscience. The list of suggestions is incomplete and is intended only to help you get started with this line of thinking.

1. Be sure your teen enjoys positive experiences in church.
2. Enjoy family Bible study together if positively possible.
3. Be a living example of the self-control you want the teen to achieve in maturity.
4. Share the burden of conscience building with other trustworthy individuals.
5. Admire the accomplishments of your teenager even if they are superior to your own.
6. Express faith in your teenager.
7. Be respectful of your teenager's good side.
8. Be sure your teenager feels heard, even if the views directly conflict with your own.
9. Try to help your teenager maintain a support system in the positive side of life.
10. Try to help your teenager maintain respect for positive, straight people or help him or her to interpret the disappointments.
11. Try to help your teenager maintain a belief in his or her ability to succeed.
12. Try to discreetly engineer opportunities for your teenager to be with positive peers.
13. Do your absolute best to keep your teenager away from the impressive propaganda of the wrong crowd, be it peers, adults, relatives, or the electronic wrong crowd.
14. Try to keep your teenager away from the addictions, or seek to get him or her help with his or her addiction.
15. Always treat your teenager justly—no matter what he or she has done. (Apply the golden rule and monitor your attitudes, actions, and reactions with "Will this heal?")

# CHAPTER 13

# IRREPLACEABLE ASSETS

**Tower of Strength 3—the family's tower:
Familyhood supplies irreplaceable assets.**

*Parents are important!*

A sixteen-year-old I'll call Dale visited with me some time ago about a problem he was having. He said, "Two forces like have hold of me and are trying their best to rip me apart. I want to party with my friends, but if I do, I have to go against my parents. I don't want to be left out, I don't want to miss out on things, and I don't want to go against my parents. What do I do?"

Crissy, seventeen, had a different problem. She said, "I hate my parents."

I asked without reacting, "Why do you hate your parents?"

She erupted: "They won't give me any space! They think they have to know everything! They don't trust me at all! They think just because they wrote their little names on a piece of paper at the bank and help pay my insurance that they can ground me from my car! . . . They hate my friends! But that doesn't really matter because my friends think they're gross anyway."

Both Dale and Crissy needed to realize the vital place their parents will always occupy in their lives. At some point in visiting with teenagers like them, I usually draw nine intersecting circles with labels. (*See* diagram on next page.)

I explain the diagram this way . . .

*Think of these circles as vital cells in your life. In order to have an all-around healthy life, you must have good health in each cell.*

*If one cell gets sick, all other cells are affected, and you become crippled to some degree. You may be able to ignore the sick cell for a while and deny that it's a problem to you, but one day you'll realize that you have been handicapped all along.*

I try to help young people see that the wisest way to live is to struggle to keep all the cells healthy and *not to sacrifice one cell to make another fat* (like when teenagers sacrifice parents to have good times with friends).

We look at one cell at a time and talk about its importance. When we come to the

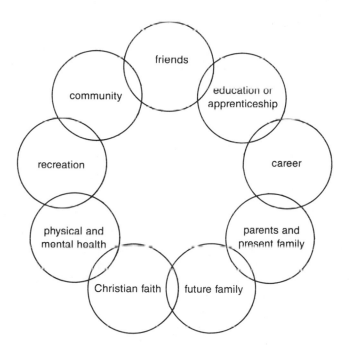

cell labeled "parents and present family," I encourage the teenagers to look ahead and see what relationship they will want with their parents in the future (when their parents become grandparents to their children, for instance).

The point is this: Parents are people whose assets can be replaced by no one.

**Fair and reasonable Christian parents are irreplaceable people.**

No matter how bad things may look to you right now, you are extremely important to your children. Remain on courteous but firm terms without becoming a doormat at one extreme or verbally brutal at the other. You have enough assets to relax a little.

In a newspaper article I wrote for teenagers, I proposed that they advertise for the parents they wished they had. I helped them compose the classified ad:

> WANTED: A new set of parents who will give me a room of my own equipped with color television, radio, stereo, telephone, and beautiful furniture. Will want unlimited access to all food supplies, access to a car with gas, and spending money furnished. Will require the freedom to come and go as I please. Am not willing to do any chores, and will not tolerate comments about my grades or friends. If interested, call (phone number).

I've used this ad in a friendly manner in counseling with young people to help them see the importance of keeping their family cell healthy and discover that their parents are not disposables. A meaningful relationship with them is vital to living a well-balanced life.

*There's no place like home.*

Children from reasonably good families have a pull toward their parents and home that they will have to fight if they stay in alienation.

Think of the televised pro football games. A football star suddenly has a live camera focused on him, and he can use his few seconds to do anything he wants. But what does he say in front of the entire nation? "Hi, Mom!"

You occupy a vital cell in your children's lives that no one else can fill. That cell is more vital and much larger than the cell their friends occupy, although they may not realize it yet.

The pull of familyhood is so powerful, in fact, that physically abused children continue to return to their parents although they know the abuse may happen again. They keep trying and trying to get their family cell healthy.

### But why won't teenagers listen to parents?

"If it's so powerful," you might be wondering, "why isn't my teenager responding to my pleas?" A generation gap? No. *An experience gap!*

There's something missing. Something is not in place yet. Your teenager is in an experience gap. He or she hasn't experienced the real world yet, and because of that, you truly are on different wavelengths.

Teens don't have enough software in their mental computers to properly judge the ill advice of the wrong crowd. Nor can they predict the low blows of chasing the party circuit. Nor can they know how their aimless escapades will make them feel in later years.

That explains why some kids aren't going to change until they go out and experience life on their own. They don't know how to appreciate their parents *because they don't know what their parents really are doing for them.* They don't have enough facts in their memory banks to be discerning and empathetic.

Think back to when you showed your children your workplace. You made the experience as fascinating as possible for them. They saw all the interesting machines you operate, and they thought, *Mom (or Dad) is so lucky to get to work here; this place is so much fun.* They don't know that you have worked with those machines so long that it is no longer fun. So, they keep on thinking that you're having a blast while you're at work and while they're slaving at school. Because of their experience gap, they don't see that you are enduring a lot for them.

The need to close the experience gap is also why parents make a mistake when they help their wayward children get out on their own and get them out of every tight spot. *They are keeping them from getting the experience that they will have to have to finally overcome their experience gap.* The road of hard knocks will teach them what they defiantly refused to learn earlier if parents don't stand in the way of the stern substitute teacher.

### You can strengthen the family tower.

Accept the challenge of building this tower stronger than you ever thought you could. How? Here are some ideas.

First, don't make any relationship-ending remarks like: "I never want to see you again"; "If you step out that door, it's over with us forever!"; "Go ahead and kill yourself, and see if I lose any sleep over it!"

You must not return evil for evil. You must not return rejection for rejection. "Do not be overcome by evil, but overcome evil with good," as the Bible commands in Romans 12:21. Always keep the relationship open to reconciliation.

Second, children need to be reminded that you have been a very significant part of their lives. Teenagers tend to forget the *great times* they've had with their families when they enter the dazzling world of adolescence. So now is a good time to bring your family picture album up-to-date. Buy some new albums and spread your family pictures around and share some memories. Or review home movies or videos at a time when your children are close enough for you to capture their interest.

By stimulating pleasant memories, you will put them back into their conscious minds, and these resurrected memories will more likely be made a part of their present decision-making processes.

But don't ruin the effort by making cocklebur comments like, "That was back when we were a happy family." Or "See how nice you used to be?" You want to remind your children of pleasant memories and of the importance of familyhood, and you shouldn't spoil it by irritating them. Take a recess from your frustration and just share an enjoyable time of reminiscing with one another.

Your misbehaving child may not warm up to this experience; it could make him or her feel guiltier. Realize that you may encounter some resistance that might feel like rejection to you. Simply get as much mileage out of the experience as you can and be content. Neglect to put the pictures away, and leave them available for a while.

Third, to close the experience gap, if you have enough control, you could have your teenager do all the work of the wife and mother for one week—all the cooking, cleaning up after meals, washing and ironing clothes, grocery shopping, housecleaning, and so forth. Be fair now. Don't make the teen do the work usually assigned to another sibling, and don't add on extra work that the adult on duty doesn't normally do.

The son of one family who did this arrived at this conclusion: "I'm never having kids!"

Parents, you know I'd want you to do this without having an irritating attitude toward your child during this week. For example, don't tease her or him about it, and prevent siblings from teasing, too. Don't make comments like, "See how much I do for you." Be quiet, remain courteous, supportive, and appreciative, and allow the experience itself to teach. Otherwise, you will get the teen's mind off the experience by his becoming preoccupied with anger toward you. It's a good idea to pitch in and work together with your son or daughter a time or two during this week when he or she seems especially weary.

Also, you need to stay busy doing the extra things you've been wanting to do. Don't sit and watch TV while your teenager slaves. Resentment will result.

Fourth, lift their sights by dreaming dreams with your children. Include yourselves in those dreams. By doing that, you become less disposable. Say something like . . .

*We, too, are looking forward to the day when we can car shop with you. We want to be able to cosign your note with you, and help you secure your insurance.*

Say . . .

*We are looking forward to your adulthood. It'll be neat when we can go to your house for a visit. We feel that you are going to do just fine. How about trying to locate somewhere we haven't lived so you can show us some new sights?*

Teenagers who are going through a period of not relating to their parents well will need some other reasons for hanging in there with them during this time. Dreaming dreams, like remembering their responsibility before God, can help them achieve stability during the family recession. (I will say more on this subject when I write about the shepherd's tower of strength in chapter 14.)

Fifth, help them experience something from their future today, and hope that they will catch a spark of new motivation. For example, arrange for them to be with someone in the career they think they might enjoy. And the more exciting the experience, the better.

If your teenager thinks she would like to be a surgeon one day, arrange for her to go on a medical mission to Mexico (instead of rebuffing her with, "That's a laugh! You have to make decent grades to be a surgeon!"). Let her actually see the joy of healing and the joy that competence can bring to one's life.

Sixth, remember that parents are projectors and children will tend to reflect the images projected. If your daily mannerisms project that things are *all wrong* between you and them, your children will tend to reflect what you've projected. You'll need to refocus.

If you project that things are going to get better, your children will have a harder time bucking your better image. By nature, they will want to reflect it, to script it. You'll be focused correctly.

There's a Scripture that has this element of truth within it. Jesus said, "For with what judgment you judge, you will be judged; and with the measure you use, it will be measured back to you" (Matt. 7:2). An old saying also communicates this idea: "What goes around comes around."

Test this at work tomorrow. Begin the day by projecting a gloomy attitude and see what your fellow employees reflect to you. At noon, cheer up and project a happy attitude, and see what is reflected to you.

I believe this projector-reflector relationship is one reason why Jesus said to "love your enemies, bless those who curse you, do good to those who hate you, and pray for those who spitefully use you and persecute you" (Matt. 5:44).

Seventh, parent like Moses' mother parented.

Parents have told me that they sometimes don't feel that their assets are so advantageous in their quest to save their children. To the contrary, they frequently feel as if they are fighting the whole world for the health of their children. My wife and I have three children—two of whom are teenagers—and I know that we are, in fact, fighting against most other influences to keep our kids from being polluted.

Moses' mother had a similar problem—only worse. She reared her son in the very middle of overt heathenism. Yet, Moses became a mighty man of God whose influence is still inspiring us today.

You can do the same as Moses' mother. Live clean and kindly in front of your children and teach them the Source of your integrity, and your witness to them can be much more powerful than your competitors (who are playing dirty).

Whether your children want to or not, their consciences will compare their "wrong crowd" friends to you and will judge them by you. Since they're basically self-serving, they cannot always put forth a fashionable front; no one can always perform at peak performance. Their selfishness will finally come slithering out so that it can be discovered and detested.

### The wrong crowd clique is really in a bind.

The kids in the wrong crowd always have to be worth what your teenager is *giving up* to get to be with them. He or she is giving up . . .

> a right relationship with God
> a peaceful conscience
> a right relationship with parents
> a high-school or college education
> a good reputation with teachers and students

The wrong crowd clique is in an even bigger bind because it has to be worth what your teenager is *enduring* for it. He or she is enduring . . .

> awkward feelings of guilt
> discomfort in the presence of good people
> a gnawing feeling of wasting his or her life
> fear of death
> insecurity about eternity

Plus, he or she may be enduring . . .

> dirty mouths
> disdain for everything good and right
> constant criticism of decent people (including remarks against
>    his or her own family)
> comments about how one of his or her lust-laden "friends" would
>    love to have sex with his or her younger brother or sister
> gross selfishness
> hypocrisy
> slavery to chemicals and sexually transmitted diseases
> seeing someone he or she likes being used
> a fugitive lifestyle
> stints in juvenile detention or adult jail
> emergency room visits

And this list is certainly not all-inclusive. *No clique can remain worth this inflated price tag.*

### Three cheers! You can compete!

You can successfully compete against the kids in the wrong crowd because for their lifestyles to be right, they have to produce at least the same quality of life that your teenager grew accustomed to in your home. Relax a little. You can win this war. You have irreplaceable assets!

Just try not to do anything that will cause your teenager to dig into a defensive position. Don't alienate him or her by your desperate reactions. You are to speak the truth with love, as the Bible says.

Do you know one thing the members of the wrong crowd have that you may not have? Do you know how they get your teenager attached to them? They listen to what your teenager has to say and make the teen feel important to them. Be sure you do, too, or they'll have this advantage over you. Whoever values the young person the most and expresses this valuing usually gets to have him or her.

### Some stand-in parents fail.

The efforts of stand-in parents break down because they can't supply the irreplaceable assets. In some situations another set of parents will decide that a teenager's defiance is all her parents' fault. These outsiders will "rescue" the teen and agree with her that her parents are inconsiderate people, reinforcing her rebellion.

The teenager supports the position of the interfering parents by dramatically telling them her side of the story. Since the interfering parents don't usually hear the other side of the story, the teenager's side seems impressive.

These ill-informed parents may be doing something very dangerous. By helping the teenager make her case against her natural parents, they may very well be setting her up to suffer from superguilt in the future. (You've already learned about the awesome danger of superguilt.)

To complicate matters, the teenager displays excellent behavior in the "rescuers'" home. She has to be on her best behavior there, or she would discredit her story. For some reason, it doesn't seem to dawn on interfering outsiders that the good behavior they are enjoying is the result of the teenager's good upbringing by the parents they are blaming and discounting. But if there's an extended illness, or if the child gets into serious trouble, or if the time arrives for college expenses to be met, the interfering outsiders almost always want to back away and tap the natural parents to supply their irreplaceable assets.

An alternative home setting can be good for teenagers and parents, but not as described here. It is good when the foster parents are purposefully cooperating with the natural parents to save both their teenager and their family.

One more thing: In some instances the only hope for a teenager of problem parents is a rescue by outsiders. I've helped in such cases. But I'm not talking about those right now. I'm talking about outsiders interfering with the efforts of fair and reasonable Christian parents.

Fair and reasonable Christian parents are so important. As such, you are irreplaceable in the life of your child. No one—not the wrong crowd, not misinformed stand-in parents, not anyone else—can take your place with your child. Your child may "go exploring" for a time, and this will be painful to you; but hold steady on standby and remain attractive as Christians. Pray and don't faint as the Bible admonishes. Your child's eye-opening journey will close the experience gap, and then he or she will finally have the mental software in place to see your irreplaceable value.

CHAPTER **14**

# AN ADULT PERSPECTIVE

**Tower of Strength 4—the shepherd's tower:
We parents have a better overview than our child does.**

*Parents are shepherds.*

'Ve named this the shepherd's tower because parents, in their shepherd roles, look after their children's basic needs emotionally, socially, and spiritually. Adolescents have basic needs that must be met on an ongoing basis in order for them to feel fulfilled. I will use only six of those needs for the sake of keeping things more manageable.

By understanding these vital needs and by helping your children satisfy these needs, you will help them have a better basis for surviving adolescence. The six vital areas include:

1. Being linked in with good people by being loved and returning love.
2. Increasing in value and feeling valuable.
3. Enjoying re*creat*ional fun.
4. Dreaming dreams and maintaining an *exciting* and *inviting* future to look forward to.
5. Gaining confidence in his or her ability to perform admirably in the adult world.
6. Receiving divine guidance, cleansing, help, purpose, and security.

These vital areas are listed without regard to the order of importance. The last should be first, of course, but it will mean more if we discuss it last.

*Shepherd by monitoring basic needs.*

The shepherd's tower is your intensive care unit (ICU), and it's equipped with six intensive-care monitoring instruments in the form of questions. As a bonus for learning how to shepherd your teenagers by keeping watch over their basic needs, you will also learn how to monitor the health and well-being of your spouse, your parents, yourself, and other significant others in your life. The same intensive-care monitoring instruments work with all age groups, with some minor adjustments. Adult needs are similar to those of teenagers. Let's admit it: To be healthy, all of us need *intensive care*-ing.

### 1. Is our child linked in with good people by being loved and returning love?

Being loved is the way we are linked to the life-support systems of others. Loving in return is the way we complete the chain.

Being loved and being loving are energy exchanges that provide the security and fulfillment of belonging, *of being linked in*. If there are linkage problems, individuals begin to shrivel.

For a health check in this vital area, ask questions like:

- Does our daughter (or son) know she is loved? Have we told her lately? Have we been actively expressing our affection for her? By our kind deeds? By our compliments? With a gift? How can we do better?
- Have her brother and sister taken a break from sibling rivalry long enough to let her know they love her?
- Should we visit our relatives to let her experience their love?
- Do her teachers like her?
- Is she feeling love from positive peers? If not, how can we help?
- If love can't be experienced from one of these places, how can we help her have a double portion from another source?

Then consider the other side of the coin:

- Does she love others?
- Does she show her peers that they are important to her?

Boom! Boom! Boom! I beat the drum at this point because peer companionship is so important at the moment. Gratifying peer group involvement for an adolescent is practically the most important thing in the whole world. Parents are put in the background momentarily since they are a constant—parents have always been there, which seems to indicate that they always will be there.

### ☐ The peer group is significant.

The peer group poses the challenge. That's where the exciting pioneering is to be done. Is your teenager healthfully involved in a positive peer group where doing right is in style and doing wrong is out of style? By "healthfully" I mean, is your teen an important part of the positive peer group instead of a mere tagalong whom the group more or less tolerates?

If your teenager is not fulfilled in a positive peer group, try to arrange for him or her to find a place where he or she can be. Search for the available opportunities.

### ☐ Church youth groups can pose special dangers.

Each church youth group has its own corporate personality, which is mainly made up of the minister of the church, the youth leaders, and the kids who participate (the kids are divided into "best friends" cliques). If your son or daughter doesn't fit in with this corporate personality, for whatever reason, you have a serious problem to help solve.

I've noticed a nonfit, for example, when the entire youth program is built around a traveling choir. Invariably, a few young people won't like music, can't sing well, don't like the regimen of choirhood, or think that church choirs are for wimps.

Without regard for their feelings, these young people are usually forced to participate by their parents, they are disciplined by the youth minister, and they are condemned for standing there only mouthing the words. Church involvement becomes painful. This treatment is not fair or just.

A church should offer variety and not try to force all teens into the same mold. Other possible youth activities could include a work team (where tough guys who don't like singing in a choir can apply their skills and muscle), a ministry team for befriending residents of a youth home, volunteering to help physical therapists with handicapped children, volunteering in hospitals, taking neglected children on a campout, and other fulfilling things.

If there is a compatibility problem between your teenager and your church, speak to the pastor and the youth leaders and see if the problem can be resolved. Problems that destroy a young person's enjoyment of a youth group could include:

- a physical bully who terrorizes your child.
- an emotional bully who is always teasing your child in front of everybody.
- cliques that won't include your child.
- youth leaders who consider your child a "problem" to be endured.
- youth leaders with whom your child has a natural personality clash.
- your child having done something so absurd or so sinful (or has been falsely accused of doing so) that he or she no longer has the respect of the youth group.

☐ *But what if your child doesn't fit in with the church youth group?*

If your child simply can't fit in with your church youth group and your church leaders can't (or won't) help you, you shouldn't force him or her to attend out of blind loyalty to your church. *You've got to help your child with the vital need for fulfillment in a positive peer group. Kids can't do without it. If they don't find this fulfillment in the positive, they will turn to the negative (the wrong crowd), almost without exception.*

May I suggest an alternative? Say to your teenager . . .

*We understand that you don't feel comfortable with the youth program in our church, and we have decided that you do not have to attend the youth group anymore. But we want two things: We want you to attend church with us as a family for worship services, and we want you to attend a Christian youth group of your choice once each week. We'll help you get there and back.*

*For this arrangement to work, of course, we would need to hear good reports about your behavior at the other youth group. If you teach us that you can't behave properly on your own, we will respond by keeping you with us so we can give you closer supervision. But we trust you; and we trust that you will do just fine.*

You will continue to worship with your children as a family, but your teenager will have a choice of youth groups. This approach relieves the pressure of church being a bad experience for your teenager, and in some cases, it helps the young person with that craving for more independence. The teen can venture out some and be out from under your watchful eye a little more (provided he or she continually *teaches* you that you can continue to *respond* with this significant amount of trust).

□ *Secular youth groups can create problems.*

Nonchurch youth groups also have corporate personalities. Sometimes the wrong crowd has overtaken an Explorer Post or a Junior Achievement company. Occasionally, a leader is a part of the wrong crowd. Sometimes a youth group can be infected by too many teenagers from the wrong crowd to earn the label of a *positive peer group*.

Putting your children with such groups means putting them under a bad influence. Investigate; be as sure as you can of the influences your children may encounter.

I talked with a teenage boy whose parents were angry because he didn't want to participate in a certain club. He confided in me, "The kids there are the very ones that my parents wouldn't let me be around if they only knew what they were like."

□ *Does your child love others?*

We've checked this question on a teenager-to-teenager level; now we need to check it on a teenager-to-adult level.

- Has the teen expressed love for parents? Teachers? Church leaders?
- Does the teen understand that adults have the same needs for affirmation as he or she does?

Teens need some help here. Remind them a week ahead of time of upcoming birthdays and special occasions like Mother's Day. Or Mom can help them shop for Dad's birthday.

Don't play the game of seeing if teenagers remember your birthday and then ridicule them when they don't (being full sure the oversight is proof positive that they don't care a hoot about you).

Generally speaking, young people require help as they go through the transition of having all their needs supplied as young children to discovering that other people have needs that must be supplied. Help them; don't harass them.

## 2. Is our child increasing in value and feeling valuable?

This is the deciding factor of whether life is worth living or not. Feeling valued helps individuals feel worthwhile and gives them something worth protecting.

□ *Be careful of how you appraise your child.*

Think of the word ap*praise*. The words *praise* and *raise* are contained in ap*praise*. To *raise* your children, you must *praise* them. To lift their self-esteem, you must compliment them.

If important people in children's lives appraise them to be of little value, and their own appraisal agrees, they perceive no reason to keep on keeping on. They may escape this self-esteem bankruptcy through associating with other "losers" to find emotional support within the losses; they may sink into drug or alcohol use, crime, or emotional problems; or they may decide that committing suicide is less painful than living. They will likely do one or more of the above.

When the people who matter in teens' lives persist in reminding them that they have become a waste, they will be too discredited to try to achieve. That's precisely the reason *you must build their self-images* at the same time you pressure them to do better.

If you succeed in convincing teens that you think they're total flops, they will avoid you like the plague, and you will have lost your ministry of reconciliation to them. What a forfeiture! Be very careful with your ap*prais*al.

☐ *Firm up your teenager by being affirming.*

Be creative. Figure out ways to af*firm* your teenager, even though you feel like wringing his or her neck instead. It is right to go by wisdom, not by feelings.

Often in counseling, I ask parents to write down all the good qualities of their son or daughter. They do this while I spend time alone with their teenager.

The parents aren't usually in the mood to do this exercise; they're more in the mood to flog. Yet all have cooperated. What I'm trying to avoid is making the teenager feel like a big flop. Swarming on problems all the time can give the effect that the object of the swarm is nothing but a mess.

When the parents return, I title their list "A Portrait in Words" and read it aloud. I openly compliment the young person on talents, good qualities, and accomplishments.

This exercise graphically points out to both parents and teenager that he or she is not all bad. There is a lot of good to ap*praise*. I do this exercise with families because I know that a teenager has to have some self-worth in order to have a treasure to protect by living a good life and to have something solid upon which to rebuild his or her life.

☐ *Affirming can make the difference.*

When an eighteen-year-old was brought in for severe drug abuse, his parents honored his good side by making up the following list:

> has a loving nature
> is courteous
> does chores well
> is easy to get along with
> cares about his appearance
> has a creative mind
> makes passing grades
> has good conduct reports
> cooperates with counseling

The positive approach helped him to be willing to enter a rehabilitation program. We are trusting for his complete recovery.

☐ *Counselors should share the responsibility for affirming.*

Counselors should also feel free to highlight a young person's good qualities. I remember a young girl I worked with for several years, beginning when she was thirteen. During one of her gallant efforts to rebuild her life, my secretary and I typed her list of good qualities on little stickers. We then stuck them onto the leaves of a beautiful silk flower arrangement. I took them to her with a letter attached. Here are excerpts from my letter . . .

> You have done well for a long time, and I am writing to tell you that I admire how well you have done. I know something of how hard it is; I was there once myself. . . .
>
> You are truly a lovely person in so many ways. I've noticed your good qualities, and I've prepared them in silk for you. Let the flowers represent your blossoming future and let the leaves remind you of your own beauty. (It's okay to rejoice in our successes from time to time.) The qualities written on the leaves are things I've noticed about you during the many times we have visited together.
>
> You and I, we've had our ups and downs in counseling. But I want you to know that I care about you, I want the best for you, and I will continue to remain readily available to you if you ever need my help.

Although this girl had had more than her share of behavior problems at home, at school, and in our community, I emphasized her good qualities to her . . .

attractive
neat
cheerful appearance
strong willed
courageous enough to try again
made passing grades
caring toward pets
willing to rebuild trust
friendly
and more

Counselors universally realize the vital importance of healthy self-esteem in young people. They enjoy their responsibility of *affirm*ing young people.

A word of caution: In using the services of a counselor, don't cause your child to feel that something is wrong with him or her. Children who get the idea that "something's wrong with me" do not have the confidence to become as successful in adulthood as children who believe nothing is wrong with them (even if they've behaved dreadfully). I've frequently referred to myself as a "life coach" to keep this from occurring.

☐ *Building self-esteem is essential.*

Feeling valued gives teenagers something to protect by being good. Think of self-esteem as self-*esteam.* This spelling contains the words *steam, team,* and *am.*

*Steam.* Your child needs a good head of steam for winning over his or her problems. A good self-esteem provides that steam.

*Team.* The *self* in self-esteem bothers me a little (as does the *self* in self-control). I don't believe anyone can have a good self-esteem all by oneself. The word *self,* quite concidentally, contains *elf,* and the word *selves* contains *elves.* The words give a hint about what happens when we are left alone. We become smaller people. We need others. Team-esteem is what we need. Our personal worth will rise when we see ourselves associated with God, positive people, and good goals. Keep these points in mind as you shepherd your teen.

*Am.* *Am* is a word that inspires thoughts of commitment. This one is for your teenager. With it, your teenager can get it all together: *"I am* going to *team* up with God and Christian friends to pump new *steam* into my self-esteem." This is the ideal, of course, and you'd love to see your teenager's change of mind-set happen right away. But you'll have to move at his or her pace rather than yours. Keep doing as much as you can do without bruising the fruit before it ripens.

☐ *Build self-esteem at home.*

One way to build self-esteem is to hang a blank posterboard on your child's bedroom wall. Write something on it like: *John is special in the following ways.* . . .

Explain to siblings that this is serious and no cutesy inscriptions are allowed (or you may want to leave the siblings out of this exercise). Start the list with several obviously good qualities of your child. Then let the list grow as you think of others.

*Warning: Do not stoop to using the poster to lash out at your teenager during an argument.* For example, don't get mad and say, "Why don't you live up to that poster over there?" Or "That poster is the biggest joke in this house!"

Here, again, is the phenomenon mentioned earlier: Whoever values your teenager the most and expresses this valuing to him or her usually gets to have your teenager.

Unfortunately, whenever some parents are trying to rescue their child from the wrong crowd, they make him feel worthless in their effort to be sure he realizes how wrong he has been. The motive is right, but the approach and outcome are wrong. The wrong crowd, on the other hand, makes him feel *valu*able and *wanted.*

Think about what you would be naturally drawn to if you were a teenager. So, what can you do?

☐ *Evaluate with these questions.*

Here are some questions to help you use the intensive-care monitoring instrument: Is our child increasing in value and feeling valuable?

- Have we subconsciously decided that our teenager is a lost cause, and could we be communicating that to him or her by our attitudes and actions?
- Are we expecting our teenager to do wrong, and does he or she realize that?
- Are we ap*prais*ing our child as *valu*able while we work on the misbehavior? Or are we out of balance by ignoring the good qualities while nagging about the bad?
- How are things going at school?
- Is there at least one teacher who has not written our child off as a loss?

- Are there young people who still offer positive interchange with our teenager?
- Is our teen getting rewards from achieving in sports, participating in a campus organization, receiving certificates honoring accomplishments, making good grades, or enjoying wholesome popularity?

- What about the situation at church?
- Does the pastor minister to our child?
- Does the youth minister see him or her as a mission field to be cultivated or as a "devil" to be cast out?
- Do peers at church include or exclude our child?
- Is our child getting attractive opportunities to develop an image reflecting the image of God?

- How are things going at work?
- Is our teenager gaining self-esteem from learning to be competent in a field of service?
- Are things going well between our child and coworkers?
- Do we appreciate or depreciate what our teen has learned?

These questions should help you spot any problem areas. Pray for ways to lift your teenager's self-esteem where needed. Be creative in your approach.

☐ *Stay out of the blame trap.*

If your questioning uncovers some shortcomings on how some adults are relating to your child, don't fall into the blame trap. Don't blame those who have gotten worn out by your teenager. Doing that will only cause even more frustration and more alienation.

Besides, it isn't always the adults' fault. Perhaps the teenager has *taught* them how to *respond* to him or her, and they are merely *responding* to what they have been *taught*, reflecting your teenager's projection. Instead of blaming, courteously request "second mile" patience from the frustrated adults.

### 3. Is our child enjoying recreational fun?

Teenagers would probably rank the need for having fun above all the rest. Think back. Remember recess? Remember how you used to sit in that elementary school classroom and wait and wait for recess? Remember the freedom and joy you felt as you ran from the room toward the playground? Remember how you hated it when the teacher raised her hand for you to come back in?

I remember a time when, as a young teenager, I would sit through each church service hoping that my parents would get caught up in a conversation afterward so that I could enjoy my friends.

I remember a time during my teen years when two of my best friends and I were trusted by one of their dads to drive his full-size John Deere tractor down the pipeline right-of-way. I can remember bouncing along on the tractor thinking about how perfectly happy I was.

I call that re*creat*ional fun because it re creates. Kids need this quality of fun on a regular basis to be happy and healthy.

By the way, are you having fun? Is your spouse? Remember to do a health check on yourself and the significant others in your life as we go along here. All these points apply to anyone you have the privilege of shepherding.

### 4. Is our child dreaming dreams and maintaining an exciting and inviting future to look forward to?

Essentially, the answer to this question involves *creating an appetite for the future* that is stronger than what's happening around kids today. Kids need a captivating reason for going against the wrong crowd and temptations.

This is making the tomorrows appear so-o-o *exciting* that they are worth sacrificing for today. The future should look so-o-o *inviting* that it is worth foregoing the illicit partying that many of their friends are into, and it is even worthwhile studying and doing well in school.

If kids don't have something *exciting* and *inviting* to look forward to, they are left with what's happening now. They are left without obvious, commanding reasons, goals, for saving themselves or preparing themselves for the tomorrows. Out of sheer *aim*lessness, they may drift into undesirable situations or adventures.

☐ *What should you do?*

As their shepherds, you should help your children have *exciting* and *inviting* dreams . . . always, always, always dreaming! You must create *an appetite for the future* within them!

Shift their focus to the future by helping them dream short-term, mid-term, and long-term dreams. Short-term dreams can happen within the month, such as a trip to a giant water park. Mid-term dreams can come true this year, such as a ski trip during Christmas vacation. Long-term dreams for the distant future include reaching age sixteen and getting a car or thinking about how they would like their adult lives to be.

☐ *Ask these questions for checking health here.*

For a health check at this point, ask:

- Is our child dreaming dreams?
- Does our child have something *exciting* and *inviting* to look forward to next week? This year? Five years into the future? Ten years?
- Or is our child's total focus on what's happening right now? Wanting to please friends? Partying?

Help your children have something to look forward to by letting them know ahead of time that you can take them skating with their friends next Saturday, by telling them about the trip you plan to take during spring break and including them in the preparations, and by taking time to talk to them about their long-term dreams.

Don't devalue your youngsters by caustically saying, "The whole world is going to be endangered when you get your driver's license!" Dream with them. Say . . .

*Yes, that'll be great. I remember when I drove a car for the first time by myself. I looked around and it was weird: I had never ridden in a car by myself before. It was great! I'm happy that you will soon be in the driver's seat. And it's important that you will have taught us to trust you by then so we will get to enjoy seeing you drive and enjoy yourself. That's what we want with all our hearts.*

☐ *Counselors should help kids dream dreams.*

We help kids dream dreams in our office. A high-school girl on the staff has the job of helping teenagers dream dreams. You can help them at home the same way. She helps them choose goals for their lives. She helps them learn the qualities of character required to reach those goals. And she helps them learn how to make their choices in view of those goals.

To make their futures really live for them—*Exciting! inviting! promising!*—the peer counselor helps them create a giant poster for displaying their dreams. On their poster, she glues their goal sheet, a maturity pledge, a brochure of the city they may want to live in when they're adults, an exterior view and a floor plan of their dream home, the sport or recreation they hope to enjoy, the career they want to pursue and, sometimes, a symbol of heaven (to add the finishing touch to their good futures).

Some of the young people have sought me out to show me their posters with great pride. They take them home and display them on their bedroom walls. Truly, this activity *creates an appetite for the future* that is stronger than the attraction of the glitter of today's high-tech sin. The future becomes *exciting* and *inviting,* worth sacrificing for, *promising!*

This exercise helps them switch from doing things because they don't want to get into trouble for not doing them to doing things because *they have their own goals in life.* This change is supposed to occur within every *maturing* young adult.

You can help your teenagers make the switch by helping them with their vital need for dreaming dreams. They require something superwonderful to look forward to if they are going to be sufficiently captivated by it to give up their entanglements.

☐ *School counselors have excellent tools for helping kids dream dreams.*

The school counselor can be of great help. Ask him or her to administer three instruments for discovering the career your son or daughter most naturally fits. The first one should reveal the careers the teen's natural interests lend themselves to. The second one should reveal the careers for which your teenager possesses natural and learned abilities. And the third one should reveal what work values are most important to your son or daughter. Integrating the results of these three instruments will help your teen discover career potential.

Some young people are really *sparked* by going through this process. They develop a *can-do* attitude. They focus their aim more precisely, and they have something worth working for and worth behaving themselves for.

## 5. Is our child gaining confidence in his or her ability to perform admirably in the adult world?

For the teenager, this means finding a spot in the adult world, claiming it, and having adults agree that he or she should have it. In other words, does the future look like it will work out okay?

From the teenager's perspective . . .

- "Can I succeed in college?"
- "Do I even want to?"
- "Do adults relate to me well?"
- "Or are they always down on me about something?"
- "Maybe I would rather try to stay at recess all the time than be with adults and risk their rude comments."

Gaining confidence in the ability to perform admirably in the adult world makes the difference between being a tagalong and being wanted and included in what is going on. Teenagers won't remain tagalongs for long. They are likely to give up on planning for a decent future and focus on present pleasures.

You've probably had the tagalong feeling. It's like the first day on a new job when you know the least about what's going on, and you are plagued with the insecurity of not knowing whether you can please the powers that be. You don't know if they'll be impressed with your talents. You wonder if you'll be rejected. You sit in the break room and listen to your new coworkers talk about experiences they've had together that you don't even know about, and you feel left out. So, you can understand the powerful effect of this feeling on teenagers.

☐ *Teenagers are people in transition.*

Gaining confidence in the ability to perform admirably in the adult world is a vital transition for teenagers. This confidence in their potential to be accepted as adults should be gradually building while they are changing from children to adults.

They aren't going to be able to make their way into adulthood all at once. But they need to see a few indications along the way that they are going to *be successful at reserving a place for themselves in adulthood.*

☐ *Learn from the old prospector.*

To remind yourself of how serious this matter is, think about the gold prospector of yesteryear. He endured the great hardships of loneliness, poverty, hard work, a steady diet of beans, tent living, and people poking fun at him. Why? Obviously, to find gold or other precious metals.

But gold for him was a means to an end. His purpose was to find gold *so that* he could catapult himself into a certain socioeconomic position. The prospector endured his hardships to try to secure himself a certain place in the adult world!

You'll remember that whenever he found a vein, he headed back to civilization to stake his claim. He was staking two claims actually: the mine claim and his claim to being a success in society.

☐ *Teenagers are prospectors.*

Teenagers are checking out the prospects of being able to stake a claim in adult society. That's one of the reasons why they will try to know more about a certain subject than their parents. They are trying to make their way into successful adulthood.

However, conflicts can result. Teenagers need to know more about a subject than their parents *so that they can feel more adult.* But parents need to continue to be the "experts" *so that they won't feel as if they have begun to slip.*

Parents who don't understand what's going on can feel threatened and can react by exclaiming: "Who do you think you are, anyway? You are just a kid and don't forget it!"

Parents who do understand can sit back and enjoy watching their young persons mature (only requiring that they assert themselves without being smart alecks about it).

Kids have to *believe* that they can find gold—a place for themselves in adult society.

This kind of emotional distress happened to me when my older son began to fish on his own. We live on the Gulf Coast of Texas, and I have taken my children saltwater fishing since they were old enough to hold a rod and reel. Shane had gotten interested in bass fishing, and all at once, he knew more about fishing than I did. He would bring home bass and laugh at my wasted efforts.

I was offended. For my own fulfillment as a parent, I wanted him to realize that I had taught him to fish and to appreciate me for doing so. Instead, he was acting as if he was somehow born knowing how, he was beating me fishing, and he was rubbing it in (I tease too, I must remember).

I finally changed my mind about this. I decided that I should appreciate the fact that he was doing something on his own and edging his way into the adult world. Once I took on my new mental posture, everything got more relaxed.

I loved watching him the day he brought home a nice catch and called a girl who was a friend of his and invited her and her mother over to eat fish with him. He fried fish and potatoes, all on his own, and served them to his guests. He was fourteen at the time (now seventeen), and he was beginning to know that he was capable of performing in the adult world.

☐ *Something wonderful just happened.*

I just took a break from writing this book because my thirteen-year-old son (now fifteen) came in to show me the boomerang he built. I said, "I don't want to merely see it. I want to watch it fly."

I left my word processor and we struck out walking to my daughter's school a block from our home. On the way, I told him, "This will be a first for me. I've never been able to make one come back. I've never even seen anyone else make one come back."

Steve pulled out some grass and threw it up to test the wind. He reared back and threw it. His homemade boomerang made the prettiest flight you can imagine and came right back to us.

I told him, "Well, that's great! I could never do that!" I wasn't manipulating him, either. I really felt that way.

He said, "Here, Dad, you throw it."

I carefully listened to his directions and gave it my best effort. It went straight up and came straight down, and a chip broke out of one end of it. I've returned to my writing, and Steve is using my marine epoxy to repair his boomerang.

I am glad that there are things that my children can do that I am not able to do, and I admire their abilities.

☐ *Use these questions for the health check.*

Parental shepherds, to check your sheep's health in this vital area, ask:

- Is our child gaining confidence in the ability to perform admirably in the adult world?
- Is our child a *contributing* member with his peer group?
- Is he beginning to see indications that he can succeed in the adult world?
- Are we giving him opportunities to know more about subjects than we do?
- Are we giving him opportunities to do things that we don't know how to do?
- Do we *admire* him for what he knows and for what he can do?
- Is he learning the basic skills required to perform in the adult world? Namely . . .

> being courteous
> being responsible
> being able to disagree agreeably
> being cooperative
> learning the work ethic and being productive
> being willing to wait for what he wants

☐ *You can't fix it all.*

I need to caution you about something: You can't solve everything. You'll have to leave some things for life itself to teach.

If your relationship with your teenager has digressed to one hassle after another so that you seem to be against him or her on everything, let go of some of the nonessentials. Teenagers can be successful even though they never learn to keep a neat room or brush their teeth three times a day or make all *A*'s and *B*'s. Step aside and assign some of these essential lessons for Mr. Hard Knocks to teach. Save yourself for the health-threatening matters.

### 6. Is our child receiving divine guidance, cleansing, help, purpose, and security?

☐ *Divine guidance is desperately needed.*

A teenage girl told me, "My friends tell me that nothing's wrong with what we do, but why do I feel so guilty?"

Teenagers have never had a greater need for divine guidance than they do now. They are in a jungle of confused values. It's hard for them to know for sure what is good and constructive for them to do. They need a way to know what is right for sure. *They desperately need this assurance and security.*

The adult world has failed teens in many ways. Never have adults given out more conflicting and confusing messages to teenagers than they do now. Parents say one thing. Teachers say something else. Adults on TV shows portray something else.

Adults in the movies demonstrate still something else. How are teens to know for sure what is right and wrong? Only through divine guidance!

But not only are they overwhelmed by confusing influences, they are also discovering some disturbing things about themselves. They think bad thoughts sometimes. They do wrong sometimes. (Young teenagers are now accosted by temptations that used to wait until adulthood.) They feel guilty sometimes. They wonder what kind of individual they are.

The Bible is God's gift to humankind, our Instruction Manual. It breaks through the confusion and can guide teenagers through the twentieth-century jungle. In the process, it will tell them where they came from, why they're here, and where they're going. Living according to the Creator's Manual ensures that life will run more safely and gives life the serene quality of being synchronized with heaven. Through divine guidance, young people can be as*sure*d!

☐ *Divine cleansing relieves guilt.*

Young people are going to make mistakes just like you and I did . . . and still do. They, too, need to be relieved of the emotional awkwardness that their guilt causes. This relief comes when they ask God's forgiveness *and do restitution.* As my pastor preached one Sunday, "God forgives us to give us our self-respect back." Kids need this as much as they need anything else.

Furthermore, young people need the cleansing that comes from forgiving others. They are getting hurt. Kids treat one another in brutal ways. Teachers and employers aren't always fair, and most of the time teenagers can't do anything about it. Parents make comments and do things they wish they hadn't. Teenagers need to unload their grudges, their burdensome feelings of anger, bitterness, and injustice—their evidence that they deserve a "divorce" from parents.

☐ *Divine help provides hope.*

Teenagers, like all people, need help beyond what anyone on earth can supply. They need help for struggling life's struggles and enduring life's tragedies, for when their dreams are interrupted. Their problems are every bit as serious as mine and yours, more so at times. They need to be supported by the as*sura*nce that God can and will help them during their roughest times.

The hope of divine help is more important than ever right now as kids wonder if they will be able to land jobs and keep them, own their own homes, and survive the gigantic national and world problems that they're always hearing about. They need the confidence of *the divine advantage.*

☐ *Divine purpose supplies answers about life's meaning.*

Kids need purpose. You probably remember going to one of your parents and asking: "Where did I come from? Why am I here? Where am I going? Am I any good? Am I likable? Am I ugly?" Children search for meaning and purpose for themselves.

One of the backlashes of the theory of evolution is that it reduces human beings to near nothingness—having no noble origin, no noble purpose, and no noble future. The process of evolution is honored as simply amazing, but the individual person is lost in the lowliness of being a mere (almost insignificant) building block.

How can teenagers feel worthwhile and purposeful when they have been taught throughout their school years that they just happened to happen, and that they are nothing more than mere building blocks for a better age that a superior race of people will get to enjoy millions of years from now? Evolution robs them of purpose.

Without Christian faith, every life on earth is like a flower—rising up to blossom, only to wilt and die for no good enough reason. We are left to the fate of an evolutionary process that carelessly leaves a trail of skeletons in the shadows behind it.

Christian faith, instead, offers young people a noble origin, a reason for living, and life after life. The Bible proclaims, "So God created man in His own image; in the image of God He created him; male and female He created them" (Gen. 1:27).

The Bible establishes the position of human beings in the cosmic scheme of things:

> You [God] have made him a little lower
>     than the angels,
> And You have crowned him with glory
>     and honor.
> You have made him to have dominion
>     over the works of Your hands;
> You have put all things under his feet. (Ps. 8:5–6)

The Bible gives Christians a position in the universe: "Now, therefore, you are no longer strangers and foreigners, but fellow citizens with the saints and members of the household of God" (Eph. 2:19).

And the Bible assures us of life after death. Jesus said, "I am the resurrection and the life. He who believes in Me, though he may die, he shall live" (John 11:25).

□ *Divine security offers eternal reassurance.*

Think of what the world is like for a new inhabitant, a child, who is just beginning to find out about it.

The evening news comes on . . .

- "Five people were killed in a plane crash."
- "A ten-car pileup on the elevated claimed the lives of three children."
- "A fire in the 100 block of Cavalcade is being blamed for the death of a nine-year-old girl."
- "Fifty people are out of work in Dallas tonight."
- "The president was quoted as saying that nuclear war could mean the complete annihilation of the United States within an hour's time."
- "Last evening was fatal for a Houston woman and her thirteen-year-old son. Their mutilated bodies were found locked in the trunk of their car. There was evidence of sexual foul play."

And in their own little world . . .

- Grandma died last year.
- A garbage truck smashed the family dog.

- A friend at school was killed in a motorcycle accident.
- Another friend is a quadriplegic and makes his way through the halls in an electric wheelchair.

These are the kinds of things that kids are discovering about their world: deaths, birth defects, diseases, tragedies, unfairnesses, disasters, potential annihilation, aging. Their own death is coming at them and they know not when. *What a world to get used to!*

I don't think we can get used to it; we have to look beyond it and *find security* in spite of it. Young people need a Christian faith for making sense out of all this nonsense, to feel eternal safety in the midst of mortal jeopardy. Young people need divine security.

☐ *The sixth monitoring instrument checks for the most vital need.*

The main ingredients of teenage despondency are home problems, personal problems, relationship problems, poor self-images, the possibility of not being able to land a job or own a home in the future, the threat of nuclear annihilation, and the mammoth size of our stubborn national and world problems—to name a few. Receiving divine guidance, cleansing, help, purpose, and security is essential to moving out the bleak clouds of despair to unveil the light blue skies of hope behind them. Hope fuels courage, and courage replaces despondency.

Originally, when we were healthy physically, mentally, socially, and spiritually, we were created in *the image of God*. Therefore, the image of God is truly *the health model*.

To be as healthy as possible, then, we all must be in the growth process of gracefully returning to *the image of God*. Jesus came to show us God's image anew, to invite us to receive Him and, thereby, to become receivers of the image of God.

Receiving divine guidance, cleansing, help, purpose, and security is the most basic of all the vital needs, although it may be unique in that it's a need teenagers may not be aware of having.

In summary, Tower of Strength 4 is the shepherd's tower: We have a better overview than our child does. I've named this the shepherd's tower because you, as parents, are shepherds looking after your children's vital needs. You have the privilege of monitoring their emotional, social, and spiritual well-being. This tower is your intensive care unit (ICU), which is equipped with instruments for monitoring the vital need areas. These instruments are in the form of questions. They are . . .

1. Is our child linked in with good people by being loved and returning love?
2. Is our child increasing in value and feeling valuable?
3. Is our child enjoying recreational fun?
4. Is our child dreaming dreams and maintaining an *exciting* and *inviting* future to look forward to?
5. Is our child gaining confidence in his or her ability to perform admirably in the adult world?
6. Is our child receiving divine guidance, cleansing, help, purpose, and security?

The more you are able to help your children satisfy needs in these basic areas, the more you are helping them.

## What about "different" kids?

"Different" kids are the ones who carry their heads in an unusual way, walk with an unusual stride, don't catch onto jokes and puns, mess up the grading curve, are in special education, or whatever. The vital area of *increasing in value and feeling valuable* is twice as critical for them. Their self-esteem gets bruised daily.

"Different" types get teased, ridiculed, and bullied without mercy. They probably are not getting positive strokes from school or church (God forgive). This alienation leaves only the family and perhaps the wrong crowd to include them.

### The wrong crowd uses and abuses "different" kids.

The kids in the wrong crowd will pull in the "different" ones because they can take advantage of them more easily than others. They need them to sell drugs to or to have sex with. They want to use them.

Most unfortunately, "different" kids are susceptible because they want to be wanted and receive attention. They can easily be deceived into massive abuse. They don't get to feel good from being popular or from being attractive or from being great at sports, and they are desperate to feel good.

Once they discover that they can have thrilling feelings through chemical use or sexual encounters, they are easily "addicted" to one or both. They are lonesome for the feelings others get to enjoy through great friendships, accomplishments, and lofty goals. These are less likely to be theirs, and they've come to know it.

These kids are fertile soil for negative things that trigger pleasurable feelings. Parents must be especially creative in helping these young people derive some feelings of value from positive things.

### "Different" types need extra love from adults.

Love them with double portions. Invite special adults into their lives who can befriend them and thrill them by joining in activities they are capable of doing. Where their peers fail them, adults can succeed with them.

Get them involved in the kinds of things that other kids know nothing about so that they can have their own special knowledge and experiences. Scuba diving, hiking into the Grand Canyon, white water trips, deep-sea fishing, and the like are the kinds of dynamite things that these kids need.

Adult companionship is much safer for them than their futile attempts with their peers. Their peers will cause them to give up and retreat, and in the riskiness of our day, their escape attempt can lead them into something with a terminal prognosis.

One family tried to help their "different" son by getting him into a camping program. What a fiasco! Camping trips for him turned into weekends of being ridiculed by others campers. Adult companionship with a sprinkling of understanding peers is more often the desirable solution.

CHAPTER **15**

# CONSISTENCY

**Tower of Strength 5—the surveyor's tower and border patrol
headquarters: We parents are to be *in charge* of
surveying situations, establishing boundaries,
and maintaining border patrol. The code
word is *consistency*.**

**A**re you a shifty parent? Or are you a *consistent* parent? These questions will
be considered as you construct this tower. This is the surveyor's tower and
border patrol headquarters. For teenagers, learning to live within boundaries is even more important than learning good hygiene. There are boundaries for everything, and living within those boundaries is called *civilized*.
Refusing to live within those boundaries and living outside social order is called *uncivilized*.

### People want and need reasonable boundaries.

Generally speaking, people want well-established boundaries, but they don't
want those boundaries to be so rigid that they can't ask for an exception or two. Thus it
is with human nature.

Think about it for a moment: In-bounds behavior and attitudes bring rewards.
Out-of-bounds behavior and attitudes cause self-induced, painful consequences.

A few months ago, a staff member said to me, "I want to be sure I'm doing my
job well. I'd like you to be more specific in my job description so that I can know when
I'm doing well and when I need to improve." Boundaries, you see, are very important.

In your job situation, you need boundaries. You may not always like them, but at
least you want to know where you stand and what you can depend on.

### Teenagers test boundaries.

Most teenagers don't like boundaries all that much, but, like adults, they do appreciate knowing where they stand, what they can and can't depend on. Teenagers will
test to see where the borders are and how strongly placed those borders are by asking
for exceptions or by venturing beyond the borders to see what happens.

When your kids ask you to let them go to a party where there will be drinking, for
example, you had better survey the situation carefully and wake up to the fact that they
are not merely asking to go to a party: *They are asking you to move your border!* The

little informal conversation is actually a summit conference. They are asking the powers that be to back off, to resurvey, to shift the boundary, to become shifty!

The next time they call for a new survey, they may say, "But you let me go to so-and-so's party, and there's going to be less drinking at this one than there was at that one!" Once the boundary can be shifted, you will be *stormed* by requests for other exceptions.

☐ *Teenagers may try to* force *you to move the boundary.*

If they crash through the boundary, their escapade is tolerated, and there are no border clashes, they have expanded their borders (without having had to request a new survey). And *they have learned how to demand even more exceptions to the rules.* Or if the fun they had while they were beyond the borders was well worth the consequences they will have to endure, they will likely offend again.

Consequently, it is this tower's responsibility to establish the boundaries, maintain border patrol, and do so *consistently,* relentlessly. This tower is the one equipped with searchlights.

### Shifting borders are frustrating.

One of the worst ways you can torture your family is to have shifting borders. I don't know of anything more frustrating than *not knowing* what you can or can't depend on, not knowing what you can or can't do, getting by with things for which you just *knew* you were going to get it, and getting griped at when you didn't know you were doing anything wrong.

☐ *Are you dependable?*

Are you *consistent?* Can your kids depend on you to come through for them? Can they depend on what you have promised them in the way of discipline or rewards? Remembering how you hated inconsistency in your past will help you realize how important it is to be *consistent* with your kids.

What if the authorities were inconsistent with you? For example, think of the way the U.S. government keeps changing tax laws. It's very frustrating, isn't it? Then you know how your children feel when you are not *consistent* with them.

### Survey the borders.

Now would be a good time for you to conduct a survey of the boundaries you've established for your teenagers. What borders have you set regarding . . .

car usage?
telephone usage?
curfews?
after-school activities?
cruising?
friends?
movies?
television?
music?

grades?
conduct marks?
chores?

Have you courteously advised your children in advance of the reward for honoring the boundaries and the consequences for defying them? Are your consequences sufficiently uncomfortable so that your children won't get the idea that the fun they could have would be worth the consequences to be endured?

Remember Tower of Conviction 8: We will be sure the discipline we choose to use is a natural consequence of the offense. Practice the art of matching the natural consequences to the offense. (I'd encourage you to review chapter 6 now.)

### *Parental* consistency *is important to youth counselors.*

Early on, youth counselors can discover if they are dealing with parents who can be *consistent*. That is the first clue to me as to how much success I'm going to have in helping a family.

If and when I discover that the parents parent inconsistently and are unable to break those habit patterns, I try to help the child in spite of the parents (without the child ever knowing my secret agenda). I don't try to involve the parents that much in the counseling after that point. The concepts and principles in this book will not work well with those parents.

I have, in fact, been careful not to invite inconsistent parents to our parent support group. They are dangerous to the group and could give it a bad reputation by using erratic disciplines with their kids and telling people that the ideas came from our group.

I've helped these parents come up with reasonable responses to their children, but things seemed to be misconstrued in their minds. I never knew whether or not they would come through with fair and reasonable procedures. So now I've discreetly redirected my efforts from helping these parents to parent more forcefully to trying to help the child in spite of the inconsistent parents. My visits with the parents and the child from then on will involve an element of negotiating a more endurable home environment for all concerned.

Instead of working toward strengthening parental authority in these kinds of homes, I tend to move toward helping teenagers dream some dreams, and I help them learn what they have to become to make their dreams come true. And then I try to get them to redefine the home as a laboratory where they get to develop the skills needed to be successful throughout their lives in realizing their dreams.

The laboratory concept helps them develop endurance. For example . . .

- If Dad parents like a dictator, teens can have opportunity to learn how to deal with a strong personality, because there will be others in the future.
- If Mom nags all the time, teenagers can learn how to deal with a nagging boss who may pop up and pop off in the future somewhere.
- If Dad and Mom are hypercritical, children can set their minds on learning to get tough enough to withstand criticism.
- If parents require a particular child to do more work than the others, that child

can adopt the mind-set that he or she will learn more skills and how to shoulder more responsibility than the others.

When young people begin to see the home as a laboratory for developing social skills, they have the potential for learning to look at things differently. They can develop a new will to live and make it in spite of their unfair homes. *They can become survivors!*

### Give your children the gift of consistency.

Give your children something they can *depend on*. Give them some boundaries and be *consistent*.

Sometimes parents are criticized for having well-established and carefully guarded boundaries; they are labeled "too strict." But I've watched the families who object to this style of parenting, and I've noticed that arguing and hurt feelings are routinely a part of their days.

Which is more humane: constant clashes over boundaries or *consistency?* Weigh which is worse: a kid frowning because he doesn't like the boundary or constant fights because parents have shifting boundaries?

Survey your situation very carefully, establish fair and reasonable boundaries, guard those borders, and do so consistently. Otherwise, you'll be found to be shifty parents and will suffer the following results: Requests for exceptions (new surveys) will rise to a *nagging* level, and you will be called on to host *summit conferences* on a daily basis; or *power plays* to move the boundaries by force will rise to a *traumatic* level.

# CHAPTER 16

# UNITY

## Tower of Strength 6—the guard's tower: We are developing a *united front*.

### *There is a great need for a* united front.

N othing will stretch you further, hurt you deeper, give you greater failure feelings, and cause you to feel more insecure in peacetime America than having problems with your teenager. That is why you must send out the cry for help and develop a *united front* for saving your teenager, your family, and yourself. The *united front* should ideally include both parents or a single parent plus select relatives, select friends, a counselor, a support group of parents who have gone through the same problems and, in some cases, legal authorities. (I'll cover those outside the family who can help you develop a *united front* in the chapters on the allies of the family fortress.)

Parents must develop a *united front* because having problems with children is just about as serious as anything can be. What's the difference between parents knowing that their nineteen-year-old son is being held hostage in a foreign country and parents trying to free their fifteen-year-old son from the tyranny of the wrong crowd and rebellious behavior? The latter is harder.

In a sense, it can be worse for the parents engaged in hand-to-hand combat trying to save their teenagers from local terrorists. Not only are their children being held captive, but the parents are stricken with . . .

    failure feelings,

      extreme guilt,

        overwhelming grief, and

          despair over not knowing what to do.

Another ingredient that goes into this dreadful concoction of emotional distress is the parents' paranoia over their other children who are being placed in jeopardy. Brothers and sisters can be influenced to do the same fun-looking but deadly things. Or they can take the offender's side against their parents. Or they can be publicly humiliated as they live under the shadow of their sibling's decaying reputation. Or any number of other things can go wrong.

*The enemies are untouchable.*

Furthermore, these parents are living near their teenagers' enemies and can't seem to stop them from torturing their teenagers. And these parents are having to watch their teenagers get hurt by the terrorists while the teens act like they love the terrorists more than they love their own parents.

These enduring parents are trying to rescue the hostages while the hostages are being rude to them and doing them wrong. A civil war is always more morbid than any other war. Yet, despite all these distresses, parents must guard their positions and maintain their strongholds with all their hearts because their children are flirting with disaster.

**A united front *in a two-parent home is Dad and Mom* standing together.**

The *front* is *united* when the father-and-mother team *agree* on how parenting should be done. If one is too permissive and the other too strict, *the team is disoriented, and each member will persistently undo the other's efforts.* The teenager will learn how to manipulate this situation and will cause complete chaos. "If a house is divided against itself, that house cannot stand," Jesus wisely said in Mark 3:25.

How can divided parents unite? Here are some suggestions:

1. Be sure you're right with God. Rally heaven behind you and go with the flow of God's promises. This is the best possible beginning for putting together a *united front*.

2. Realize how important it is to put aside your differences and become united. Reread the beginning of this chapter.

3. Use this book as your point of agreement. If you both agree to go by the concepts in this book, both of you can win without giving in. Losing your children is too big a price to pay for getting your way.

4. Find a counselor who can basically agree with the content of this book, and let him or her help you develop a *united front*. (See the comments in "What's a single parent to do?" and in chapter 23 on counselors in the last part of this book.)

5. If there are no counselors close to where you live, seek out a strong parent or a strong set of parents who know how to take a fair stand and stick to it. Ask them to be supportive. Be sure they read this book and agree with its concepts and principles.

6. Join a support group that agrees with this book, and the group will strengthen both of you in the same direction. The support group can help divided parents come to closer agreement.

Some divorced parents have attended our group for the purpose of learning how to put on a united front so that their children would be parented the same way in both homes. They sat on opposite sides of the room; nevertheless, they were learning how to cooperate in parenting to the rescue.

If there aren't any support groups in your area, search out two or three couples of good character and invite them to meet with you once each week. Take turns teaching one another the information in this book, and assist one another in applying the concepts and principles to individual parent-child issues. But please honor the following request: Don't invite people to meet with you until you have read the chapter about the support group for parents.

7. Learn who your allies are, learn how they can rein*force* your posture and convictions as parents, and learn how to form an alliance with them to develop a stronger united front. Your allies include school personnel, a youth and family counselor, the police department, the juvenile probation department, inpatient treatment centers, and homes outside your home. (A chapter on each appears in the last part of this book.)

## How can single parents present a united front?

The most difficult civil wars are the ones in which single parents have to fight with one of their children, for that child's life, all alone, with little or no support from the other parent . . . or with the other parent being a part of the problem. The parenting assignment becomes even more complicated in such cases.

My heart goes out to these hurting single parents. Half the team is missing, and they must perform in the Super Bowl trying to rescue and control their kids. They yearn for someone with whom to talk things over. They'd love to have someone on their side when they're in conflict. It would be luxurious to have someone beside them when they have to say "no." Without companionship, their decisions come hard, and carrying through isn't easy.

Single parents are often still shaken by the death of a spouse or by the turbulence associated with a divorce. Either way, they're not up to fighting a civil war. They are in the stages of grief or loss. They've been left behind or rejected. They are emotionally drained.

If the spouse has died, they may get mad at the person for dying and leaving them to deal with the kids alone. Then they feel less than human for being angry with a dead person. They may question God, "Why did You let this happen to me?" And in this emotional state, they have to parent! Like a locomotive with a full head of steam, problems with children keep coming straight at them.

If the parents are divorced, either they've been rejected, or they've torn themselves away from someone they had committed their lives to. Either way, they are emotionally worn and weary. If they were rejected, their children's rejecting-like attitudes and actions sting like hornets. These parents need love, friendship, and support from their children. Instead, the self-concerned kids act like they couldn't care less: They are hateful to them, they argue with them, they scream at them, they refuse to do what they say, and they may turn around and blame their parents because things are such a mess at home.

Although I've stood beside many of these parents, I've never developed a tolerance for this cruel abuse. I've been aghast at times! I love these people who need extra help to understand their hurts, consider their problems, and develop a *united front*.

Divorced and widowed individuals have to go to work and act as if everything's okay while they leave their misbehaving children at home unsupervised and have a neighbor watch the home to see who comes and goes while they're at work. Single parents continue to have to do the housework, cook meals, keep the family's books, help with homework, and fix or pay for everything that breaks.

Divorced persons have yet another giant complication with which to contend: The wrong parent may have received custody of the children. I feel that domestic courts, generally speaking, have deserted traditional values and have become disoriented, left without a standard of values on which to formulate decisions. Jurors are selected from a disoriented American population, and they are often overly permissive. Consequently, the halls of "justice" have become unpredictable—sometimes moral and just, sometimes amoral and unjust, sometimes immoral and unjust. Judges can do practically whatever they want since appeals to overturn their decisions are so expensive and time-consuming.

But if justice was honored and the most wholesome parent received the children, then there is the complication of having to give them up to a less wholesome environment every other weekend, a week at Christmas, a week during spring break, and a month during the summer (or whatever else is decreed in the divorce papers). During these stays, the ex and the new spouse (or, unfortunately, the live-in) and the grandparents may be indoctrinating the children against their custodial parent, and the children may be allowed unwise freedoms, such as cruising or attending wild parties. How do the custodial parents undo what is done? How do they tame the wild streaks when the children return home?

At our office, we have group therapy for divorced people. I recently attended their meeting, and I asked the thirty participants what their biggest problems have been in parenting their children after the divorce. A sampling of their answers follows . . .

"Allowing my children to be raised in an atmosphere I don't respect, and only having them every other weekend and at intermittent times. Worrying that my influence may not counteract the environment they are subjected to." (This was written by a father.)

"Having to send my children to their father every other weekend when his new wife (whom I don't like or respect) will be taking care of them. I worry about his and her influence on them. Also, I have difficulty making all the decisions about everything myself."

"Trying to get through to them and correct them on the weekends I have them for visitation. To be able to communicate with them."

"Being alone during problems, and not having someone there to talk to about the problems. Being a recovering alcoholic, looking back, I wasn't really there anyway very much during my practicing alcoholism."

"It's very difficult to handle the emotional ups and downs that my children have after they return home from their weekend visits with their father."

"Time. Finances for all the things they want. Disciplining—my son is hard-headed and doesn't want to listen to me."

"Time management. Adjusting to remarriage of my ex. Children's playing one parent against the other. My tendency to try to outdo the other parent."

"Finances. Making major decisions without anyone to help, such as when they should date and where they can go and not go. Never having time to myself at night."

"Having nobody to back up my decisions. Teenage children are tough by yourself."

"Not having the support of another person—not money, just a father."

"Feelings of not knowing what actions to take with kids and not having anyone to talk with and share with so I won't be wrong. I struggle all the time to work and keep house and buy groceries and cook meals. Tired of this."

"Being very tired much of the time, not having a lot of time to spend with my son talking or sharing time with him, listening to him and enjoying him. Finances are also a struggle—providing him with the things he needs and some things he just wants. Also it's difficult seeing him without a Christian man as a role model at home. Not seeing the example of a loving relationship."

"Being responsible for everything—all the running around that a teenager requires."

"Having to take care of the bills, washing, and cleaning house."

"Having to discipline them, and they threaten to go to the other parent's home if they don't get their way."

"Trying to explain to the child why Mom and Dad don't live together anymore."

"I worry about the balance or lack of it when raising my three-year-old. . . . I go through periods when I wonder if I am a good mother, am I being strict enough."

"My greatest problem with my teenage daughter was getting her to love and forgive her father when he would not give her any attention at all. Fathers really need to pay their children extra attention when they are not with them all the time."

"Helping my children cope with the absence of the father figure—the rejection they feel, the loneliness and the bitterness."

"To protect my ex-husband's reputation with the children and to protect the children from the harsh truth of the things their father does. . . . I fear my children will want to someday live with their dad and maybe blame me for leaving him."

"Being 'up' for my children all the time. Trying to make their father look good in their eyes when he has done us wrong."

"Having an only child, the most difficult thing is being mother, father, sister, brother, and friend and not enough emotions for me, let alone her."

"I had to move in with my parents, so there have been three bosses to the kids for the last four years. Mom and Dad are very *set* in their ideas. I have had to forfeit much of my independence."

We also have group therapy for widowed people at our office. I recently attended their meeting, and I asked them what their biggest problems have been in parenting their children since the death of a spouse. Their answers follow . . .

"Making decisions. Disciplining them and making rules stick. Making financial decisions—I tried to buy them happiness."

"It is difficult to feel you are giving the same amount of attention—especially during prime time—and the financial difficulties when they started driving. Now college."

"One child wished that I had died instead of her father. I gave the children too much. Also, I've had no one to back me up, and no one to discuss discipline problems with."

"Knowing how much responsibility to give my children and knowing when to give it to them."

"Helping my children to get in touch with their feelings. To get over their anger."

"My daughter felt like her father deserted her by dying, and she hated me because of displaced anger."

"My grown son distanced himself from me, having a hard time accepting his dad's death."

"Trying to keep them from being the 'adult' to the other siblings."

"The neighborhood children teasing my children because their father is dead."

"My children have not been tolerant of my grief and the way I handled it. They did not understand why I couldn't just begin my life again after two months."

☐ *What kinds of misbehaviors have single parents been trying to deal with?*

A research scientist told me how his sixteen-year-old daughter had completely humiliated him: "We were going down a rural highway, and she was driving. She asked me if she could spend the night with a friend. I told her that tonight wasn't a good night. She got mad, pulled over, got out of the car, and began to walk down the highway." She wouldn't get back in the car until he pleaded with her at length and told her she could go ahead and spend the night with her friend.

An industrial secretary brought her son in because he had been drinking home brew and harassing schoolteachers.

An abused mother came in with an injured nose. "He refuses to cooperate, and he becomes violent when forced to do something he doesn't want to do. He has been abusive to both me and his younger brother," she said in anguish.

Another exasperated mother sought help after her son was arrested at the mall for trying out a cigarette lighter on a cassette tape in a store.

Other presenting problems include: "He ran away because he said he was bored with being grounded."

"When she doesn't want to do something, she walks out on me and goes over to her friend's house."

"He and his friends had a party while I was out of town, and his so-called friends stole $1,200 worth of my things."

"She missed the bus on purpose and refused to let me take her to school."

"He lies around all day watching R-rated movies on cable TV and won't do his chores."

"She ran up a phone bill of $600 talking to her boyfriend who moved out of state two months ago."

☐ *What's a single parent to do?*

1. Be sure you're right with God. Rally heaven behind you and go with the flow of God's promises. This is the best possible beginning for putting together a united front.

2. Help yourself to emotional health. Find a pastor, a counselor, or a good friend who understands what you've been through and will empathize with you until your heart's content and won't become frustrated because you're taking too long to get over it. Widowed or divorced, it is natural to grieve. Give yourself permission to grieve. It's okay. Think of how some of the Old and New Testament folks worked at grieving. You don't need to go that far, but actively grieve until your heart's content. (The other

option is to suppress your emotions and stretch out your grief over the years, which is not healthy.)

3. Finish reading this book. Reread it until you are familiar and equipped with its contents.

4. Look for a support group of parents who subscribe to concepts and principles in agreement with this book. They can be a powerful addition to your united front. A father from the divorced group wrote: "My greatest help has been knowing other people who are single parents and being able to observe what they do."

If there aren't any support groups available, find three or four people of good character who are suffering as you are. Invite them to meet with you each week, and take turns teaching one another the information in this book. In a later chapter, I outline what a parent support group is, how it functions, and how to put one together. But please honor the following request: Don't invite people to meet with you until you have read chapter 24 about the support group.

5. Secure a competent counselor to help each of you individually and all of you together. Your children need help in recovering from the death or the divorce. Some times a child's defiance is completely based on a misunderstanding that had happened during the breakup of the home.

A counselor can help you use the monitoring instruments in your intensive care unit—in your shepherd's tower. An alert counselor will invest time in the other children—the ones who tend to get ignored because they aren't causing trouble.

Invite your counselor to monitor your home life. Your counselor should be someone who can offer direction to both you and your children. He or she should allow you to call him or her at home during crises. (You need to be careful not to abuse the privilege.) Be sure your counselor can agree with the basic concepts and principles in this book. I know some singles can't afford to pay a counselor. Look for one who charges on a sliding scale. (In chapter 23, I provide information on how to select a counselor.)

6. Find a good friend who can help you cope with your defiant child, your other children, and your own needs. This friend could be one or both of your parents, your pastor or youth minister, a layperson in your church, a teacher at school who has taken a special interest, a neighbor, a grandparent or other relative, a friend from work— anyone who cares enough to give time, who has dependable Christian values, who expresses wisdom and common sense in handling problems (and who basically agrees with the concepts and principles in this book). This person will provide companionship and be a vital addition to your united front. Try not to fight the battles alone. As a woman from the divorced group wrote, "I have a good friend who has been a great help—listens well and prays mightily."

*Note:* I am not talking about a live-in boyfriend or girlfriend. Don't expect to rescue your child from doing wrong if you're modeling wrong. My first suggestion was to harmonize with heaven and flow with the promises of God.

*Important inside information:* A solid, well-balanced Christian friend or relative has the potential for being as effective with your child as a counselor. What is a Christian counselor anyway? He or she is a solid, well-balanced Christian who courteously shines the wisdom of God on persons' problems and on their lives and uses gifts, training, experience, and professional tools for doing so. A quality friend has all of these except the professional tools and experience. Dedication and sincerity can partially compensate for what's lacking. Don't discount the redeeming value of a *good* friend.

7. Find an adult to be a big brother or a big sister to your child and make him or her a part of your united front.

For a single mother raising a rebellious son, a big brother figure can provide heroic help and help his charge learn the ways of manhood. And for a father raising a rebellious daughter, a big sister figure can provide heroic help. While they're together, she'll help the girl know how to fix her hair, apply makeup, buy school clothes, and learn how to care for feminine hygiene needs.

8. Learn who your allies are, learn how they can rein*force* your posture and convictions as a parent, and learn how to form an alliance with them to develop a stronger *united front*. (See Part V.)

### Be careful of the games some parents play that destroy a united front!

Parents are people, too, working through all kinds of emotions and passages of life, and it's easy to slip into slouchy postures as parents. This can happen so gradually that you may not be aware that you've begun to do something you should not be doing. To illustrate what I mean, here are a few games that I've seen parents play.

☐ *Some games have subliminal messages.*

*Like me the most.* A parent's secret agenda: "I'll let you go more places. I will buy you more things. I will grouch at you less. Just like me the most."

*Let us agree.* A parent's secret agenda: "We feel closest when we're agreeing about how worthless your other parent is."

*Eavesdrop.* A parent's secret agenda: "I'll act as if I don't even know you're overhearing me, and I'll tell my friend all your mother's (or father's) faults so that you can know them without my actually telling you."

*More power to me.* A parent's secret agenda: "You are going to spend the weekend with your grandparents (and while you're there, they are going to tell you that I'm right about how disgusting your mother [or father] is)."

*Live here, not there!* A divorced parent's secret agenda: "I'll treat you like a king (or queen); I'll give you anything you want; but please don't live with your mother (or father)."

☐ *Some games have outspoken messages.*

*We need to pray.* "Your father (or mother) is not a Christian. We need to pray that God will save his (or her) filthy soul, if that's possible. I've got the whole church praying!"

*Who can cut the deepest?*
- "Don't be lazy like your father (or mother)!"
- "You're just like your mother (or father)!" (This comment is made after the child has done something wrong.)
- "Your dad (or mom) told me he's (or she's) sick of you!"
- "If it weren't for you, we wouldn't be getting a divorce!"
- "If I had a decent kid, I wouldn't have a drinking problem!"

• "You had better be nice to me; I'm the only thing that's keeping your mom (or dad) off your back!"

*U-tote-em.* Parent to child: "I'm depressed and confused. I don't know what to do about your father (or mother). Let's trade places. I'll tell you my problems, for a change, and you tell me what I should do." (A child is being called on to carry adult-sized problems, and possibly to side against one parent in favor of the other.)

*Find fault.* One parent to another: "If you hadn't done what you did, our child wouldn't be having problems today!"

These examples of "games" are merely intended to stimulate your thoughts; you can probably think of more. This mental exercise will help you monitor yourself to see if something preventable is standing in the way of you parents presenting a *united front* that is healthy, consistent, and loving to your child. (You might want to review chapter 2: "Developing a Proper Posture.")

# CHAPTER 17

# CONFIDENCE

**Tower of Strength 7—the guide's tower:**
**This book, *Relief for Hurting Parents*, and supportive counseling**
**build our confidence and, thereby, our *courage* to continue parenting.**

**A**nd you must keep on parenting! Who is going to parent your children if you don't? But how can you keep on parenting when you've been through so much already? How can you maintain your resilience? Your zeal? Your position? Your marathon endurance? Or if you haven't maintained it, how can you get it back together?

This tower of strength says you need a guide you can trust. You have been abused as parents and cast into a dark wilderness that you may never have explored before. You are trying to figure out how to cope with stubborn, unmerciful teenage problems. You are unprepared for what's happened: You didn't know to prepare because you never dreamed it would happen.

You need a guide to give you *the gift of direction*. Knowing which way to go and what you should do builds your *confidence*, and *confidence* boosts *your courage*.

I trust that this book has struck a harmonious chord in your common sense and has revived your *confidence* in your ability to parent effectively as strong, *confident parents*.

Confidence (in the way you are parenting) + Self-control and Integrity = COURAGE

You must not be sidelined as in*valid* parents, disoriented and washed out with feelings of in*timid*ation. You must refuse to be benched!

My hope is that you will find this book to be a tower of strength for you and yours. As I wrote at the beginning . . .

*This book is dedicated to and written for*
*all fair and reasonable parents—and those who aspire to be.*

### You need help to grow stronger.

I went to a Galveston doctor once who noticed symptoms of stress within me. He advised me this way: "Buddy, everything you're doing is very important. You must keep doing it all. So, what you're going to have to do is to become a stronger man."

I was thrilled with his advice. I had expected him to tell me to cut back. I found his advice to be a challenge, and I became a stronger man.

I would like to pass his advice along to you: *Each of you must become a stronger parent.* One way you can do this is to thoroughly digest the concepts and principles set forth in this book. Make them natural parts of your response patterns. Also, surround yourself with support by being with people who agree with these principles.

### I would love to spark a spark.

I hope I have sparked a spark within you that you will fan into a warm flame of renewed courage for taking a stand and continuing your rescue operations for saving your teenager.

I pray that I have helped you become stronger and I hope I have . . .

relieved a portion of your pain
improved your parenting posture
helped you wade through in*timid*ations
salvaged a portion of your self-esteem
given you ways of checking your attitudes and actions
warned you of grave dangers to avoid
reinstated your confidence in your common sense and uncommon sense
   (common sense + divine anointment = uncommon sense)
lifted your convictions to towering heights
built your strengths even stronger
provided abundant en*courage*ment
handed you new tools to use
reprogrammed a few of your reflexes
suggested specific ways for you to deal with specific problems
urged you toward a more meaningful relationship with God
helped you get a better grip on forgiving

### You are capable of parenting.

A man esteemed in the medical profession and I were riding down the highway together a few years ago. Out of the clear blue, he began to tell me what a terrible father he had been. "I can't believe I was such a lousy parent," he wailed. Noticing how distraught he sounded, I glanced over at him. He was clutching the steering wheel with eyes staring and tears trickling down his face.

I couldn't believe it! His son was in a prestigious university with a 4.0 average and job recruiters pursuing him. His daughter, although she had had some problems, was married to a successful craftsman, and she was doing well. In addition, this man had been a dedicated churchman, community leader, and husband.

But there he sat mourning his failure as a parent. I asked him how he had come to his conclusion. He said he had sat in on a seminar* on how to parent children. He said, "The leaders showed me how I had done it wrong."

*Of course, there are good seminars for parents, and I like to see parents become more capable by participating in them. I only urge you to be cautious. Watch for the dangers I've cautioned about here. Test what you may be taught with the principles of this book. There's no use putting yourself through what my friend went through.

This is a danger in listening to some counselors. They inadvertently seem to want to remake parents into counselors. What happens far too frequently is that they cause parents to feel incompetent to parent at all! Parents get the feeling that they have been doing it so wrong for so long and there's so much to learn that they end up dis*couraged* rather than en*couraged*, as my friend was.

My purpose is to help you realize that you *are* capable of parenting. The key word is *balance:* blending an understanding heart with firm discipline. This word has been constantly on my mind as I have been developing this material. *Balance* is the unique ability to blend speaking the truth in love with compassionate justice—my definition of fair and reasonable Christian parenting.

Speaking the Truth in Love + *Compass*ionate Justice = BALANCE

This book, *Relief for Hurting Parents,* and supportive counseling will help you achieve balance in your parenting. Achieving balance will build your confidence and, thereby, your *courage* to keep on parenting. This is the guide's tower, Tower of Strength 7. Parents, please parent!

---

### The seven towers of strength for strengthening our positions as parents and persons

We need strength to consistently stand by our convictions. Therefore, we are erecting towers of strength at the very corners of our family fortress. These towers are our energy sources for maintaining our posture, standing by our convictions, and continuing our salvaging efforts. As such, they stand taller than our towers of conviction, and they supply us with the confidence, courage, and faith needed to parent our children.

1. *The Creator's tower:* Our child is God's child, too.
2. *The chaperone's tower:* Our child has a *guard*ian conscience.
3. *The family's tower:* Familyhood supplies irreplaceable assets.
4. *The shepherd's tower:* We have a better overview than our child does.

   In our shepherd roles, we look after our children's basic needs. This tower is our intensive care unit (ICU), and it is equipped with intensive-care monitoring instruments. These instruments are for monitoring our children's health and well-being in vital areas. The instruments are in the form of questions:
   (1) Is our child linked in with good people by being loved and returning love?
   (2) Is our child increasing in value and feeling valuable?
   (3) Is our child enjoying re*creat*ional fun?
   (4) Is our child dreaming dreams and maintaining an *exciting* and *inviting* future to look forward to?
   (5) Is our child gaining confidence in his or her ability to perform admirably in the adult world?
   (6) Is our child receiving divine guidance, cleansing, help, purpose, and security?
5. *The surveyor's tower and border patrol headquarters:* We are to be *in charge* of surveying situations, establishing boundaries, and maintaining border patrol. The code word is *consistency.*
6. *The guard's tower:* We are developing a *united front.*
7. *The guide's tower:* This book, *Relief for Hurting Parents,* and supportive counseling build our confidence and, thereby, our *courage* to continue parenting.

# — PART IV —
# Essential Strategies

The top priority of my life has always been to receive the truths of God, meditate on them, and apply them to the issues of modern times. This is why I've done my best to be true to God's wisdom in this book.

A unique way to check my concepts and principles to be sure they are in harmony with God's wisdom is to insert them into the story Jesus told about the prodigal son. The results of this quality-control measure are pleasantly reassuring. Chapter 18 displays the comparison. As you read it, you will have an excellent illustration of how to apply the concepts and principles you have learned.

Chapter 19 will show you how to put everything you've learned in a positive parenting package. You need to *integrate* the seven commandments for parental posturing with the fifteen towers of conviction and the seven towers of strength. You can use all this information to *orchestrate* a rescue and recovery operation for salvaging teenagers who are in trouble. I will give you a fill-in-the-blank form and a formula to assist you with this.

Chapter 20 is for expelling saboteurs from your family fortress. Trespassers have penetrated your home, and they are out to destroy your gallant efforts to rescue and recover your child. You must find out who or what they are, how your family is being infiltrated, and you must expel the aliens, if at all possible. ■

CHAPTER **18**

# CHECKING YOUR POSITION

The Bible assures you that you will be blessed if you walk "not in the counsel of the ungodly" (Ps. 1:1). A good way to check the principles and concepts presented in this book is to see how compatible they are with the story Jesus told about the prodigal son.

### Jesus told an appropriate story for abused parents.

Jesus showed how He empathizes with abused parents when He told of the prodigal son. The story lives in Luke 15.11–32.

Jesus began His story with the father cutting his son loose.

*Tower of Conviction 1:*   *We are breaking through denial and admitting that our child is, in fact, ignoring our guidance on purpose.*

The young man had asked for his inheritance so that he could leave home and go his merry way. His father complied. He allowed his son to leave pre*maturely*.

*Tower of Strength 2:*   *Our child has a* gu*ardian conscience.*

(*Note:* This doesn't mean that parents should give early inheritances today. Don't forget to be careful about inflicting superguilt.)

I wonder if this father was tempted to compromise his moral values and say, "No, you don't have to leave; I'll let you party some if you'll just stay here"? If he was, he didn't give in. His convictions were foundational roots for his child, and he didn't want to get root rot. Without firm roots, children lose their orientation of where to return to, to get right and to be right.

*Tower of Conviction 4:*   *We have the right and are responsible before God to require our child to live as a good citizen in our home— to live a decent, legal, cooperative, and productive life.*

*Tower of Conviction 5:*   *We must raise our child consistent with how he or she will have to become to be successful in the real world.*

*Tower of Conviction 6:*   *We refuse to be conned by our child.*

*Tower of Conviction 7:*   *We will cause our child's tools of in*timid*ation and manipulation to become useless.*

*Tower of Strength 5:*   *We are to be* in charge *of surveying situations, establishing boundaries, and maintaining border patrol. The code word is* consistency.

What would drive a father to allow his son to leave? If he compares well with fathers who have talked to me, I would say that he had tried everything he knew to do, but still the son rejected his guidance. He had talked and disciplined and perhaps had had someone else talk to his son, and nothing had helped. The son just kept abusing his family with one disappointment after another. The father acted in harmony with "Will this heal?"

*Tower of Conviction 8:*   *We will be sure the discipline we choose to use is a natural consequence of the offense.*

*Tower of Conviction 9:*   *We are* responders, *and our child is the* teacher. *We will* respond *fairly to what our child teaches* us.

*Tower of Conviction 10:*   *We will allow our child to experience the pain of his or her own wrong choices.*

*Tower of Conviction 15:*   *We will continue to or begin to set good examples of self-control before our children.*

Then, there was the older brother and the parent's concern for him. Father may have wondered, "Will the wayward one tell him how pleasureful waywardness is and sway him, too . . . and I'll lose both of them?"

Also, Dad knew that big brother was watching him deal with his younger brother. Maybe Dad wondered if his older son was also learning how far he could push him or deciding whether or not Dad was a decent parent.

As if all these pressures weren't enough, the wayward one showed his dad that a lot worse could happen. He apparently sold his portion of his father's goods. The father found himself wondering if the good future he had slaved to save for his youngest son was about to be poured down the drain. It was the ultimate slap in the face.

*Tower of Conviction 1:*      *We are breaking through denial and admitting that our child is, in fact, ignoring our guidance on purpose.*

*Tower of Conviction 2:*      *Our child does wrong because of his or her choices, not because of mental illness or physical problems.*

*Tower of Conviction 8:*      *We will be sure the discipline we choose to use is a natural consequence of the offense.*

*Tower of Conviction 9:*      *We are responders, and our child is the teacher. We will respond fairly to what our child teaches us.*

*Tower of Conviction 10:*      *We will allow our child to experience the pain of his or her own wrong choices.*

*Tower of Conviction 15:*      *We will continue to or begin to set good examples of self-control before our children.*

The son split. He left his father behind with trampled dreams . . . wondering what he had done wrong . . . wondering how his son could so easily reject and discard the family's treasured values . . . wondering what the parent business is all about, anyway: You give your child the best part of your life, and then he "divorces" you and leaves you mourning the death of your dreams for him.

Jesus didn't mention the mother. But I think I can presume, from my experiences with hundreds of parents, that if there was a mother in the home, Mom and Dad didn't always agree on discipline. Perhaps the strains and stresses had driven them apart. Maybe she had said to him, "If you hadn't done such and such, he probably wouldn't have turned out this way." They may have screamed in the privacy of their own minds: *Can we ever be happy again, together?* Or perhaps they agreed enough to pull in closer to each other, forming a united front.

*Tower of Strength 6:*      *We are developing a united front.*

Failure, defeat, disappointment, depression, fear, embarrassment, betrayal, and frustration toward the wrong crowd made up the mixture of emotions that must have harassed this good father. He most likely asked God's forgiveness for his feelings, but to his dismay, he probably kept feeling the same way. He may have tried to get involved in something to get his mind off his plight for a while, but he couldn't stop thinking about it.

As his son had become "addicted" to peer pressure and pleasure pressure, Dad likely became preoccupied with the pressure of concern:

- Is my son all right?
- Does he ever think about what he's done to us?
- Does he love us at all?
- How badly will he get hurt?
- Will I ever see him again?
- Has he completely forgotten all the good things we taught him?

This pain-stricken father may have thought of baring his soul to one of his friends. Perhaps he didn't do it, though, because he didn't want to confess that he hadn't been able to handle his son. He probably remained lonely.

*Tower of Strength 7:*      *This book* Relief for Hurting Parents, *and supportive counseling build our confidence and, thereby, our* courage *to continue parenting.*

I imagine he went about his business out of habit. He frequently caught himself staring beyond his associates, thinking about his son. Tears seeped into his eyes and threatened to chase one another down his cheeks in front of everybody.

Those days were absolutely miserable. He felt just like someone had broken off a piece of him and had thrown it away. He may have thought, *This is worse than if I'd lost him to death. If he'd died, at least I would have been left with pleasant memories of his life.*

His only thread of hope was in a Scripture that he repeated again and again: "Train up a child in the way he should go, and when he is old, he will not depart from it" (Prov. 22:6).

Perhaps he started out to search for his son. Maybe he packed up his donkey for a journey, but changed his mind along the way and returned to his partially empty home.

His logic had won over his heart. He allowed his son to feel the pain of his own wrong choices without interference from his father.

*Tower of Conviction 10:*    *We will allow our child to experience the pain of his or her own wrong choices.*

He didn't short-circuit nature's way of asking for a course correction—*pain!* Behavior changes for the better when the pain of doing wrong becomes greater than the pleasure received from doing the wrong. He didn't try to dig his son out pre*mature*ly. He resolved to keep on waiting and hoping and praying.

*Tower of Conviction 3:*    *Our child can change . . .*

*Tower of Conviction 13:*    *We will not give up on our child.*

He didn't interfere with the stern substitute teacher known as Mr. Hard Knocks, either. This teacher was confirming everything he had taught his son.

*Tower of Conviction 5:*    *We must raise our child consistent with how he or she will have to become to be successful in the real world.*

*Tower of Conviction 10:*    *We will allow our child to experience the pain of his or her own wrong choices.*

Due to the son's lack of experience in living in the real world—because of the experience gap, not because of a generation gap—the young man did not have the capacity to appreciate his family's contribution to his life. *He had not experienced the real struggles of the real world.* His parent (or parents) had been trying to reason with him from the overview of experience, but he had been arguing from his perspective of inexperience, of having seen only a partial picture of what life is all about. His experiences had been limited to living in a protected home environment.

*Tower of Conviction 5:*    *We must raise our child consistent with how he or she will have to become to be successful in the real world.*

*Tower of Strength 4:*      *We have a better overview than our child does.*

The son hadn't realized that when he took to the road with his tingling feelings of freedom, the road he had taken was the road of hard knocks. Mr. Hard Knocks fills in the experience gap, and young people get to see more clearly—the hard way.

Pain pressured the boy to think about what he had done. It all came clearly into focus while he sat in the bottom of a hog pen so hungry that he was coveting the pods the hogs were eating.

*Tower of Conviction 10:*   *We will allow our child to experience the pain of his or her own wrong choices.*

*Tower of Strength 2:*   *Our child has a guardian conscience.*

He made the decision to forsake the wrong crowd, to repent, to return, and to honor his father for a change.

*Tower of Conviction 3:*   *Our child can change . . .*

*Tower of Conviction 11:*   *We will see the wrong crowd as family enemy #1.*

*Tower of Strength 3:*   *Familyhood supplies irreplaceable assets.*

He decided to return home. One reason why home looked inviting to him was because his father hadn't erected any barriers by making negative challenges when he left. He hadn't said, "If you walk out that door, you'll never set foot in my house again!" Or "Go ahead, leave, but I warn you, you're too stupid to make it out in the real world!" Or "If you leave, it's over between us!" No negative challenges. No grudges. Open arms, instead.

*Tower of Conviction 13:*   *We will not give up on our child.*

*Tower of Conviction 15:*   *We will continue to or begin to set good examples of self-control before our children.*

The father understood a principle I have come to understand: Whoever values the child the most and expresses this valuing to him or her, usually, eventually, gets to have the child. Even when the son seemed most undesirable, the father valued him! The son had had to walk through his father's love and kindness to leave him. This memory made him know he could return home and straighten up his life. Home remained attractive to him.

The wrong crowd was in a terrible bind.

*Tower of Conviction 11:*   *We will see the wrong crowd as family enemy #1.*

To hold onto him, the wrong crowd had to stay worth what he was sacrificing to be with them. He was giving up his home, his right relationship with his loving family, his right relationship with God, his peaceful conscience, his inheritance, and his security. He was having to endure the rash selfishness of the wrong crowd and the disappointment of backlashing pleasures.

*Tower of Conviction 10:*   *We will allow our child to experience the pain of his or her own wrong choices.*

*Tower of Strength 1:*   *Our child is God's child, too.*

*Tower of Strength 2:*   *Our child has a guardian conscience.*

*Tower of Strength 3:*   *Familyhood supplies irreplaceable assets.*

The son decided that the price tag of staying with the wrong crowd and sticking with illicit pleasures was ridiculously inflated. The cost was unbearably painful. He rebelled against the wrong crowd, and he walked away from them, toward home.

*Tower of Conviction 3:*   *Our child can change, and it's our responsibility as parents to give him or her a decent opportunity to improve.*

His father was on the lookout. He saw the young man coming. His horrid emotions peeled back and a jubilant father was resurrected! It was like being released from the prison of "not knowing."

He literally ran for his son!

Hugged him!

Kissed him! (Will this heal? Yes!)

Gave him new clothes!

And prepared him for a first-class opportunity to put things back together again. Dad was tuned to God's symphony of forgiveness, and he had a forgiving state of mind.

His joy swelled into a party spirit!

His son had finally returned and only the best of every party favorite could match his joy!

They partied and partied!

His other son was astounded by the extravaganza and was also somewhat bewildered. Common sense said that Daddy was supposed to be mad and engulf the selfish brat in a storm of verbal condemnation, but there he was pouring love all over him, *valu*ing his son.

*Tower of Conviction 13: We will not give up on our child.*

*Tower of Conviction 15: We will continue to or begin to set good examples of self-control before our children.*

*Tower of Strength 4: We have a better overview than our child does.*

The elder son wasn't as in tune with God's symphony of forgiveness, and he faced his father with what he believed to be an injustice: "This son of yours wastes all your property on prostitutes, and when he comes back home you kill the prize calf for him!" (Luke 15:30).

*Tower of Conviction 12: We will strive for cooperation, not "happiness."*

The father answered symphonically, "Your brother was dead, but now he is alive; he was lost, but now he has been found" (Luke 15:32).

*Tower of Conviction 14: We will help our child have opportunities for spiritual conversion (a change of mind-set).*

*Tower of Strength 5: We are to be in charge of surveying situations, establishing boundaries, and maintaining border patrol. The code word is consistency.*

Nothing counts like the health of your children. People who haven't been through losing a son to the wrong crowd and to self-destructive behaviors and attitudes can't understand this, but the good parents who have are willing to withstand any critical looks and remarks while they hold their child safe with them once more.

And you can be sure of this: Your child is going to have to go against the tide of true love to keep walking away from you into sin. To walk into sin is to wade out into the muck away from both earthly and heavenly parents—because your child is God's child, too!

Be *nice* while being firm, and he or she will be more likely to get homesick and come home. In the next chapter, I'll give you a formula for applying a proper pressure setting for helping your child.

CHAPTER **19**

# ORCHESTRATING RESCUE AND RECOVERY

**T**his chapter reviews and builds on what you've learned in the previous chapters, and it will show you how to ad*minister* rescue and recovery (R and R) operations for your misbehaving teenager, if you happen to have one. The same concepts and principles apply to guiding teenagers who are basically behaving themselves.

Every fortress must maintain a carefully designed rescue and recovery strategy, and your family fortress is no exception.

### The seven essential strategies of R and R work *in concert*.

Your rescue and recovery plan involves seven essential strategies of R and R that must occur simultaneously, constantly, consistently, persistently, and relentlessly—*in concert*—as you seek to rescue and recover your children or preserve your children.

### 1. Keep *compassionate pressure* on your children to act responsibly.

The positively best thing you can do for your children is to raise them consistently with the real world. Future employers, future families, and God Himself will not put up with . . .

> rudeness
> selfishness
> extreme sloppiness
> dishonesty
> disloyalty
> irresponsibility
> tantrums
> chemical abuse

or with those who . . .

> often search for loopholes
> refuse to listen

refuse to follow instructions
sneak around
fudge on the rules
hide to avoid doing their parts

or with those who are hateful to their providers. And if you allow these misbehaviors, *you are helping your children prepare to fail and be rejected* throughout their lives. You are right if you keep positive pressure on your children to act responsibly.

Be strong! Be consistent! It is not best for your children for you to indulge them as no one else will ever indulge them again.

### 2. Discover and correct contributing factors of offensive behavior or attitudes as much as possible.

While you are applying pressure for responsible behavior, it is essential that you search for any causes of the problems and try to correct them. For example, all along I've stressed the importance of getting a thorough physical examination for your children to be sure there is no physical cause for uncivilized behavior. Also, I've been outspoken about the need to cut off the negative reinforcement of the wrong crowd. Remember that the wrong crowd is family enemy #1. Other causative factors could include parental expectations being too high, parents favoring one child over another, problems left over from a divorce, child abuse, or unsuccessful or negative experiences at school, to name a few.

### 3. Provide a reassuring atmosphere to encourage children to change for the better.

Suppose you made a series of giant mistakes at work, and the boss came down on you really hard. He called you a stupid idiot, and he made fun of you in front of your fellow workers. And suppose he said to you, "Okay, even though you are the least productive employee I've ever had, I'm going to waste my time and give you one more chance to do better. But I'll tell you right up front that I don't think you've got what it takes to do better!"

How would you feel? Would you want to do better, or would you be too hurt and too angry to try? Would you feel that you had been given a decent chance to improve? Would you say that he had given you a re*assur*ing atmosphere for doing better?

Then don't make the same awful mistake with your children. Excluding them from all family activities, making caustic remarks to them (or to other family members about them), prophesying failure, not trying harder yourself, and the like are ways that the decency can be drained out of the opportunity to change. Children will not change until somewhere along the way they are provided with a re*assur*ing atmosphere in which to change.

As I wrote earlier, you will probably get what you expect. If you expect failure, a teenager will pick up on that intuitively, and he will more likely lower himself to meet your expectations. If you expect success, a teenager will be more encouraged to succeed. In psychology, it's called scripting. Be careful about what script you hand your teenager to follow.

*Compass*ionately scrutinize your child's world and demand that the environment offer a re*assur*ing and supportive atmosphere favorable for succeeding in changing for the better.

Here are the elements of a re*assur*ing atmosphere and of a decent opportunity to do better:

- The parents have taken on new poise by read*just*ing their posture in cooperation with the seven commandments for developing the proper posture as parents.
- The parents have become more competent and confident by adopting the convictions expressed in the fifteen towers of conviction.
- The parents have become stronger and more composed through building or re*model*ing the seven towers of strength, as much as possible.
- The parents have recognized the *Trojan horse* for what it is and are shutting off the moral and spiritual pollution issuing from his belly (this point will be discussed later).
- The parents have come to know who their allies are, and they are beginning to welcome as many of these rein*force*ments as they need: school personnel, counselors, ministers, friends, relatives, a support group, police officers, juvenile probation officers, and others. (See Part V, "Your Allies.")
- The parents have stopped hoarding grudges and punishing and have started disciplining instead. They have begun to provide an optimistic grounding structure (or some other plan) through which a child can reteach trust and reestablish a positive relationship within the family and the community.
- The parents have come to realize that remedial efforts for life-dominating problems, such as alcoholism, drug dependency, habitual criminal behavior, gambling, promiscuity, "addiction" to the wrong crowd, and the like, must be as intense and supportive as a program like Alcoholics Anonymous.

## 4. *Offer abundant encouragement for improvement.*

You may not be in any mood to do this if you have been abused by your teenager, but it is essential to R and R. You must recognize your son's or daughter's good qualities and compliment them.

Have you ever known anyone who thought you had no redeeming qualities? Were you drawn to that person? Or were you repulsed? Did you want to do what that individual wanted you to do? Or did you want to say, "Get lost"?

It's a fact: *Your children will find you repulsive and they won't want to please you if they think you think they're all bad.* Use this knowledge to motivate yourselves to see their roses and comment on their beauty instead of always nagging about their thorns.

While you keep the pressure on them to do better, you must compliment their progress. One of the best ways to motivate children to do better is to notice their good points—their good attitudes, their good behaviors, and their good accomplishments. Doing better must have its happy rewards since young people are giving up instant pleasure for delayed fulfillment—a BIG assignment!

**5. *Constantly monitor the general health of your children's lives by using the intensive-care instruments in the shepherd's tower.***

Tower of Strength 4 asserts: We have a better overview than our child does. And this means that parents can oversee children's lives for the purpose of helping things be better for them.

This tower is your intensive care unit (ICU) and contains intensive-care monitoring instruments for keeping check on your teenager's social, emotional, and spiritual health. The instruments are in the form of questions. To use them, ask:

(1) Is our child linked in with good people by being loved and returning love?
(2) Is our child increasing in value and feeling valuable?
(3) Is our child enjoying re*creat*ional fun?
(4) Is our child dreaming dreams and maintaining an exciting and inviting future to look forward to?
(5) Is our child gaining confidence in his or her ability to perform admirably in the adult world?
(6) Is our child receiving divine guidance, cleansing, help, purpose, and security?

(*Note:* The more you are able to help your child improve the condition of these vital areas, the more you are helping your child.)

**6. *Model the self-control you are encouraging your children to mature to.***

Modeling self-control is hard. You feel desperate, and your natural tendency is to do desperate things. But you can't afford to react that way. It is subversive to your parental purposes. Values are caught more than they are taught.

The *self* in self-control bothers me. You need team-control! This team needs to include your Good Shepherd (Christ), other adults in your family, your pastor, and other parents who have been through what you're going through. If you're having control problems, don't be reluctant to ask for help.

**7. *Arrange opportunities for children to spiritually convert to a new spiritual and mental focus for their lives.***

If your children are misbehaving, they are revolving their lives around the wrong focal points. If they change their focus, they will change their choices, and they will change their attitudes and behaviors.

Defiant and rebellious teenagers need to convert . . .

- from pursuing evil to pursuing good
- from having everything in common with the wrong crowd to having nothing at all in common with the wrong crowd
- from being self-indulgent to becoming others-minded
- from being unmotivated to caring about their contribution to the world
- from living only for this world to living with their viewfinders set on the eternal perspective

These points describe much of what is meant by Christian conversion.

*These seven essential strategies for R and R must be constantly* in concert.

These essential strategies for rescue and recovery must occur simultaneously, constantly, consistently, persistently, and relentlessly—*in concert.*

Keep reviewing, being sure that all essentials for the rescue and recovery operation are in place and relentlessly working. I've provided you with a summary of all this information in formula form and in tool form. Feel free to invite a counselor to help you if you need to.

## Use the formula for a proper pressure setting for orchestrating a rescue and recovery effort.

You must keep *compass*ionate pressure on your children to act responsibly. Your pressures must be pressing in the right direction for rescue, recovery, and reconciliation—creating an atmosphere that will sustain living rather than dying. Love leaves you no choice but to press your children toward regeneration and to break them away from degeneration.

But how do you apply consistent pressure in a positive, constructive, and attractive way? The following formula systematizes what you've already read in this book. It's another way for you to digest and make use of the concepts and principles.

You've got to become more and more magnetic while the road of hard knocks becomes more repulsive. Your beautiful harbor as a family can be pulling your teenager toward you while the ugliness of sin will eventually shove your child away from it and from the bad guys. The formula shows you how to pull while letting sin shove so that your child can finally be freed of his or her entanglements and entrenchments.

---

### The proper pressure setting for rescuing, recovering, and reconciling with your teenager

EQUALS:

The *magnetic pull* of your love and your familyhood

PLUS

The *moving power* of your intercessory prayers and of those of your closest friends

PLUS

The *warm neon welcome* that radiates from your shepherds' hearts and your intensive care unit

PLUS

The *lighthouse beacon* built within kids' natures that directs their return to their roots—their heritage and your uncompromised and dependable values

PLUS

The *relentless nudge* of the teenager's ever-present *guard*ian conscience

PLUS

Your *beckoning assurance* of forgiveness and acceptance

PLUS

Your *standing offer* of an *attractive* and decent opportunity for redemption

PLUS

The *open arms* of Christians who clearly want him or her to return
to their circles of friendship

PLUS

Your *removal of the barrier* of harbored grudges and bitterness
that you've purged through forgiving your wayward child

MINUS

The *no-man's-land* of any caustic comments from family members

MINUS

The *interference* of solvable causative factors of defiance,
wrongdoing, and alienation

MINUS

The *erosion* of the evil influence within the *Trojan horse* by no longer
allowing him to empty the contents of his stomach in your home

PLUS

Your son's or daughter's *awful ride* on the road of hard knocks

PLUS

The *repellent* of the stench of disappointing and souring sin

PLUS

The *shove* of your child's guilt, insecurity, and homesickness

PLUS

The *rejection* of those who are rejecting their God, their families, and their
country, and who will finally reject your child—finally unmasking
and showing their *repulsive* selfishness

MINUS

The *blockade* of the terrorists—the wrong crowd.

Reread the formula and see which elements you can have some control over and which ones you can't. Do what you can where you can and wait for the other factors to do their work. This serenity prayer is a good way to pray as you work the formula...

*God grant me the uncommon sense to patiently wait for the pressures I cannot apply, to kindly apply the pressures I can while remaining as attractive as possible, and grant me the courage, control, and endurance to keep my balance. Amen.*

And be patient. Patience is a tool! I write that with an exclamation point because you must learn that you are taking action when you are patiently waiting for the rest of the formula to do its work. Some people have a strong urge to charge ahead because they feel that they might not be courageously standing up for what's right if they don't. To them, I say: Do not equate patience with ineffectiveness or weakness.

Being patient is a form of action; it's a tool in your toolbox just like establishing boundaries is a tool in your toolbox. So, be sure that all the pressure settings you can control are being adjusted properly and apply the tool of patience to the others. One day, I trust, most of the formula will come together, and the stage will be set for rescue, recovery, and reconciliation.

The eighth element in this formula—the *open arms* of Christians who clearly want him or her to return to their circles of friendship—is one for which you can enlist help. Take this formula to your pastor or youth minister, point out the eighth element, and request the help of your church in providing that element of the formula.

Now, as you work on what you can of this formula (becoming as magnetic as you can), and while you patiently wait for the rest of it to work (for wrong to become more and more *repul*sive), use the following form to orchestrate a rescue and recovery operation for your teenager.

## Use this form to orchestrate the seven essential strategies for rescue and recovery.

I have put the seven essential strategies for R and R into a question format for you. Fill in this form every few days. Before long, you will learn to implement the strategies spontaneously without this form.

1. Keep *compassionate* pressure on your children to act responsibly.

    A. Are you doing what you can to apply the formula for a proper pressure setting for orchestrating a rescue and recovery effort?      ☐ Yes  ☐ No
    B. Which elements that you can impact need your attention?

    _____

    _____


2. Discover and correct contributing factors of offensive behavior or attitudes as much as possible.

    A. These may include the wrong crowd, negative adult influences, bad mental programming from the electronic wrong crowd, medical problems, poor self-image, parents favoring another child, parents' expectations too high, leftover problems from a divorce, or others, such as . . .

    _____

    _____

    B. Have you found any contributing factors? If so, what are they?

    _____

    C. What are you doing to alleviate their influence on your children?

_____

_____

3. Provide a re*assur*ing atmosphere to encourage children to change for the better.

A. Are you giving your teenager the benefit of the doubt and optimistically expecting him or her to do well this time? *(Remember that it's human nature to script the expectation, to reflect the projection.)*     ☐ Yes  ☐ No

B. Have you taken on new poise by read*just*ing your posture in cooperation with the seven commandments for developing the proper posture as parents?
☐ Yes  ☐ No
If your answer is no, which ones require attention?

_____

C. Have you become more competent and confident by adopting the convictions expressed in the fifteen towers of conviction?     ☐ Yes  ☐ No
If your answer is no, which ones require attention?

_____

D. Have you become stronger and more composed through building or re*model*ing the seven towers of strength?     ☐ Yes  ☐ No
If your answer is no, which ones require attention?

_____

E. Have you recognized the *Trojan horse* for what it is, and are you shutting off the moral and spiritual pollution issuing from his belly? *(See chapter 20.)*
☐ Yes  ☐ No

F. Have you come to know who your allies are, and are you beginning to join hands with these rein*force*ments? (See Part V.)     ☐ Yes  ☐ No

G. Which allies are presently rein*forc*ing you?

_____

H. Have you stopped hoarding grudges and punishing and started disciplining instead?     ☐ Yes  ☐ No

I. Have you begun to provide an optimistic grounding structure (or some other plan) through which your teenager can reteach trust and reestablish a positive relationship within the family and the community?     ☐ Yes  ☐ No
Briefly describe your plan:

_____

_____

*(This plan may involve admitting your teenager into a treatment center or having one on standby, if he or she becomes willing or desperate enough to enter one.)*

4. Offer abundant encouragement for improvement.

A. How have you complimented and encouraged your child this week?

_____

_____

B. If you haven't done this, how can you correct this undersight?

_____

_____

*(The best way to motivate children to do better is to notice and compliment the good they do—their good attitudes, their good behaviors, and their good accomplishments. Doing better must have its happy rewards since young people are giving up instant pleasure for delayed fulfillment—a BIG assignment!)*

5. Constantly monitor the general health of your children's lives by using the intensive-care instruments in the shepherd's tower.

These instruments are in the form of questions. They are . . .

A. Is our child linked in with good people by being loved and returning love?  ☐ Yes  ☐ No
If so, with whom?

_____

If not, here's how we will seek to help:

_____

Does our child have a loving and positive adult to listen to and to respond to him or her?  ☐ Yes  ☐ No
If so, who is this vital person?

_____

If not, here's how we will provide this very important person:

_____

B. Is our child increasing in value and feeling valuable?  ☐ Yes  ☐ No
If so, how so?

_____

If not, here's how we will seek to help:

_____

C. Is our child enjoying re*creat*ional fun?  ☐ Yes  ☐ No
If so, how so?

_____

If not, here's how we will seek to help:

_____

D. Is our child dreaming dreams and maintaining an *exciting* and *inviting* future to look forward to?  ☐ Yes  ☐ No

If so, what is *exciting* and *inviting* in his or her near future? _____

This week? _____

This month? _____

And in the distant future (captivating dreams)?

_____

If not, here's how we will seek to help:

_____

E. Is our child gaining confidence in his or her ability to perform admirably in the adult world?    ☐ Yes  ☐ No
If so, how so?

_____

If not, here's how we will seek to help:

_____

F. Is our child receiving divine guidance, cleansing, help, purpose, and security?
☐ Yes  ☐ No
If so, how so?

_____

If there's a problem in one of these areas, here's how we will seek to help:

_____

_____

*(Note: The more you are able to help your child improve the condition of these basic needs, the more you are helping your child.)*

6. Model the self-control you are encouraging your children to mature to.

    A. Are you modeling the self-control you are encouraging your children to mature to?    ☐ Yes  ☐ No
    If you are, how so?

    _____

    If not, how are you planning to improve?

    _____

7. Arrange opportunities for children to spiritually convert to a new spiritual and mental focus for their lives.

    A. What opportunities did you arrange last month?

    _____

    B. What opportunities are you arranging this month?

    _____

    This year? _____

# CHAPTER 20

# EXPELLING SABOTEURS

**Y**our family fortress is being penetrated by trespassers. These enemies are out to sabotage your good posture, your towering convictions, your growing strength, your moral and spiritual influence, and your gallant efforts to orchestrate a rescue and recovery operation for your teenager. Or they are out to destroy your efforts to prevent your teenager from getting into serious trouble. Everything you do is in danger of being undone.

The worst news is that you or your children are the ones who are assisting the enemies into your home. These enemies are riding in the belly of the *Trojan horse*. You've got to discover the enemies and expel them from your fortress—if at all possible. Welcome to "Operation: Search and Expel."

### We have pulled the *Trojan horse* into our family fortresses.

Many parents have asked me, "How did our child become a stranger to us?"

Numerous parents have said, "We can't understand it. We don't know how our child got to be this way. We don't see how he could be raised in our home and turn out to love the things we're against and hate the things we believe in. He's like a stranger to us. We just can't figure out how this happened."

A parade of parents have expressed this bewilderment. They're asking, "How did my own child turn against me?" "Where did I go wrong as a parent?"

I tell them that one of the biggest problems is the *Trojan horse*. Most parents have pulled the enemies right into the middle of their homes, and some don't even know it! These parents have become tolerant or comfortable with their enemies while the enemies *slowly but surely* alienate their children from them and from what they hold dear. *The* Trojan horse *could be making strangers out of your own children,* and it may be undoing everything you are desperately trying to do.

### Review the story of the *Trojan horse*.

Around 1200 B.C. the city of Troy had been under attack by the Greeks for ten years, but they could not conquer the city. Troy was strong. Time and again the Trojan forces had driven the Greeks back to their ships.

The Greeks had suffered heavy casualties. They were about to fail. Then they came up with a novel plan based on deception. They built a huge wooden horse, hid warriors inside, placed it outside the walls of Troy, and sailed away in their ships as if they were finally giving up and admitting defeat.

The Trojans saw the retreat and discovered the horse. A prophetess named Cassandra and a priest named Laocoon warned them not to pull the horse into their city. But Sinon, a captured enemy among them, convinced them that they should pull it in because the horse was sacred and would bring them protection.

They pulled the *Trojan horse* into the very midst of their fortress, celebrated their apparent victory, and fell asleep. While they slept, the Greek warriors slipped out of the belly of the horse, opened the city gates, and let in the rest of their warriors. They slaughtered the drowsy Trojans! Burned their city! Showed no mercy!

Without realizing what they were doing, the Trojans had destroyed themselves with the *Trojan horse*. They had pulled their enemy right into their midst.

## We are destroying our families with today's *Trojan horse!*

We or our children have pulled the *Trojan horse* into the very center of our family fortresses just like they did in Troy. We are asleep to its danger just like the Trojans were.

- The morals of our children are being slaughtered.
- Our values are being burned.
- Our children are being turned into strangers.
- And history is repeating itself.
- We are being no smarter than the ancient Trojans.

On second thought, maybe the Trojans were smarter than we are. We see that our kids are being damaged somehow, some way, and still we don't recognize the *Trojan horse* for what it is.

## The enemies are inside the *Trojan horse*.

How many of you reading this book would knowingly take in a house guest who would tell your children about his sexual escapades? Who would brag to them about how he took off his lover's clothes, how he made love to them in bed, how delightful the experiences were and how right they were?

Or how many of you would let your thirteen-year-old sit in the corner of your neighbor's bedroom and watch him seduce his girlfriend?

None of you.

But that is exactly what your children can watch on television! And that's on regular television. Nudity, actual intercourse, and profusely filthy language are not unusual on pay TV or satellite.

Unmonitored TV viewing is one of the enemies in the *Trojan horse*. The TV sits there in the middle of your family fortress making strangers of your children, programming their values to be different from yours.

What are your views on affairs? Homosexuality? Guys and girls just living together? Abortion? Violence? Materialism? Chemical abuse? Patriotism? Does your

TV agree with you in front of your children? If not, what are you doing with that *Trojan horse* in the middle of your family? Start *watching* what you're watching!

Christian families who would not break the Ten Commandments are entertaining themselves by watching other people break those very commandments! The TV is teaching your children to break The Ten Commandments. Watch what they are watching! Sin is contagious!

Now watch for the more subtle things about TV:

Do you believe Christian living should be top priority? Is it evident on the shows your family views?

Should partying be more important than integrity? How is it on the shows you watch?

Should money and what money can buy be the whole quest of life? Is it on the shows your family watches?

Beware: The uncontrolled TV sprang from the belly of the *Trojan horse,* and it may be right in the center of your home radiating contradictions to what you hold dear. Do your kids have TV's in their rooms, too?

### *The uncontrolled stereo is in the belly of the* Trojan horse.

The rock stars and the country stars and even the easy listening stars often directly oppose the traditional Christian moral values that you love. They are teaching your children to disagree with you. The headsets your kids wear look like futuristic, mental programming devices! And they are!

My younger son, who is fifteen now, decided this week that his youth-counseling father needed to become more informed. Steve said, "Dad, you're just not in touch with how bad things are." He took me to a music store and gave me a tour of the rock releases. It was depressing. I assumed things had gotten less explicit since AIDS had become such a threat. Not so. Go see. Find out what programming your children are receiving if they're followers of certain rock groups. Two of the groups that sing immoral lyrics toured near our area recently, and their T-shirts are being worn by local high-schoolers on our campuses.

### *Certain books and magazines are in the belly of the* Trojan horse.

It never ceases to amaze me how Christian families have rationalized themselves into believing that "mild" pornography is harmless. For example, a family needed counseling because the husband and father had become sexually involved with someone other than his wife. Come to find out, his wife had subscribed to his "mild" pornography for him (which they were also allowing their sons to read). And these parents were active leaders in their church.

Truly, you must wake up to the dangers of the poisons leaking out of the belly of the *Trojan horse!* But pornography is not the only problem. Other books and magazines can also be a big problem. For example, some magazines glamorize the lifestyles of celebrities, many of whom are exactly opposite of what you want your children to become. Why give them exposure in your home? The "nice" magazines are displaying glossy contradictions of your values to your children, and you are possibly the one who ordered their counterpublicity into your home.

Or how about the magazines that contain articles like these: "How to Enjoy Better Sex with Your Spouse or Lover"? Or *lover?* Do you agree with sexual encounters outside marriage?

Magazines like these are subversively telling your children that you are probably wrong about your moral standards. They are undermining your family values. They are influencing your children to doubt the *valid*ity of your Christian faith. They are helping your children become strangers to you!

You must stop this from happening. The *Trojan horse* looks tame, but he's wild. He will, in his deceptive and subversive way, rear up and eventually destroy your home if you don't take a stand and take control.

### Children's memories, replaying the movies they see at the theaters, are in the Trojan horse.

They see the movies outside your home, but they bring them home and replay them in their minds. Some researchers have indicated that the subconscious mind doesn't know the difference between imagined experiences and actual experiences. Both are recorded with the same intensity. If that's true, the mental replays of the flashy movies they've seen are every bit as destructive as the TV, maybe more so.

It would be impossible for the vast majority of movies to be more opposed to traditional family values and Christian values than they are. Nevertheless, parents routinely loan their kids out to the movie theaters. Don't be surprised, then, when you find that your children have become strangers to your belief system and defy you.

For the most part, theaters show movies that are directly opposed to everything you stand for. They portray . . .

> materialism
> rebellion
> deception
> irreverence
> the occult
> horror scenes
> violence
> illicit sex
> extreme profanity
> vulgarity
> excessive drinking
> drug abuse
> disrespect for authority

Everything you're against is glamorized in multimillion-dollar ways on the big screen.

Don't be uninformed. Go to the movies and see how your children are being programmed against you. My children and I have walked out of PG-rated movies. We don't even try to go to PG-13's.

If you're serious about knowing what's tearing your kids away from your values, go see for yourselves. Take in the teen movies, especially, and see what the movie industry is teaching your kids to be like. And while you're at it, survey the cartoon movies. Producers are now injecting immoral themes into cartoons. In *Howard the*

*Duck,* for example, a girl is shown in bed with the cartoon-character duck trying to seduce him. I was angry to see the implication of attempted bestiality in a children's movie; our family walked out. Low has gotten lower.

Many parents do not feel that their children's values are affected much by what they see on TV and at the movies because these parents don't believe their own values are affected. There's a difference: Most parents' were programmed twenty years ago. *Children's moral values are being programmed right now.*

You do have a choice about who programs your children. Use your right to choose, and be choosy, very, very choosy.

### There are other enemies in the Trojan horse.

The kid who is spending the night with your child may be in the *Trojan horse.* The kids on the phone with your child may be in the *Trojan horse.*

Your family is being desecrated by an alien force if your kids' friends are saying such things as:

- "How do you stand it? Your parents are so strict!"
- "C'mon, spend the night with me. My parents will let us go. They're neat! They don't care what I do."
- "My parents wouldn't make me go to church! I'd tell them where to get off!"

Know your kids' friends, and try to avoid such disruptive, counterintelligence operations.

Your child's brother or sister may be in the *Trojan horse.* A brother or sister who glamorizes sin to his or her siblings is an enemy in your home.

Investigate. It's humiliating to be infiltrated by the enemy when a member of your own family pulled him inside your family fortress.

Take a few moments to finish this sentence: Other enemies in the *Trojan horse* in our home would include . . .

I'd like to dedicate the conclusion of this chapter to parents of younger children. Since values are caught more than they are taught, children are molded by the models displayed before them. As they say in computer talk, "garbage in, garbage out." Protect your children's mental software from computer virus by casting out impressive immoral models. Bravely expel the *Trojan horse* from your home, to the best of your ability.

# ══ PART V ══
# Your Allies

**R**emember some of the old Western movies? The fortress would be about to collapse when over the hill came the rein*force*ments from the cavalry and saved the day! Your family fortress can also receive help from rein*force*ments. These are other authorities who will rein*force* your rescue and recovery operation to save your teenager. You should do your best to add these reinforcements to your *united front*.

The last portion of this book will introduce you to these allies, inform you of how to work with them most effectively, warn you about how a few of them might betray you and hurt you and your teenager, and offer guidance on how to be selective of persons you will trust for assistance. ■

CHAPTER **21**

# INTRODUCTION TO THE AUTHORITIES

**What rebellious teenagers *don't want* is exactly what they will get.**

**W**hen teenagers break the Ten Commandments and no longer honor their fathers and mothers enough to be obedient to them, they will suffer the natural consequences: What they *don't want* is exactly what they will get. They will get more authority hovering over them, and the authorities will ask more questions and impose more rules. Rebellious teenagers are crusading for more independence, but they will get less. Concerned authorities equals more hassle. That's just the way the world works.

*If they disregard and disobey their parents* and hot-rod the car, for example, they will finally get caught and will find themselves involved with a legal authority—*the police*.

*If they become more rebellious and rebel against the police*, too, they will be ticketed again and again until another authority, *the insurance company*, will step in and cancel their insurance. Mr. Hard Knocks will discipline them by requiring them to insure with companies that handle only bad risks. And Mr. Hard Knocks will charge them a fortune for their insurance! Nontrusting authorities equals more hassle. Thus . . .

$$\frac{\text{STUBBORN}}{\text{MISBEHAVIOR}} = \frac{\text{MORE}}{\text{AUTHORITY}} + \frac{\text{MORE}}{\text{RULES}} + \frac{\text{MORE}}{\text{QUESTIONS}} \; minus \; \frac{\text{DESIRED}}{\text{FREEDOM}}$$

*If teenagers become even more rebellious and rebel against both the police and the high-risk insurance companies,* a bigger authority, the state, will step in and take away the driver's license. Mr. Hard Knocks grounds them, and no amount of pleading, manipulating, or intimidating can change their plights. So it is with Mr. Hard Knocks in real life.

*If they disregard and disobey their parents and aren't dependable in their employment,* the other authority will fire them. Disappointed authorities equals more hassle.

*If they disregard and disobey their parents and run around with the wrong crowd,* authorities will identify them with that group and assume they're like the others. They will expect them to do wrong, and when they do, the authorities will have less patience with them. Suspicious authorities equals more hassle. Why less patience? Because the authorities already don't like the crowd they are running with (due to the abuse they've already received from people like them), and because authorities know that if individuals are entrenched with the wrong crowd, they likely will not do better. Trying to help them will most probably end with frustration from having failed with them. Why risk failure?

*If teenagers disregard and disobey their parents and drink illegally or do drugs,* they will eventually get caught because they can't always win when gambling with not getting caught. When they do get caught, they will discover that their rebellion has introduced them to new and bigger authorities. They will find that frustrated authorities equals more hassle . . .

- principals expel them from school.
- police officers arrest them.
- juvenile authorities jail them.
- judges order them around.
- probation officers supervise them.

Thus . . .

MORE AUTHORITY = MUCH MORE HASSLE AND MUCH LESS FREEDOM

## Meet your allies.

These authorities are your allies. They are your rein*force*ments! These other authorities will rein*force* what you have taught your children throughout their lives. You should do your best to add these rein*force*ments to your *united front*.

*Don't be against your reinforcements!* Don't storm the police station ranting and raving about the arrest of your child. Don't go to the school and harass the principal about disciplining your child. Don't tell the juvenile probation officer that you don't need anyone to tell you how to run your family.

Remember Tower of Conviction 1: We are breaking through denial and admitting that our child is, in fact, ignoring our guidance on purpose. Break through denial and cooperate with your allies.

### It Is as your child chooses.

If your child chooses to do wrong, that choice means he or she has chosen to bring unto himself or herself the consequences of doing that wrong. Authorities are only *responding* to what your child has chosen. Their day would have gone better, actually, if your child had not forced this crisis on them.

### Thank God for reinforcement from the reinforcements.

You have been teaching your child that doing bad turns out bad, so *let your teaching be true*. Thank God that someone else—a more authoritative authority—is taking a turn teaching your child the very lessons that you've been trying to get across.

Don't mess up the lessons by siding with your child against the authority or by having an I-told-you-so attitude. Instead, be a courteous onlooker and appreciate the break from being the only one telling your child what's right and wrong.

Of course, as an observer, you should constantly evaluate what's happening, and if you find the unusual case of an authority bullying a teenager, you must step in cautiously (behind the scenes, if possible) and adjust toward justice. You'll wisely do this without leaving the impression that the injustice justifies the teenager's wrong behavior.

## Actively form alliances with the allies.

Your rein*force*ments are schoolteachers and principals, school counselors and private counselors, the employers of your children, the police, juvenile probation officers, inpatient treatment centers, foster homes, and county youth shelters. Check out your allies. You've never really considered them much before. You haven't needed to. Now, though, they are your rein*force*ments, and you need to get to know them better.

*Warning:* People who are hurting terribly, like you, tend to be so caught up in their own problems that they are blind to the problems and needs of other people. The urgency of securing help can push aside tact and patience. However, inconsiderate attitudes and actions toward your allies will cause them to be less attracted to helping you.

## The word is *diplomacy*.

The first step to good diplomacy with your allies is to understand where they are coming from before you approach them. Walk a mile or two in their moccasins, as the saying goes.

I want to help you do that. I've done the research for you by interviewing educators, police officers, and juvenile probation officers, and I'll present my findings in the next few chapters.

Each chapter will follow the general theme of understanding the allies' positions. We will look at their secret frustrations in their work, what parents do that irritate them, what parents do that they appreciate the most, and how you can help them serve your family. Understanding your allies better will help you know how to approach them more diplomatically and more constructively.

In summary, your family fortress needs allies on the outside. You have your towers of conviction and your towers of strength in place, and now you need some allies to help you parent your children. They rein*force* you and should become a part of your *united front,* if possible.

You also need some allies to keep yourself in a coping frame of mind. You'll need your church, perhaps a parent support group, perhaps a counselor of your own. I'll provide information about those allies as well.

PROPER POSTURES + CONVICTIONS + STRENGTHS + ALLIES = emPOWERed PARENTS

CHAPTER **22**

# THE SCHOOL

T he school is your closest ally. Next to you, teachers and school administrators are in contact with your children more hours than anyone else. Teenage problems usually surface at school, which often means that parents and school officials are thrown together to work for the betterment of the child. It is essential, therefore, that you learn how to work effectively with school personnel.

As a means of better understanding how to diplomatically approach teachers and administrators to gain their respect and support, you should be aware of their frustrations and preferences. Then you can be more successful at forming an alliance with them.

## Consider these points *before* approaching school officials.

In preparation for this chapter, I interviewed school superintendents and principals and asked them two questions on your behalf: (1) How would you like parents to approach you when they come to deal with the problems their teenagers are having at school? and (2) What approach have parents used that you have found to be especially disturbing or counterproductive?

The educators indicated that parents need to consider some *matters* before they make their first approach to school officials. They suggested at least three things that need to be understood.

### *Parents and administrators want basically the same thing.*

They want things to go well for the student.

A superintendent expressed it this way: "Parents can make their best approach to school personnel by remembering that teachers and school administrators have the same goals as they do. We are not adversaries of the parent or the child. We want each individual student to have good experiences in school."

Since parents and school personnel have so much in common—both focusing on the well-being of the same young person—they should have a good start toward making excellent allies for one another.

**School administrators are limited in how far they can go in helping
a particular student.**

A principal said, "Parents need to understand that we are limited in the degree of the individual concessions we can make due to our responsibility to the student body as a whole and to all other parents. Furthermore, we are limited by state laws and by school policy. We are not free to do anything we want without regard to these other considerations."

**Parents should avoid jumping to conclusions before they speak
with school officials.**

A superintendent said, "The assumption that school officials are picking on the child or somehow 'out to get the child,' almost without exception, proves not to be true."

## Question 1:  How can parents most effectively approach school officials?

**Parents should start by going to the school official originally
involved in the problems.**

A superintendent advised, "Try to solve it at the level where it occurred, with the cast of characters who were present at that time. This keeps the problem from getting bigger than it deserves to be.

"If and when parents bring problems to me," she continued, "I always begin by asking them if they have been to the teacher involved."

She said, "If parents find the problems can't be resolved on that level, then it would be appropriate for them to appeal for help to the next higher level. If it's an academic problem, they should approach the counselor. Otherwise, they should go to the principal."

The superintendent's office should be the last place people turn, according to this respondent. But when the problem does reach her office, she knows what she will do. She explained, "I try to get everyone together because it's only together that we can work toward resolutions. My role is to resolve the stalemates. My role is to open up and assist communications—not to say it's his fault or her fault. I believe that few people want to purposefully hurt someone. We have the same goals."

**Parents should approach school personnel with open minds.**

Their purpose should be to get a clearer view of the situation, to better understand everyone's point of view, and to work together as allies for the well-being of the young person.

The superintendents suggested that a good approach would be to say:

*I am here because I care about my child and my child is hurting; but I realize that there are a lot of things involved, and I would like to find out what they are and see what we can do.*

A principal asserted, "I don't think it's proper for parents to come here in a defensive mood. They should come with the goal of seeking understanding first. We are trying to be fair to everyone involved, based on the evidence before us."

Another commented, "Parents should come to the school open to the possibility that their child has done something wrong. Some say, 'My kid is innocent. Why are you mistreating my kid?' But all they know is what their child told them—they haven't heard the teacher's perspective or ours."

"If parents are so defensive that they have gone blind to any other point of view, the atmosphere gets so charged with anger that level-headed discussion can't be accomplished," a principal said.

A superintendent made the point that he knows teachers can make mistakes, "but still the wisest and most constructive approach is for parents to begin with the attitude of believing that school officials want what's best for the child."

### Both parents and teachers need to be trained in how to give and receive negative feedback.

A superintendent said that people should understand that criticizing a single behavior is not a condemnation of the whole person, be it student or teacher.

A principal said, "We are not trying to pronounce their child bad, or the parents' parenting skills defective. We are just trying to make a needed adjustment."

One of the superintendents looked at it from the parents' perspective: "Parents are concerned that if they give negative feedback, their child will receive retribution in some form from the teacher. This simply should not happen. One of my goals is to forge a stronger working relationship between families and school personnel."

But I would like to add: If retribution does happen, parents are obligated to their children to help them find relief from a condition so unjust and so painful that it could turn them off to school and to achieving.

Worse yet, if you realize that your children are being mistreated and you don't take up for them, they will feel abandoned by you; they will feel that you were against them when they needed you the most. The relationship between you and your children could be permanently damaged. After such a catastrophic disappointment, your children may stop caring whether they ever please you again.

Kids who have done wrong and done wrong and done wrong scream for fair treatment at every point of conflict. Their insides are shouting: "Please! Notice that someone else is wrong for once!" Taking up for children, when it's appropriate, tells them that you still care and haven't given up on them and that you're still fair-minded.

Remember that an adolescent's cry for justice seems to be stronger than the sex drive. Consequently, if your child is being treated unjustly, you must seek relief for him or her.

Be diplomatic as you disagree with the powers that be; after all, you don't want to lose your ally over one disagreement. Try to disagree agreeably.

Abiding by these suggestions will help you move into a good position for seeking relief. Administrators will appreciate the properness of your approach, and the atmosphere will be more conducive to changing things for the better.

### Question 2: What approaches by parents have you found to be counterproductive?

One answered, "To me, as a superintendent, the most frustrating thing that can happen is for someone to call me and tell me about a problem and then try to swear me to secrecy, not wanting their name mentioned. We have to open it up and deal with it if the problem is to be solved."

The superintendents were disturbed by either of two extremes: "I know it happened just as my child told me." Or "My kid is always in trouble, and I'm not surprised at anything he does."

A principal had comments on the first of those extremes. He said, "When a parent tells me, 'My child won't lie,' I realize that I don't have an objective parent with which to work."

A principal said he doesn't like it when parents arrive at his office issuing threats, or when they don't want him to get the teacher's input.

A principal said that it bothers him when "we spend a lot of our conference time talking about the school's reaction to the problem rather than what the student did wrong—the child is left out."

The purpose here is not to say that school officials are usually right and parents are usually wrong. The purpose is to help you understand how school personnel feel and think so that you can approach them constructively. Teachers and administrators can be very important allies for your family.

This chapter is in no way a thorough treatment of this subject. However, it clues you in on how to put forth your best effort toward winning school authorities as allies to your rescue and recovery operations. You'll need their rein*force*ment.

CHAPTER **23**

# YOUR COUNSELOR

**A**nother ally you should consider is a counselor with experience and connections, one who specializes in youth and family problems. He (or she) can be an important addition to your *united front*. He can offer experienced guidance because he has gone through the territory of teenage troubles with many families before you. He should be able to help you know how to make connections with other allies since he is involved with them on a daily basis. And he should be able to help you keep coping, to tie a knot at the end of your rope and hang on.

(*Note:* A psychologist suggested I make it clear that I use the word *counselor* here as a general term to include psychiatrists, psychologists, and professionals who hold master's degrees.)

### A man-to-man talk for fathers and husbands.

Men are generally more hesitant to seek counseling than women are. Men tend to feel that going to a counselor is akin to admitting that they don't know how to help their own families. The comment I've heard so often is: "I don't need anybody to tell me how to run my own family."

But men should consider seeing it another way. Turning to a counselor for help is no different from turning to any other professional when you need expert help. When you take your car to a mechanic or your bookkeeping to an accountant, you're doing the same thing you're doing when you turn to a counselor for help with your family: you're turning to someone who knows more about your problem than you do because that's where the individual's training and experience lie.

Some men hesitate to go to a counselor because they feel he or she will get on their case about something. In general, most competent counselors have a very tolerant attitude about the past and are more concerned about the future. We've all made serious mistakes; we have that in common. Sincere people are willing to correct their mistakes and prepare for better tomorrows.

Some men don't go to a counselor because they're afraid the counselor will find out about something embarrassing. These men should remember two things: (1) Counselors are like doctors; they've already seen and heard almost anything they can see and hear; and (2) counselors are people, too, and they've had embarrassing things happen in their own lives.

When a man comes to me for counseling, I respect him more. It takes a big man to turn to another person for help. I'm confident that other counselors realize this as well.

## What should a good counselor be able to do for you?

He or she should . . .

- be understanding of the pain you are feeling and help you learn ways of coping with it.
- help you keep private matters private.
- help you improve your skills for parenting a defiant child.
- help you chart a course of corrective action, a rescue and recovery plan for seeking to save your teenager.
- help you monitor the progress of your R and R operation and recommend needed adjustments.
- counsel with your teenager and with your family.
- stand in for you with your teenager when he or she is too turned off to you to hear what you have to say.
- help your marriage survive the complications teenage problems can impose on a family.
- put you in touch with key people among other allies.

If a professional youth and family counselor is unavailable, seek help from your minister or youth minister. Some of these men and women are also competent to help families in trouble.

## How do you choose a counselor?

Be absolutely sure you find someone who counsels in harmony with the basic tenets of the Christian faith, who can agree with your towers of conviction, who is wise enough to examine the family system, and who is wise enough to consider any possible physical causes of the teen's misbehavior.

The counselor must be both realistic and thorough.

Never be shy about asking a counselor about his (or her) counseling philosophy. Ask how he will plan to handle your case. (Don't forget to be diplomatic! You want to form an alliance of rein*force*ments.)

Show him this book—the posture you are assuming and the convictions to which you are holding—and ask him if he can agree with its basic concepts and principles. This is one of the best ways to see if you're going to be compatible in your thinking. If you are *not,* keep looking. You can't put on a *united front* with a counselor who is at odds with your posture and convictions.

As fair and reasonable Christian parents, you don't want to try to get your teenager to own up to his or her misbehavior and become responsible for it while a counselor tells your child that the problems are mostly your fault because you're too strict, too religious, too old-fashioned, or too establishment-oriented; or tells your teenager that his or her problems are all inherited or are entirely due to some past trauma; or teaches him or her that practically anything is okay so long as you're comfortable with it and no one gets hurt; or stamps your teenager with a psychological label and offers no constructive help.

Membership in or credentials from professional associations do not necessarily assure quality. No matter what important papers are displayed on the walls of counselors' offices, their personhood, their values, and their gifts and skills matter the most.

I need to alert you, though, that one way some teenagers manipulate their way out of counseling is by giving a bad report on the counselor. Kids know your values, they know what you would find offensive, and they know how to alarm you about the counselor you've chosen.

If and when you get a bad report, call the counselor and check it out. If it turns out to be a con job, your child needs to see that the manipulation attempt will not work, and the counselor needs to know that the manipulation was attempted. If the bad report turns out to be true, you may need to turn to another counselor.

It's okay to change counselors if you decide you should. Your child needs to see you stand up for what you believe, and the counselor needs to be reminded that certain approaches are offensive to people with traditional Christian values.

## Diplomatically ask questions.

In addition to being sure you and your prospective counselor hold to the same posture and convictions, you'll want to be sure you agree on basic values. You'll need to diplomatically ask a few more questions. Some counselors are bothered when their competency is questioned, but you must not let that stop you. Selecting the right counselor for your child and your family is one of the most important decisions you will make. You are choosing someone as important as a heart surgeon. In a sense, the counselor will be a heart surgeon counseling the very "heart" of your teenager and your family.

Here are some questions you should ask:

- In your counseling, do you honor traditional Christian ideals and values?
- Are you a Christian? What church do you attend?
- What is your stand on premarital sex? Extramarital sex? Abortion? Smoking pot? Using drugs? Teenagers drinking alcohol? Sixteen or seventeen-year-olds coming and going without asking permission from their parents? How about the importance of teenagers finishing school before they leave home? And ask about whatever else is important to you and yours.
- Do you follow a counseling approach that holds that people are responsible for their own attitudes and behaviors?
- If you discover that ours actually is a case where two (or one) basically reasonable parents are trying to pull their rebellious teenager away from the wrong crowd and from self-destructive behaviors, how will you go about helping us rescue and recover our child?

- How much and how often do you involve the parents in counseling?
- Do you mind if we call you periodically to see how things are going and to receive an updated overview of your treatment plan for our child?

### This is not the place to compromise.

Don't accept a counselor's statement that personal beliefs don't matter because he or she is a professional and counsels objectively. That isn't true!

The counselor's values (or lack of them) will come through verbally or through body language or through the "feeling" in the office. If you've selected the wrong counselor, he or she can assist the wrong crowd in turning your child away from you while you're paying him or her a fee to betray you.

Almost all counseling involves moral and spiritual values. How about your problems with your teenager? If they are related to moral and spiritual values, you must select a counselor whose values are basically in harmony with yours.

A woman asked me if I knew anything about a certain John Doe, Ph.D. She wanted to know if it would be advisable to take her son to him. I didn't know Dr. Doe, but I called a Christian doctor friend and inquired about him. He answered, "Well, he's not a Christian, and he doesn't attend church, but he's so professional and objective that it wouldn't be a problem."

I relayed my findings to this mother, and I also told her about a Christian psychologist she could consider. She decided to go with Dr. Doe.

She took a seat in his office and immediately noticed a book lying on his desk that had to do with the uniqueness of open marriage. Their conversation confirmed that they didn't share the same values. She left and sought other counseling.

## Here are three true examples of how people were hurt by counselors.

A couple went to a counselor with their daughter and noticed that he cursed as he talked. That bothered them, but they figured he was trying to establish rapport with their daughter.

He saw their daughter many times alone, and they were pleased that she liked him so much. Then they discovered why: He was reinforcing her rebellion against her parents by agreeing with her that having sex with someone you truly love is okay and that smoking pot is not all that bad. He counseled her that she needed to be very cautious with her smoking because some Americans are still narrow-minded.

The parents realized what was going on when their daughter lost her temper and screamed, "My counselor told me that you need counseling more than I do!"

They called the counselor, and their worst fears were confirmed. He had been deprogramming and devaluating the Christian values that they had so lovingly taught their daughter, and they had paid him a lot of money to do it. They felt betrayed by the counselor.

A young woman came to me for counseling because she was hurting from the consequences of partying and being promiscuous. We met several times. I gently sought to help her understand that she couldn't begin to feel good about herself until she began to live in harmony with her values, recover her self-respect, and reestablish a good reputation among her significant others. I was discreetly recommending a complete change of lifestyle, and I was offering her abundant support for doing so.

During a mood swing of not wanting to give up her old ways and old friends, she went to a secular counselor. He heard her story and told her that casual sex is not a moral issue. He told her that one reason she was suffering was because her significant others were imposing "puritanical" values on her.

She returned to me saying, "I can't go to a counselor who thinks it's all right to sleep around! Even I know that's wrong, as messed up as I am!"

Last Christmas, I received a letter from her. She drew a happy face representing herself, and beside it she wrote: "Jesus is Lord. He disciplines those He loves." She closed with: "How we grow over the years! Joy to you and your family!"

Unfortunately, this woman had a setback. As I was doing my final rewrite of this book, I received a phone call from her. She told me she had fallen back into her old ways but had been recently released from a residential treatment center. We need to keep her in our prayers.

A married couple came to me for counseling. He had had an affair, but had ended it, and was pleading with his wife for forgiveness. She was not opposed to reconciliation, and I began to work toward that end.

Meanwhile, they went to another counselor to get a second opinion. They reported to me that he said, "I would not necessarily recommend this to you—I mention it only as one of several options—but if the wife were to have an affair, it would even things up so that the two of you could start over again on equal footing."

My response was, "Please don't accept that advice. You cannot heal by inflicting more hurt."

But the wife did have an affair!

Apparently, she had been looking for a rationalization. She ended up moving in with her new flame, deserting her husband and their children. The marriage was torn asunder, and the husband was left bitterly wondering how he could have been so foolish as to pay a counselor to "finish off" his marriage.

What's the problem here? The problem is that counselors who don't honor traditional Christian moral values have no standarized set of values and their advice may go against those values you uphold. You don't know what is going to be communicated in their private offices.

## A counselor can become a key ally and friend for your whole family.

Carefully choosing a counselor is the prerequisite of assuring that you gain an ally. Your purpose is to rally together a *united front* of people who are going to be "with" you and who will provide you with reinforcement for your rescue and recovery operations for saving your teenager. To be united, you and your counselor have to be reasonably close in your value systems.

By the way, when I speak of a *united front,* I don't mean that you are going to gang up against your child. I mean that you are going to come together *on behalf* of your child; you are putting together a *united front* for the sake of your child.

*It's okay for a counselor to courteously confront you.*

Parents need to be courteously confronted if they are making an error that is further complicating their problems. I have counseled many parents, and I don't enjoy confronting them about what they may be doing to hurt their situations. But courteous confrontation is sometimes vital for initiating the healing process.

Allow yourselves to be constructively criticized. After all, your most important treasure, your child, is at stake.

The possibility of problems within and between parents is the reason why it is good to find a counselor who approaches youth and family counseling by examining the system at work within the family. At times the family system itself produces the problems.

The scenario goes like this: A child is placed in a treatment center and gets better. But when he comes home, the malfunctioning family system, which contributed in some degree to his problems in the first place, is still malfunctioning and aggravates the same problems in him again and nearly all is lost.

A counselor who knows how to discover destructive family systems can help families resolve them and stop the perpetual damage being caused by them.

## Seek referrals before you select a counselor.

Referrals from people you trust are usually a safe approach to the selection process. Your minister, the school counselor or principal, the family physician, or a police officer (those who are solid Christians) will likely be able to put you in touch with the right agency and the right person. It's especially nice when they know of people who have used the counselor being recommended. They can phone those individuals (if they will go the extra mile for you) and ask them to phone you and give you their opinions.

But no matter who makes the recommendation, investigate the counselor for yourself. You are choosing a "heart surgeon." Use the information in this chapter and your own good intuition to interview and choose a responsible counselor.

## Monitor counseling.

Monitoring counseling should be easy because you should be involved in counseling with your child. If you're fair and reasonable people, the counselor should want to work with you to help you orchestrate your rescue and recovery operation for your child. In addition, the counselor will want to give you guidance on how to be more successful in dealing with your child and in communicating with him or her.

But how can you monitor what's going on between the counselor and your child when everything is so confidential? Counselors see the confidentiality issue as sacred, and some even take it to the point of not talking to parents at all and they may act surprised that you'd even inquire. Don't allow that. Your child is your responsibility, not theirs. When you stop paying, counselors become absent from the picture, but you have to deal with your child the rest of your life. Things *are* confidential between counselor and client, and confidentiality *is* sacred; yet counselors *can* clue you in on how things are going without being unethical, if they will.

These are my suggestions for keeping in touch with what's going on in the counseling office . . .

1.  Ask your child an open-ended question like, *How did things go in counseling today?* But don't press. If your child chooses to talk with you about it, you can pick up some clues from what is said.

2.  Call the counselor and say something like,

*I respect the importance of confidentiality and I wouldn't ask you to tell me anything confidential, but I would like to know how things are going. What is your treatment plan at this point?*

3.  If the counselor is evasive or rebuffs you, you can change counselors, but if your child really likes the one he or she is with, you'll be reluctant to change. Then you may opt to go to your trusted family physician, sign a medical release form, and ask him to do the checkup for you. Counselors aren't quite as free to be evasive with doctors as they are with parents; doctors are on the same professional level with them, and doctors send them some of their referrals. If your counselor is unwilling to be cooperative with your physician, ask your physician's opinion about the wisdom of staying with that particular counselor.

4.  Make it clear to your child's counselor that there are certain matters you want to know, period. You could say something like:

*It's very important to us to know if our child is under a serious threat of any kind. For example, if he is suicidal, we want to know; or if he is taking a drug that could be lethal, we want to know. Will you tell us if you find that our child is under a serious threat of some kind?*

In making this request, you are not asking too much. The American Psychological Association's "Ethical Principles of Psychologists" says under Principal 5:

Psychologists have a primary obligation to respect the confidentiality of information obtained from persons in the course of their work as psychologists. They reveal such information to others only with the consent of the person or the person's legal representative, *except in those unusual circumstances in which to do so would result in clear danger to the person or to others.* Where appropriate, psychologists inform their clients of the legal limits of confidentiality. [Emphasis added.]

5.  You can request to be present at the beginning of each session. You can request ten minutes to give a family report, to mention any concerns you have about attitudes and behaviors in your home, to be available for any family matters that need to be discussed, and to deliver some compliments when they are deserved.

You will want to protect your child's rapport with the counselor by not causing him or her to feel that too much is being shared between adults. A suspicious child may quit trusting the counselor and may stop sharing on a confidential level, greatly handicapping counseling. You need to be like the mother of Jesus: She was good at quietly pondering things in her heart.

# CHAPTER 24

# THE SUPPORT GROUP

**P**arents, you need to be understood.

You need the friendship of someone who can identify with what you're going through, someone who knows how to care, someone who really does understand.

You need to let your bottled-up emotions flow in the form of talk and tears. Talk and tears are T and T for relieving emotional distress.

You need support for figuring out how to help your child, for implementing your plans, to help you continue wanting to help your child!

You need your confidence regenerated, your courage boosted, and your stamina renewed.

You need to be taught how to survive in this strange, cruel wilderness of family problems, in this eerie jungle of confusion and frustration.

And you need someone to rejoice with you over the victories! To applaud you when you've done well!

We meet these needs in our counseling agency through our parent support group, which is named Parenting Within Reason (PWR). The name emphasizes the balance we diligently seek to maintain, and the initials are the abbreviation for *power*.

We have found the companions we get to be with in this group to be wonderful reinforcements deluxe. The participants say that it is one of the best allies a parent could have.

In this chapter, I'll tell you how a group like ours functions, and I'll briefly outline how one can be started in your community.

### Companionship ranks highest in support received.

I asked several abused parents what had helped them more than anything else. I thought the parents in our parent support group would list God as their greatest tower of strength, since ours is a Christian counseling center, but they didn't.

Each person listed the support group. It was unanimous. The understanding people who had moved up beside them and who were standing shoulder-to-shoulder with them near their battlefields had become their greatest stabilizing factor. Here are a few of their comments:

- "You can say what's bothering you, and they understand. I finally feel understood."

- "Because of the group, I was able to maintain my self-control during confrontations."
- "I relaxed a little and didn't stay angry all the time."
- "We were able to regain confidence in ourselves as parents."
- "If we hadn't been coming to the group, we would have killed that boy when we caught him in our daughter's room in bed with her. We're serious! This group saved his life, and it saved us from a prison term!"

## God mostly helps people through people.

The parents' testimonies about the life-preserving help that they've received in our group are in line with my belief that God mostly helps people through people. When we are going through our roughest times, God helps us by putting the right people near our pathway—people He has been preparing for years to be qualified to help us during our crises.

Praying people sometimes don't recognize God's answers because they are looking for some miracle to drop out of the sky. They need to begin to also look for a person (or persons) to walk into their lives—someone God has been preparing and wants to provide for them.

Parenting Within Reason has accomplished some incredible feats. I would like to give you a few examples.

One night, a set of parents had another major disagreement with their seventeen-year-old son. He ended up walking out of their home. Their fifteen-year-old son, angered by his perception that they had been mean to his brother, pulled a knife on his dad. A set of PWR parents took the fifteen-year-old into their home and let him cool off a night or two with them. The elder brother called his parents and wanted to come back home. Instead, they had arranged for him to stay a week with still another set of PWR parents. During the separation, they sought family counseling together, and they were reunited at the end of the week.

In another situation, a businessman's daughter had been leaning toward illegal behavior. He and his wife turned to our group early to learn how to become stronger parents. They established companionship with members of the group, and they learned some of what you've been reading in this book.

Then, their daughter fudged too far and ended up in juvenile detention. The traumatized mother couldn't stand the thought of her daughter spending a night in jail. Her natural reflex was to run and get her, kiss her, and say everything would be all right (as she had done throughout the girl's childhood). In spite of knowing Tower of Conviction 10 (We will allow our child to experience the pain of his or her own wrong choices), it seemed she would rescue her daughter pre*mature*ly.

She called one of her newly found friends in the group for support. Our veteran explained that her daughter had also been in juvenile detention (JD). She told her it was a clean facility where both a male guard and a female guard were on duty together at all times. "The horror stories you hear about jails are not true of our particular JD facility," she assured her.

This woman didn't sleep a wink that night, and people from our support group gave her companionship during her vigil. With this en*courage*ment, the mother was able to support her husband's decision to allow their daughter to experience the natural consequences of her crime, and they let her serve her one night in jail.

This event happened several years ago, and the daughter has never been back to jail. She is graduating from high school this year as an honor graduate.

(In PWR, we normally assign support people to parents who are in a crisis or who are facing a sizable challenge with their children. It's a standard service provided by our group.)

Still another family had to go to court over a crime their son had committed. The parents were embarrassed and afraid. A set of parents from our PWR group accompanied them to court and sat beside them, in companionship with them, throughout the proceedings. The parents were greatly comforted by these understanding peers.

### Huddle up with helpers.

Huddle up with helpers. Develop some supporters and expand your *united front* to include this grand ally. God will help you through your ministry to one another. Keep building the guard's tower taller and stronger: We are developing a *united front*.

### But what if you have no support group in your vicinity?

If that is the case, there are at least three ways you can go. You and your spouse can bind together to form a support group of two. You can chart your course with this book.

Or you can develop an informal support group composed of family members and close friends who will read this book with you and agree to support you in harmony with it. These individuals must be the kind of people who can understand your objectives and work toward those same objectives with you. They can give you companionship and support you emotionally. They can help by providing an alternative place for your teenager to be (in preference to his or her hitting the streets). They can help by steadying the teenager when your presence is not effective in that way (for whatever reason) and by being individuals to whom the teenager can unload problems or share feelings.

Or you can become the key to forming a parent support group in your community. The manual is in your hands. But please don't take the lead unless you have a well-established reputation for being a Christian and being a "together" person. The way this group will be received in your community will largely depend on the first individuals who represent it. If you don't think you qualify to lead in starting a group, then you can be a catalyst for starting the group: Put someone else in front and support him or her diligently.

### What is a support group like?

A support group like Parenting Within Reason (PWR) is a group of parents who have formed a companionship of mutual support based on the concepts and principles contained in this book. Teenagers are not allowed to attend the meetings.

The group finds a youth and family counselor who agrees with the concepts and principles in this book, will attend their meetings, and will provide individual and family counseling. This counselor will not take over the group. This is to be a self-help group. Instead, he or she is to be there as a quiet monitor and as a resource person for the group.

*As a monitor,* the counselor will see some of the teenagers in private counseling and will be at meetings to be sure teens are being properly and appropriately represented to the group by their parents.

For example, my monitorhood was very important in a case where a woman came to the group to seek support for forcing her sixteen-year-old daughter to be more receptive to her fourth marriage. She accused her daughter of being rebellious and inconsiderate. In talking with her daughter in private counseling, I discovered that the girl wasn't being rebellious at all. She was just saying, "Mother, I can't emotionally handle another of your marriages. Can't you just let me get through two more years of high school before you bring another stepdad into my life?" Had I not been there, the group would have heard only the mother's side of the story and may have supported the mother in putting inappropriate pressure on her desperate and pleading daughter.

*As a resource person,* the counselor, being trained in both psychology and Christian principles, will be a wonderful source of information and guidance. As the ally with connections, he or she can help parents know where to turn (or not to turn) for additional help.

For example, one of the parents in our group recommended a counselor I knew was not against smoking pot or having sex outside marriage. I cautiously and courteously advised against him and saved this family from a disappointing (and an expensive) wrong route.

*Note:* The counselor's attendance at the meetings should be without cost. But parents should expect to pay a fee for private counseling.

*Another note:* Be sure the counselor has been selected in harmony with the guidelines for choosing a counselor provided in this book. Be absolutely sure to check with several families who have received counseling from this counselor. The actual reputation of the counselor is the true test. In checking the reputation, you are not looking for someone who succeeds in all situations (since success is controlled by the clients as well as by the counselor); you are looking for someone who uses reasonable counseling procedures and counsels within the perimeters of traditional Christian moral values.

## How about the agenda?

Every meeting contains the following elements:

1. The meetings are two hours in duration. The first hour is for teaching, and the second hour is for applying the teaching to individual situations, sharing with one another, and supporting one another.

2. The meetings are presided over by a parent (or a set of parents) who serves as volunteer coordinator for a period of six months.

3. Before the meeting, participants gather early for coffee and fellowship.

4. The meetings begin promptly at the appointed time with a reading of the towers of conviction. These are read at each meeting *without exception.* This discipline keeps the convictions before the group and helps new participants digest them.

5. A chapter or portion of this book is taught at every meeting—perpetually. Once the group makes it through the book, the process begins again. Immediately before starting through the book again is a good time to advertise for new members.

Parent volunteers do the teaching. The concepts and principles must be so thoroughly digested that they become reflexively reproduced in thought and conversation and action. If a portion of this book is not taught at every meeting, the group will inadvertently drift away from its concepts. One of the most tempting temptations will be for the group to digress into informal opinion sharing rather than holding fast to these concepts and principles. When participants become familiar with these ideals, everytime someone mentions a concern, the commandment, conviction, strength, or principle that applies will instantly spring from someone's lips. The group must learn to talk the talk.

Our group had fun videotaping the volunteer teachers of this book. This helped in two ways: The videotapes were checked out to new people who needed to digest the material immediately, and the videotapes were used instead of "live" teachers the next time we went through the book. Watching one another on video added the pleasantries of home movies and bound us closer together as a group.

6. Allow each parent or set of parents to give a one- to three-minute summary of the reason for coming to the group (no one should be forced to share, however). That way the parents in attendance can identify others who could be most supportive of them. There will be parents of thirteen-year-olds, parents of seventeen-year-olds, parents of adult children, and so forth; there will be parents of runaways, parents of children with discipline problems in school, parents of children who are making poor grades in school, parents of pot smokers, and so forth. These folks need to find one another.

These three minute summaries also serve to assure parents that their's is not the only family in trouble. Sharing at this level stimulates and hastens companionship.

*An extremely important note:* We stress at each and every meeting that everything said in our meetings is to be held in the strictest confidence. Stories are not to be retold, even with names changed. Violation of the confidentiality rule causes automatic and immediate expulsion from the group. Fortunately, we've had to expel only one couple.

7. The coordinator announces how the small groups will be formed. We try to assign people who have similar problems to be in small groups together. This is done before the break so that people can go immediately to the small groups at the end of the break.

8. Break for coffee and fellowship.

9. The small groups convene. (A new support group doesn't break up into small groups because its members are few. When numbers increase and veterans develop, it will be appropriate to break up into the smaller groups.) The small groups are led by veterans of the program, and they meet for forty-five minutes. Their purpose is to . . .

- let each parent or set of parents share specific problems.
- receive suggestions on how they might handle their problem(s) in harmony with the seven commandments for developing parental posture, the fifteen towers of conviction, and the other concepts and principles within this book.

- make a commitment to the most appropriate suggestion.
- receive a promise of companionship from those who want to stay in contact with them throughout the week as they follow through on their commitments.

*Note:* Small group coordinators must require strict adherence to time limits so that each parent or set of parents has time to participate.

10. The large group reconvenes, and each parent or set of parents announces a commitment and who the companions are going to be.

11. The group unites in reading the seven commandments for developing the proper posture as parents.

12. The meeting is closed with prayer.

Here is the agenda for the meetings:

A. Coffee and fellowship before the meeting
B. The reading of the fifteen towers of conviction (5 minutes)
C. A teaching from *Relief for Hurting Parents* with discussion (30 minutes)
D. Each participant reports on why he or she is in attendance (20 minutes)
E. Break (5 minutes)
F. Small-group meetings (45 minutes)
G. Announcements of commitments and companionship (15 minutes)
H. Reading of the seven commandments for parental posturing
I. Dismissal in prayer

**Guest speakers are to give and receive.**

A guest speaker can be used during the first hour. Having a guest speaker will help the group in at least two ways.

First, the speaker can introduce the group to the thinking, procedures, and help of various allies.

Second, the group becomes visible to representatives of the agencies who visit you, and they will learn to respect the group more. And it is hoped that they will talk up the group to their associates in other agencies. They will likely be more helpful to your members when called for help. That is why they should be encouraged to stay for the whole meeting. Otherwise, they may leave during the break after they speak, causing the group to lose half the purpose for having them in.

When guest speakers are present, the teaching time for the book is reduced to fifteen minutes, and other agenda items are compressed as well. Nothing is eliminated because the guest speaker needs to see what happens in the meetings: *He or she must see the dynamics of the group!*

We have found it unwise to have more than one guest per month. The participants need all the time they can conserve for doing their work together. They have important concerns to deal with, and they should not be slighted. Their crisis may not be able to wait another week to be considered.

## What's involved in starting a new group?

*Do not put an announcement in the local newspaper* inviting people to help you start a new parent support group. The only way to have a good group is to start with a core of Christian people who are aspiring to be fair and reasonable parents, because the core you start with will chart your course.

So, you should start small and grow slowly. Invite a select group of parents to your meeting place and begin with them. As you start the group, you and your new companions will hear about others who are having misbehavior problems with their children. Ask them to join you. But try your best to invite only people who have *the capacity to be consistent* and who will not use the group as a tool for oppressing their children or who will not conflict with your group's moral standard.

For example, I went to observe another parent support group in Houston while doing research for developing our own. A set of parents there were trying to decide the stand they would take with their two teenage daughters. The mother told the group, "We've decided that our girls can spend the night with their boyfriends on weekends but not on school nights, and this seems to be working out pretty well."

The father objected mildly, "I don't think that I'm all that in favor of them having sex with their boyfriends all weekend like that."

The mother laughingly said, "You weren't against it when we were doing it!" The whole group laughed with her.

If you want to grow faster than you are growing, go to your school counselors, principals, and ministers and explain that you are looking for new participants for your group; ask them for referrals. Be open and tell them that you are looking for members who have the capacity to be consistent and who have the ability to receive new information without distorting it.

Once you get your core established, you have charted your course. If someone joins who doesn't agree with the values of your group, he or she will usually leave, and your group will be self-cleansing. If not, you must sharpen your diplomacy skills without compromising your values or purpose.

If you decide to start a new group without carefully selecting its charter members, you will likely have to be prepared for the trauma of requiring people to leave your group. Be prepared to see the group's quality degenerate before your very eyes and be prepared for your group to get a bad reputation with your allies due to the outlandish things being said and done by those erratic ones among you who distort your output.

Here's another story that illustrates the problems this can cause. A juvenile probation officer called me from the courthouse and asked, "Do you tell people to quit feeding their children if they're misbehaving? We have a teenage girl here who hasn't had anything to eat for twenty-four hours. The parents say that they are taking your advice by not feeding their daughter."

I assured the officer that I've never advised starvation. I say that between-meal snacks and desserts are family privileges and that if kids don't do their part in the family, they shouldn't expect to get all family privileges. But I've never advised parents to withhold adequate nourishment.

The point is this: The group is hurt in one way or another by people who can't seem to get their own acts together or who can't reproduce something without distorting it. Be careful. Work with people who can be worked with. Let the others get their help somewhere else. They need intensive individual counseling so that they can be encouraged at their own pace and monitored more intricately. This outcome cannot be achieved in a group like Parenting Within Reason.

Once your core group establishes the kind of organization you are, a desirable phenomenon happens: People will hear about your reputation, and people who hold to your standard will want to associate with you. Those who don't will usually want to avoid you. Numbers are not important. A group of around ten members is a nice size. Quality help is what's important, and that's why you should start your group with quality control as your top priority.

### Parenting Within Reason groups may be duplicated.

A Parenting Within Reason support group for parents can be a part of your community. Caring individuals may feel free to use the name if you wish. I only request that you be true to the concepts and principles of *Relief for Hurting Parents*. I am claiming no ownership to the name, but I will not and cannot be responsible for what happens in the groups or as a result of the groups since I will have no supervision privileges.

Last evening, I attended a reunion of the parents who helped form our parent support group several years ago. They organized the dinner on their own and invited me to enjoy the evening with them. They told stories about how much the group had meant to them during their times of crisis. We felt a warmth and depth of friendship that is rare in these busy times. Support. We've learned the rich meaning of the word.

CHAPTER **25**

# THE POLICE

**G**ood diplomacy begins with understanding, and understanding nurtures mutual respect and mutual support. In this chapter, I will help you better understand the position of the police department, the law enforcement ally.

### What is it like to walk in a police officer's boots?

I interviewed three police chiefs, a captain, and a juvenile investigator. I asked them three questions on your behalf: (1) What frustrates you about dealing with juveniles? (2) What annoys you about the way their parents present themselves to you? and (3) How can parents best cooperate with the police in helping them to help their family? Their answers will clue you in on how they are thinking and how you can best approach them to gain them as allies and have their badge of rein*force*ment to fall back on.

### Question 1: What frustrates you about dealing with juveniles?

In response to this question, the peace officers made the following comments:
"Parents aren't supervising their children."
"Either not enough supervision or too much supervision; we see both extremes a lot. The parents of the kids we handle can't seem to find a happy medium with their children."
"Parents aren't monitoring their children. We have kids who steal a new $300 bicycle, and the parents don't even question them about it when it shows up at home. In one instance, a kid stole a microwave and took it home. The mother set it up and started using it, and she never questioned the child about where and how he got it."
One officer said, "Seeing kids in trouble is in itself frustrating."
But another said, "I don't find it any more frustrating than working with any other person who has broken the law."
An officer complained, "The law itself is frustrating    the way the law is structured not to take hardly any action on juveniles—juveniles who need some kind of disciplinary action taken. A juvenile is involved in a crime, and the law and the people who administer the law don't recognize juvenile crime as being as serious as an adult crime when really there is no difference. If something is ripped off, it's ripped off just as much if the offender's age is sixteen or thirty-six."

"I don't get my expectations too high to begin with. I know, going in, that the most they will get is a consequence involving supervision by a juvenile probation officer."

"You just say *juvenile*, and my officers' eyes cross and their hair stands on end. They simply dread dealing with these cases."

### Why do many officers dislike working with juveniles?

Early on in my interviewing process, I noticed dread among police personnel about working juvenile cases. I was curious enough to ask the police chiefs why so many of their officers did not like to work with juveniles. They replied . . .

"It takes so much time. It can take a whole morning or even a full day just to take a confession because of the steps that have to be followed, and after that nothing may come of it."

"The load of paperwork connected to each arrest is greater than with adults."

"Why put out the work when before you can get your paperwork over to the juvenile probation department, the child is already gone and back on the streets? It often takes repeated offenses before anything is done of a penal nature. . . . It's a thankless sort of thing because after you've done all you can do, nothing much is going to happen to the juvenile."

"A kid can sit across the desk and give you a red-eyed cussing, and there is nothing much you can do about it."

"They don't like having to deal with the parents. They don't know how to handle the parents when they get irate," a police chief reflected.

"It seems that most of the juveniles we handle have been shown by example that what they are doing wrong is not all that bad. Our permissive society spins off teenage problems."

"We get frustrated because the sick family system that is causing this problem is still limping along making the problem worse and bigger."

"Male officers fear that teenage girls might make an accusation against them," a police chief noted.

### One police chief objected to what the others had said.

He countered, "The present system works for me. Let me tell you what I hope to accomplish when I arrest a juvenile.

"First, I want to gain restitution for the offended party.

"Second, I want to put this individual in a work program within the community so that he can feel the effect of undoing what he has done to society.

"And third, I want this child to discover that there are uncomfortable consequences for committing a crime.

"I can accomplish this within the present system."

### Other findings are significant.

I discovered that those who were well versed in juvenile law were not intimidated by how complicated it is. Those who weren't were. Many people in law enforcement were especially frustrated by trying to deal with status crimes—running away from home, skipping school, and breaking city curfews. The consensus of opinion was this:

"We get very little support from those who make the laws and from those who administer the laws. And the parents themselves are on-again, off-again. Our best efforts are probably going to come to naught."

I find this disturbing because leaving home without permission, skipping school, and breaking curfews are problems parents are trying to deal with much of the time, and this is where they need the most help. It's too bad the police are also finding themselves in a no-win position with the same matters. This ally of yours can't always rein*force* you.

### Question 2: What annoys you about the way the parents of offending juveniles present themselves to you?

The police chiefs and the officers said:

"Parents being on the defensive. Before you even tell them anything, they say, 'My child couldn't and wouldn't do anything like that!' "

"It irritates me when parents immediately assume that the police are the enemy, assuming a defensive position against us. If parents would realize that we are not out to hang their child and begin to cooperate with us in helping their child, things would begin to progress better."

"Denial. We can have evidence laid out before the parents, and the child can be sitting beside them saying, 'Yeah, Mama, I did it,' and she'll reprimand the child saying, 'No, shut up, you didn't either!' The parents are the most difficult thing about juvenile cases. They refuse to believe that their child is involved in a criminal case."

"As soon as I get the juvenile in the office with his parents, I can tell you within five minutes whether or not the juvenile will be a repeat offender. I can tell by the attitude of the parents. If parents defend their child in the face of clear evidence that the child did something wrong, I figure he will be a repeat offender."

"The nonchalant condoning of the crime is what aggravates the heck out of me. You run across this more and more. Like, 'What's so wrong with that? He's just being a kid.' Parents sometimes take the side of the kid (in front of the kid)—no matter what he has done wrong. On the other side of the coin is the frustrating attitude, 'Well, I don't care what you do to him. I'm through with him.' It leaves us not knowing what to do with the child from then on. Parents need to take a walk down the middle between these two extremes."

"After we pick up a child repeatedly, then the parents begin to say we are picking on their kid."

"The police are expected to become involved in things that should have been handled between parents to begin with. They call us in and I ask, 'Have you talked to the [other] kid's parents?' . . . and they haven't. We don't need to be involved in things that can be settled between cooperating sets of parents."

"In dealing with runaways, we've found that parents know where they are 50 percent of the time but won't go to them and demand that they come home. Instead, they call the police department and tell the police to do it for them. They should make their own try first. . . . Also, parents fail to inform us when a kid does return home. We touch base with them, and they say, 'Oh, she's been home for two days.' That's maddening!"

"We can't do as much as parents think we can. We have very specific guidelines from the state Juvenile Probation Commission that we have to follow in dealing with runaways."

"I've known parents to laugh at peer pressure and brush it off like it's no big deal, but peer pressure is one of the worst things a kid has to contend with."

"I hate it when parents are too severe with their children and quote the Bible to justify their meanness."

"I'm terribly annoyed by the way the parents don't demand respect from their children. They allow them to cuss them in my presence, and then turn to me and say, 'See how terrible he talks to me?'"

### Question 3: How can parents best cooperate with the police in helping them to help their family?

Their various answers were:

"Cooperate with us. I would say nearly half the parents don't cooperate well enough for us to help them help their children. The parents who are cooperative are so, I think, because they realize that whatever their child is doing out in the community is reflecting on them. They know they are responsible."

"Sometimes parents aren't in the mood to cooperate because an officer approached them with a horsey attitude. We have our own problems to deal with."

"Every time we work with a child who has torn up some property, we request restitution. If parents have had a complacent attitude about what their child is doing, when you hit them with restitution, it gets their attention really quickly. They begin to get involved with their child. Also, you get the child's attention. When he begins to have to fix up what he has messed up, he thinks twice about messing something else up."

"Admit the mistake and help the child learn from it and go on without becoming negatively set against that child. Parents aren't going to change the fact that it occurred, but they are more likely to make it through if they will give their child a chance to change."

"Parents need to get themselves and their kids into some type of counseling, some type of mediating service where they can find some common ground and repair what they've torn down and start from there. Just because parents are parents, they are not always right. Just because kids are kids, they are not always wrong. A mediator can help them come out of the trees so that they can see the forest."

"If parents find a joint in their child's room, they should bring that out in the open where it can be dealt with. You either solve that at home by talking with your child, or if the kid is belligerent and says 'You can't do anything about it!' then ask for our help before it gets worse. . . . I can admire a mother and daddy who marches in this police station with the child and sets him down and makes him tell us about it. That takes a lot of guts. Sweeping it under the rug allows it to grow worse."

### Select a police officer who can help you with prevention.

In my experience, most police departments have an officer who is especially good at relating to and talking to juveniles who are leaning toward doing wrong.

I would encourage you to call your local police department and find out who that officer is; then request he or she visit with you and your teenager. A uniformed officer can have an excellent effect on teenagers in helping them reconsider both their friends and the route their lives are taking.

Do not present this visit to the teenager as if it is punishment. Instead say . . .

*Since you have begun to make choices that could get you arrested and placed in juvenile detention, we feel it is important for you to get a preview of our local system of justice. We want you to be aware of all that could be involved in the route you have begun to take. So, we are going to talk with a policeman together . . . or separately, if you prefer.*

Parents have sometimes decided to take this a step further, and they have included a visit in a juvenile probation department and to a juvenile detention facility. I'll talk about this department as your family's ally in the next chapter.

CHAPTER **26**

# THE JUVENILE
# JUSTICE SYSTEM

I n this chapter, I will help you better understand the position of juvenile probation departments, the supervisory ally.

**The juvenile justice system should rein*force* parental authority.**

Parents who find themselves facing an appointment with representatives of the juvenile probation department concerning a crime committed by their teenage son or daughter feel awful about the whole ordeal. Intermingled with their sadness, embarrassment, and anger over their teenager's crime, they now have to open up their parenting methods to inspection by strangers (who may or may not be competent), want to or not, and comply with court orders, like it or not.

In spite of the trauma in progress, I'd encourage you to see the people in the juvenile probation department as allies in helping you parent your children and try to respond to them in a diplomatic manner.

Children who refuse to be decent and legal American citizens and cooperate with their parents invite more authority into their lives—enter the rein*force*ments—enter the juvenile justice system and the juvenile probation department. Each time a higher authority enters the picture, children are accosted by more rules, less freedom, and more interrogations.

$$\text{MORE AUTHORITY} = \frac{\text{MORE RULES} + \text{MORE INTERROGATIONS}}{+ \text{CLOSER SUPERVISION } \textit{minus} \text{ FREEDOM}}$$

Or in the words of teenagers: "More hassle!"

MORE AUTHORITY = MORE HASSLES

If you and your allies keep at disciplining your teenager and keep at it tirelessly, your misbehaving teenager may finally decide that the escapades aren't worth the hassle. I've seen this come true for several families.

In other words, behavior changes for the better when the pleasure of doing wrong is no longer worth the pain to be endured. It's okay to be sure the natural consequences of wrong behavior bring hassle after hassle after hassle. The more natural the hassle and the less parent-inflicted it is, the better lesson Mr. Hard Knocks will get to teach.

## Understand the function of the juvenile justice system.

In Texas, the juvenile justice system judges the situation and issues court orders as to what the state requires of the teenager and his or her family in seeking to rescue him or her from a criminal lifestyle.

The juvenile probation department is the arm of the court charged with being sure court orders are carried out.

I talked with five juvenile probation officers (JPO) in three probation departments in as many counties, and I'll be telling you what they told me. Your state's juvenile justice system may be different in some ways from the one in Texas, but the following information will still be relevant.

## Question 1: What are some secret frustrations on the job?

You'll notice that there's a wide variety of thoughts and feelings in these responses of juvenile probation officers:

"Lack of enough resources to help in all the varieties of ways that help is needed."

"Enough money: Treatment programs for alcohol or drug abuse or for psychiatric care are priced clear out of reach in many cases."

"Lack of time to be as thorough as we'd like to be with each child."

"We find it hard to get our cases through the courts because they are so tied up with adult felony cases that could go beyond the statute of limitations causing them to have to be dismissed; there's no statute of limitations on juvenile cases in Texas and these can be pushed aside, and are."

"The District Attorney's office often assigns its newest attorneys and police departments often assign their newest officers to juvenile cases because these are considered Mickey Mouse in comparison to the big felony cases."

"Disagreements between higher-ups and/or courts on how a particular child's case ought to be disposed of."

"The court has judicial immunity. The JPO doesn't have. The JPO gets blamed and has to take it. The court is not so accessible."

"Returning a child to a home where the warped family system is going to hurt the child again."

"When children are getting the blame when it's really the parents who should be put in jail."

"I am so sick of people coming in and saying, 'We don't drink, we don't carouse, we go to church, and this kid is giving us these problems.' I'm so tired of this that I get blue in the face. They, in this way, are using the child as the focus of the problems of the family. In this way, they are avoiding looking at and addressing the other root problems that need to be addressed."

"The parents won't admit that they, too, have problems, like marital problems or alcohol problems [or parenting problems]."

"When children are being locked up simply because you can't find the parents so that you can make other arrangements."

"Parents not thinking they have the time or not taking the time to work with their child."

"Listening to the parents' criticisms when they are really mad at the system but dump on the JPO."

"The aggravation of having to deal with status offenders [runaways, truants, violators of city curfews]."

"There's an idea which prevails with the public that seems to say: 'When it comes to juvenile offenders, if you show them some love and give them a hug, they'll be okay.' Some of these kids are criminals in every sense of the word, and cookies and milk are not going to turn them around. Fifty percent of all crime in America is committed by juveniles."

"We have the same coworker problems as any other workplace."

"County politics."

"Our salaries are too low."

## Question 2: What annoys you about parents of adolescent offenders?

They answered:

"Parents having already let it go too long. They didn't start early enough, when things first began to go wrong. They stayed in denial too long."

"Blaming everybody else and everything else for their kids' problems . . . not being consistent . . . not keeping in touch."

"Not supervising their children and giving them too much money. . . . they need to earn much of their money."

"Having a know-it-all attitude."

"Parents being too busy to want to be involved to the extent they need to be to help their teenager with his or her problems."

"Denial as expressed in the attitude of: 'Why are you picking on my son? He hasn't done anything!' In some cases, kids confess to a crime, and their parents still refuse to believe it, saying, 'You did no such a thing!' "

"Parents sometimes refuse to see that their child is mirroring them. For example, parents will be complaining about how disrespectful their son or daughter is while I sit there listening to them respond the exact same way to their child. The child learned hateful and rude attitudes from his or her parents and is reflecting them back on them."

"Refusing to accept and carry through on recommendations made by the JPO."

"I'm frustrated when the first words out of parents' mouths are, 'What can you do with this child?' and they want me to become the proud mother of a bouncing fifteen-year-old that they have created. They want to bow out, lock, stock, and barrel. . . . they want us to fix everything in quick order when it took fifteen years for their child to develop the problems he or she is having."

"Giving up on counseling and the healing process too quickly . . . standing up counselors . . . discontinuing counseling without notifying us."

## Question 3: What first impressions of the family are important?

They replied:

"The amount of concern the parents show."

"Are the parents together? Are both parents and the child willing to be involved in making things better? I'm alert to the fact that single-parent families can give only about half the supervision needed."

"I first begin by wondering if these parents are going to be consistent or haphazard. About half the parents don't follow through like they should."

"The parents' willingness to participate. Willingness to be supportive of the recommendations that come out of this office. Their willingness to keep us informed."

"I look for the amount of respect the parents have for themselves, my department, and the courts. I notice everything, including the way they dress."

"I want to know at the very beginning: Does the child recognize what he or she did to be wrong? Does he or she recognize that he or she has caused hurt to someone else? Does he or she care about that?"

"I observe the child first. I am first of all concerned about the child and the offense. Is this unusual for this child? What is the child's track record like at home? At school? At work? With peers? Is chemical abuse present with the child or in the home? Is the child experiencing success somewhere, like in sports, band, or some club?"

"As I interview a family, I'm ascertaining: What kind of help does this family need?"

### Question 4: What are the first things you look for in a family to see if it is a healthy one?

These responses will help you know how to put your best foot forward with this ally:

"Supervision."

"Communication. Do they talk and hear? Is it yelling, or do they talk?"

"Parent and child interaction or lack of it."

"Are they blaming and overblaming the child?"

"Are they blaming everyone else to avoid looking at the possibility that they have problems themselves?"

"The amount of involvement with the child."

"Are they actively loving and caring about the other members of the family?"

"It's important to me that the family is honest and open, letting the 'doctor' have a look without finding it objectionable."

"Family values and lifestyle."

"Do they attend church together?"

"How supportive of the children are the parents?"

"The absence of chemical abuse (including alcohol) in the home."

"Relating to one another constructively rather than destructively."

"School being a fulfilling experience in the children's lives."

"The willingness of the child to do better."

"The willingness for this family to seek help for themselves."

### Question 5: Do you have any preconceived notions about families involved in teenage problems?

They said:

"Every situation, regardless of how similar it looks on the surface, is different.

Some kids do something only because it is fun. Others are trying to survive a bad home situation. Others are rooting into a criminal lifestyle."

"We feel like it is the parents' fault until they prove to us differently." (Only one JPO said this.)

"Breakdown of the parental role. Parents can divorce each other, but they can't divorce their kids."

"The majority of the cases I have dealt with over the past ten years showed a lack of parental guidance, supervision, and support."

"More times than not, the parents need more counseling than their children do. Around 60 percent of the kids we handle, for example, have one or both parents with alcohol problems."

"Every situation is different. To me there is not one reason why there is delinquency. I do not see it primarily as the parent's fault; I feel that children are responsible for their own behavior."

## Question 6: How can parents help you help their children?

I said, "Let's say the parents take the stand of seeing your department as one of their important allies in rescuing and recovering their teenager. How can they be supportive of your efforts with their child?" The juvenile probation officers' answers will help you know how you can best cooperate with them. For your convenience, I've condensed them into the following list.

First, *break through denial.* "They have to go ahead and accept the fact that their child really does have problems," an officer stated.

Second, *cooperate with what is being suggested by the JPO or the court.* As a chief probation officer said, "Parents should cooperate even if we have to go to court and restitution gets involved. We have a lot of resistance to children paying for the damage they have caused. Parents should make their kids earn the money, even if it's merely doing extra chores around the house, and pay their own restitution."

One JPO described his favorite parents to work with: "The best parents I work with are those parents who have a balanced view. They stand by their child, wanting him or her to be dealt with fairly and justly, but at the same time they want their child to be required to make things right. Their attitude is that they want to do everything they can to help the probation department help their child."

Third, *follow through and do so consistently.* As an officer said, "Accept the recommended counseling and treatment program, be consistent, and give it time to have an effect."

Fourth, *keep in touch and keep the officer informed, reporting any change.* If a recommendation is not working out, the probation officers want to know; they don't want parents to stop carrying through on the recommendation without reporting it.

If there is progress, they want to know. If a child begins to violate the rules of his or her probation, they want to know. A JPO said, "Some parents won't report, say, an hour's violation of curfew because they don't want to get their child in trouble again. They just let it slide, and it slides right back into big trouble."

Fifth, *understand the position being occupied by your child's JPO.* One said, "Don't use the probation officer as a threat to the child. Use him for what is intended.

He is there to monitor and supervise the situation, to offer assistance, and to help them utilize community services. Don't use him as a surrogate parent."

Another said, "Try to realize that the court put their child on probation, and the probation officer is not there to be blamed but to carry out the court's orders and to help the family. I personally see myself as more of a caseworker than a policeman." (By the way, the perceived role of the JPO differs with each officer and each department.)

Sixth, *hang in there.* An officer said, "Be consistent and dependable in discipline, promising rewards and punishments, and coming through as promised."

Seventh, *be alert to a family system that fosters the behavior objected to.* An officer encouraged, "Be somewhat introspective and see for yourself if there are some problems in the family dynamics that are causing the misbehaviors of the child. You have the private view of your family that no one else gets to have."

Eighth, *get the child active in positive peer groups.* An officer recommended church youth groups. "There they get moral education and better kids to relate to," he said.

Ninth, *get the child involved in positive activities so that he or she can feel successful.* Clubs and sports were suggested.

Tenth, *realize that it's going to be a slow, constant battle.* An officer observed, "There will be some progress and some setbacks along the way. Expect both."

## What if you disagree with the recommendations?

I anticipated that readers would like to know what they can do if they disagree with a JPO's recommendations. To my question, an officer replied . . .

"The juvenile probation officer has the clout to override what the parents want if their child is on probation and assigned to him or her; but generally speaking, the JPO will work with the parents to find something they will commit to willingly, give their best effort to with a positive mental attitude, and stick with it."

He continued, "If the parents object to what the JPO is recommending and he or she refuses to change the recommendation, their only appeal is directly to the judge. Appealing to the judge is a maneuver that is possible, but again, they have to realize that the burden of proof is on them to show the judge why they disagree, and why the plan they are offering is better than the one recommended by the juvenile probation department."

But almost unanimously, the officers said that their recommendations are negotiable since they want the parents to feel comfortable with their plan of action for helping the child. The parents are the ones who must carry through and try to make it work on a daily basis. If they disagree with it, there will naturally be a lack of commitment to it. This has a good ring to it, doesn't it? It means that JPO's are also interested in developing a *united front* for controlling and helping the misbehaving child.

I asked what parents could do if their teenager was assigned to a counselor they didn't prefer. A chief juvenile probation officer answered, "My experience is that a JPO or a court will not require a certain counselor. The parents will be allowed to choose their own counselor so long as the individual has acceptable credentials."

This same officer expressed his feelings further: "I would never require a family to go to someone they didn't want to go to because it sets things up for failure."

There's still room for concern here, though. Another JPO replied quite differently. She said, "If we have made counseling a part of their order of probation, and the counselor is specified in the court order, the JPO can force them to go to that particular counselor or they can be reported to be in violation of probation to the judge."

If parents disagree with a court-ordered part of the probation, they would have to return to the designated judge to request a change.

## Why are psychological tests sometimes given to children in trouble with the law?

Parents have wondered about psychologicals being required by juvenile probation departments. On your behalf, I asked why these are required.

One said, "To give us some clues as to how we can develop a plan that will be best suited to the needs of the child."

Another said, "To rule out or to discover the presence of serious psychological problems."

And another: "Placement centers almost always require a psychological before they will accept a new resident."

Each officer agreed that psychological testing had been a helpful tool for them more times than not.

One officer volunteered his synopsis: "I've been in this work for eleven years. I have found some psychological testing to be startlingly accurate, and yet, some of it hasn't been worth the paper it was written on. It is not so scientific that there is not room for variations of opinion when it comes to subjective interpretations."

## Juvenile probation departments usually operate in one of three ways, or in a combination of the three.

One chief juvenile probation officer told me that there are three ways juvenile probation departments see themselves . . .

1. They see themselves as public servants, here to help. They will give it their best try. They will discern what's best for the child, map out a plan, and help the family make it work.

2. They see themselves as police officer types, and they go strictly by the book. They have a stereotypical police officer's mentality, and their motto seems to be "keep yourself protected at all times."

3. They see themselves as a referring agency. They prefer to send the family somewhere else for all their help.

I trust that this inside view of the juvenile justice system and the juvenile probation department will help you better understand how to try to form an alliance with them that will rein*force* your family's effort to rescue and recover your teenager.

CHAPTER **27**

# COUNTY YOUTH SHELTERS

f a child runs away from home and is picked up, authorities may decide that conditions in the home are too emotionally charged for the child to be returned to it. Consequently, they may place him or her in the county emergency youth shelter—an ally that may help you or hurt you—for up to thirty days or more.

The nature of this ally varies so much from county to county that there's no way to tell you how to best deal with the one in your county. Some shelters are extremely helpful to families. Others are extremely harmful. Still others are in between those extremes.

*Important note:* I am only discussing shelters in relation to their role with rebellious teenagers. I am not discussing shelters in their role of sheltering children who have been emotionally, physically, or sexually abused or neglected.

You need to do some local research to find out what the emergency youth shelter is like in your county. Checking references is the best way of knowing what on earth you're dealing with. This will be easy to do if you are in a support group for parents of troubled teens because other parents will already know from experience.

## What's right with good shelters?

*Good shelters reinforce the basic, reasonable rules enforced by most families.*

Well-run shelters provide good supervision and require residents to keep their space neat and clean, do their chores, make good grades, and be respectful of house parents. They require them to be decent, legal, cooperative, and productive American citizens. Their privileges are based on their cooperation and performance. These shelters forbid them to smoke cigarettes or pot, do drugs, drink alcohol, be sexually active, use profanity, possess lewd magazines, and so forth.

It is absolutely wonderful when a shelter rein*forces* the home this way. Teenagers who have trampled on parents' values and walked out on them are faced with the inconvenience of being away from family and friends while having to keep the very same rules. That's very good.

This kind of shelter is a key ally in restoring children to parents with a new resolve to be fair, for a change.

*Emergency youth shelters can give parents and teenagers a break for reevaluating their family situation and their role in it.*

Battle fatigue is a very real problem. Trying to fix something that refuses to stay fixed can cause parents to become so frustrated that they just stay generally mad. Being perpetually mad ensures that things are going to get worse before they get better. Furthermore, it's dangerous; someone could get hurt.

Teenagers tire out, too. They need to get away from the battleground, and from the counterintelligence being pumped into them by their peers, and get some space for thinking . . . alone.

Parents and teenagers need time to rest. To back off. To cool off. To reconsider. To receive counseling. To reunite. And to try again.

Parents have been more tied down than when the teenagers were toddlers. They have never parented so intensely in their lives. They need to back away awhile and regenerate their own personhoods and their marriage relationship. I've seen the countenance of worn and weary parents take on a new radiance while their children were safe in an emergency shelter. They've acted like they were on vacation from being tortured.

*Teenagers get a glimpse of the truth that acting in uncivilized ways often ends in institutionalization.*

Offending kids of reasonable parents need to become aware of the principle of cause and effect. The fact is, in this world, we are either in control or out of control; and if we are out of control, we have to be under someone else's control. Doing wrong, being rude, acting irresponsibly, and refusing to cooperate carry an inflated price tag. Belligerent teenagers somehow, some way, need to discover this essential truth, and the sooner, the better.

*Teenagers may have the good fortune of meeting house parents or other adults at youth shelters who can have a reconstructive influence on their lives.*

I have seen a few cases in which the right person has single-handedly turned a teenager around and headed him or her in the right direction. This doesn't always happen, but when it does, it's an immeasurable blessing!

*House parents may have more ability to discipline than parents do.*

In some arrangements, the juvenile probation people and the shelter people work closely together. If a teenager breaks the law, he or she is promptly shuttled to the detention facility, and that's that for a night or two. The relationship of cause and effect is made more obvious.

*Good shelters can help children learn more about how to be successful in a community setting.*

A shelter is a community setting where everyone has to work together to keep the home functioning properly. Many of the shelters use a point system in which residents earn points for good attitude and behavior and for being responsible. They lose points for unacceptable behavior. They have to buy privileges with points. Attending a movie costs 500 points, for example. If the resident hasn't earned 500 points or has lost too many points, he or she has to stay behind and hear about the movie when the qualifying kids return. Positive peer pressure comes into play in good shelters.

House parents and counselors involved with shelters often use a reality therapy approach to counseling (see chapter 1), which is one of the best approaches they could use.

### Youth shelters can teach kids how important it is to be with people who love them.

Shelters can seem like youth camps at first. There are always kids around to play pool with, study beside, talk to, and listen to music with. Then reality finally begins to soak in. It dawns on them: "Nobody here truly loves me. They're all paid to take care of me." Nothing can take the place of being with people who love you. Familyhood supplies irreplaceable assets, according to Tower of Strength 3.

### Youth shelters can keep kids off the street.

If the only choices are to be at home or on the streets, many kids would choose the streets. Youth shelters provide a third alternative, and a much safer one.

### Shelters can help keep kids in school.

Young people who have literally had it with their parents—although it may be more their fault than their parents'—will often drop out of school and give up on trying unless there is another alternative other than living with their parents. A shelter can again be that essential alternative.

### Shelters can allow the family pressures to subside so that family counseling can be more effective and have time to make a difference.

It's tough to teach communication skills to people who would rather beat on each other than talk. Counselors are amazed occasionally at how much worse off a family can become in only one week! There are times when people have to separate before the healing process can begin.

### Shelters can buy time so that more permanent foster care can be arranged.

There are times when families have to admit that relationships have broken down so badly, personality styles grate against each other so totally, and so much damage has already been done that their family is not going to be the best place for the child to be redeemed. The best thing for the mental health of everyone involved is to separate. In such a case, parents and children need to admit as much and be courageous enough to work out a different arrangement. This alternative arrangement may be in place for the rest of the child's school years.

The county youth shelter can serve as a safe holding place for the child until arrangements can be made with relatives, friends, or others for foster care. Some Christians feel called of God to provide such homes.

Good shelters can help more than I have room enough to mention. Good shelters are among the greatest allies for caring parents, and I thank God for them.

## What can be harmful about shelters?

*Youth shelters can introduce teenagers to more members of the wrong crowd.*

Kids are in emergency youth shelters because they have problems, their parents have problems, or both. And who is the biggest enemy to rescue and recovery attempts for teenagers? The wrong crowd—so much so, in fact, that we are calling the wrong crowd family enemy #1. The wrong crowd is the greatest reason why kids take wrong turns in life and become "addicted" to their wrong turns.

Who are going to be your child's new "brothers" and "sisters" at the youth home? Some of them will be kids who are or have been involved with the wrong crowd.

Add this grim reality to the fact that sin is contagious, and you have the very situation you've tried your best to avoid! You may have forbidden your teenager to be with his old friends, and in a youth shelter he would likely be living with some of the same kinds of people.

Your child's dark side may very well be supported by new friends at the youth shelter. They will probably exchange phone numbers.

*Shelter leaders may allow the residents to do things against the value systems of your family.*

Some shelters allow the residents to smoke. Others allow them to attend movies that you wouldn't approve. Some allow videos you wouldn't allow in your home. Some don't provide close supervision.

Others let kids date on school nights. Who decides if your daughter's date is someone you'd want her to be going out with?

Some shelters take their kids to churches you wouldn't want your child to attend.

*Shelters and juvenile authorities may provide a teenager with a counselor who is not of the parents' choosing.*

There may not be a lot you can do about it, either. Your child might be fortunate and get a counselor who agrees with your traditional Christian approach to life. Or he or she may get one who thinks kids' problems are always the fault of the parents. If you've had your teenager in ongoing counseling with a counselor, that counselor may or may not be allowed to visit with the child in the shelter.

*Since some shelters are so psychology oriented that they avoid religion altogether, they have reduced their ability to get quality house parents.*

House parenting doesn't pay much. Successful people who are Christians will become house parents without regard to the low pay if they see a vision of what they can do for the children they serve. But if and when they are rebuffed, where will shelter administrators find quality house parents? It's a problem.

*House parents come in all varieties, and some of them can do a great deal of harm to the parent-child relationship.*

A teenager and a house parent click and boom! The teen begins to pick up his or her values, and the parents are more "outside" than ever. Some house parents may get their strokes off of believing that they could parent your child better than you have. Their proof is that they have readily won his or her friendship.

The trouble often is, one way house parents help teens improve is to compromise the reasonable expectations. The kid is dipping smokeless tobacco, dressing outlandishly, forsaking all goals, still hating his parents, still entrenched with the wrong crowd, laughing because his parents can't make him go to church anymore, but he is holding a job at a fast-food place, is attending school more regularly, isn't being quite as rude, and seems happier. And house parents like these wonder why you never learned to parent as wisely as they.

## Investigate your alternatives before the crisis occurs.

Teenagers who are so rebellious that they are out of control pose a special problem. Your ability to work with them in your home is overthrown by them. As if that isn't bad enough, they may involve you with forces not of your choosing. One such force is the county youth shelter. My experience with youth shelters leads me to offer the following recommendations:

1. Placing a child in a shelter needs to be seen as practically a last resort.

2. You may be able to avoid involvement with a shelter by having a foster family on emergency standby in case you need them. An alternative home, provided by parents within the parent support group, is superior to the youth shelter and can be better than relatives or friends (if the child is in control enough to stay in a home). It can be better because the parents of this alternate home subscribe to the same convictions for raising children, and they share the same textbook: *Relief for Hurting Parents*.

3. Before a crisis hits, make it your business to know the reputation of your county's youth shelter and find out how its program works.

4. If your child enters an unwholesome youth shelter, go to the persons in authority and courteously request that your child be transferred to your alternative foster home. Securing permission for this transfer might not be a problem since it's costing either you or the county a lot of money to keep the child in the shelter.

5. If the shelter has a bad reputation and your child is uncontrollable, you must decide if you want to go to the expense of transferring your child to another program, such as a wilderness camp.

Familiarize yourself with what's available in your state when you begin to feel the first tremors, without waiting to see if the earthquake is really going to hit. Seeking out programs takes time. (A potential by-product of beginning your search early could be desirable to you: Brochures about residential treatment programs coming into your home through the mail tend to let an adolescent know how serious you are about wanting him or her to behave in a more civilized way. Teens tend to find the presence of such brochures a little eerie.) Watch for church-sponsored programs. Some of them are excellent and are offered on a contribution basis or on an adjusted-fee basis.

6. If your child would be out of control outside the youth shelter and you have't been able to develop an alternative controlled setting, you will have to cooperate with what his or her misbehavior has brought upon you and yours. If this is the case, you will have to look at the evidence before you and make some decisive decisions. You will be facing questions like the following:

- Should we visit our child in spite of his or her rudeness?
- Or would it be better to have a complete separation for a while?
- Should we provide him or her with a counselor?
- Or should we use the one associated with the shelter?
- What should be the conditions for reopening negotiations for our child to return home?
- What are we willing to furnish our child during the stay there?
- What are we going to request in the way of reports from the shelter.

7. If the shelter has a good reputation and its reputation proves to be genuine, thank God with all your heart and work closely with this superb ally and receive its rein*force*ment.

CHAPTER **28**

# TREATMENT CENTERS

**E**arlier, I wrote that selecting the right counselor for your child and your family is one of the most important decisions you will make. You are choosing someone as important as a heart surgeon. In a sense, the counselor will be a heart surgeon counseling the very "heart" of your teenager and your family.

In this chapter, we take on a matter even more serious. You are choosing not only a "heart" surgeon but also a "brain" surgeon. In choosing an inpatient treatment center, you are trusting your child's heart and soul to strangers. You will take your child there, turn your child over to them, and drive away, and it will probably be against policy for you to have contact with your child for a few days. They will have access, without your presence, to your child's mental programming, and their purpose will be to adjust it to what they perceive to be an acceptable way to think and live.

Nothing could be more serious than choosing a treatment center. You'll be trusting as you've never trusted in your whole life. Therefore, you should investigate first. Treatment centers are potential allies that have to be investigated before you hire them to probe and attempt to reprogram the heart and mind of your child and, to some degree, your family. The effective ones are treasures. The ineffective ones are molesting families by building false hope, wasting the family's desperate rescue attempt, and draining away their savings. (Before you spend all your savings on treatment programs, you should review my comments on superguilt in chapter 7.)

My best guidance and the theme for this chapter is: You should investigate treatment centers carefully and thoroughly, make your selection, and then step out of your investigator's role and form an alliance of trust with your child's therapists. The therapists will need your trust because you are embarking on a tempestuous journey together.

### Be prepared; investigating will come hard.

The fact that you will be squeezed between the desperate condition of your child and your own battle fatigue may mean that you won't feel like taking on a thorough investigation. You may be tempted to compromise too much.

You'll be nose-to-nose with the question: What could be worse than my child being out on the streets or in detention, or doing drugs, or taking a chance of getting AIDS, or attempting to commit suicide, or being a threat to the family?

What's worse? Wasting your effort to rescue your child from self-destruction by

219

placing him or her in a defective treatment program is worse. It's worse if he or she becomes more messed up after admission than before admission. It's worse if he or she is at a more desperate spot a few weeks after release. I've never heard of a facility giving refunds or volunteering to make restitution to a family for letting them down or doing them wrong.

### Why consider the child's admission to a treatment center?

Let me explain something that may appear to be inconsistent. I'm writing about how to choose a treatment center that will be an ally to you and your family in spite of the fact that the first and second towers of conviction state that defiance is rarely a mental problem. Why? Because suicidal gestures, dangerous behavioral problems, criminal behavioral problems, severe drug or alcohol addiction, and the like effectively close off all your options except the treatment center.

For example, coming off drugs often requires detoxification, and detoxing is most safely done under medical supervision. Also, chemically dependent persons rarely win over drugs without a treatment program. The only other alternative for them is to attend thirty meetings in thirty days (meetings like Narcotics Anonymous or Alcoholics Anonymous) and remain faithful to attend weekly meetings thereafter—and/or to have a heart-changing Christian conversion and a deliverance from their bondage. This latter alternative needs to be affirmed by a support group on a very regular basis to maintain the victory.

### How do you find a treatment center that you can trust?

How do you prejudge the effectiveness of a center? What questions do you ask? How do you check references? How do you determine if the unit you are considering forming an alliance with is friend or foe?

When and if your child is placed in a unit, how do you monitor what is being done with your child? Who at the unit can you call for progress reports? What questions do you ask when you call? How much parental involvement do you have a right to expect?

These are the questions I hope to help you with. I'll try to make it as easy as I can for you; you probably haven't been involved in anything like this before. The discussion will be limited to treatment centers that deal with stubborn behavioral problems and substance abuse, however. My comments do not necessarily apply to psychiatric units dealing with severe emotional problems, mental disorders, or mental illness.

I relate the following stories to cause you due alarm and to impress upon you the importance of careful investigation before you hand over your child to strangers. You may readily accept medical personnel and their advice, but you can't do that in this case. There are more adolescent treatment centers that conflict with Christian values and principles than honor them. There are more that are nonproductive or counterproductive than productive.

Residential treatment centers for substance abuse, for example, have sprung up and are springing up everywhere. Invitations to attend their open houses are continually coming across my desk. Why so many? There are two reasons. First, because the need is there, and hospitals want to serve their communities. Second, because many hospitals are hurting financially. Hospitals are saving themselves by developing treatment centers, which are a way to fill empty beds and to generate new cash flow.

This is good *and* bad. It is good because we need more treatment centers. It is bad because competition for outstanding alcohol and drug counselors has been stiff, and many centers have had to settle for less competent ones to move ahead and get their centers open and operating.

You may find this hard to believe, but believe it anyway: "Successful" substance abuse treatment centers have about a fifty-fifty success rate of getting kids off chemicals and their staying chemical free. The success rate is much lower in other treatment centers. The poorly staffed ones, those without tried-and-true programs, and those that don't emphasize aftercare are going to be tragic disappointments most of the time. Again, you must carefully investigate to find the effective ones.

The success rate is lowest with kids who don't want help. As one mother put it, "The chances of a child staying clean are poor unless the child comes to you and says, 'I want to go,' no matter what the hospitals tell you."

Another mother wrote me a nine-page letter when she learned that I was writing about this subject. Here is an excerpt from her summary of experiences with treatment centers:

It's tough, Buddy, but the bottom line is, do they want to be in a recovery unit and want to *work* at changing their lives? It cost us a lot of money to learn we wanted our daughter's recovery, but she did not. Perhaps parents have to go through the financial, physical, and emotional pain to come to this point.

Both mothers had had contact with several treatment programs as they tried to rescue and restore their children.

Several parents have said to me, "Our son (or daughter) was worse off when he came out of treatment than when he went in." And they were thousands of dollars poorer. Families have said, "Our child came out smoking and cursing." Other families have said that their children returned to them with worse attitudes, telling them off and screaming, "I have a right to express my feelings, and I don't have to do what you want! Kids have rights, too, you know!"

A Texas pastor recently told me about some parents in his church who had had their daughter in a treatment center. They decided that they didn't like what was going on, and they tried to take her out. But the psychiatrist refused to discharge her, and he prevented her discharge via a legal maneuver.

I did a training session for the staff of our county's Children's Protective Services not long ago, and a caseworker told me that they had received a call from a psychiatrist requesting that they forbid a set of parents from removing their adolescent daughter from his treatment program. Upon investigation, they found that there had not been any child abuse or neglect within the family nor did there appear to be reason to suspect that there would be any; the doctor only wanted to keep her in his program, and he was fighting the parents to do so.

One set of parents had their son in three treatment programs. Three weeks after his release from the last one, he was back on drugs. They had spent $100,000 on treatment expenses; their insurance company paid $80,000, and they paid $20,000. Now in debt and emotionally exhausted, they've placed themselves on standby while their son continues his self-destructive course of drug abuse. They are hoping and praying that he will bottom out, reach for help, and stop doing drugs before he kills himself or hurts someone else.

I've known of cases where adolescents never detoxed during the treatment program. Drugs were being smuggled into the hospital, and they used drugs throughout treatment.

A young woman who volunteered to help me talk with adolescents had had a bad experience in a drug treatment center when she was a high schooler. One of the male counselors would drop by her room at night and put her to bed with kisses and caresses. At the time, she found it romantic that a professional found her attractive, but as she looks back, she sees how the situation completely destroyed any growth she could have experienced. She was so totally preoccupied with him and jealous over who was getting his attention at the moment that she gave little thought to getting better. Her parents' effort to save their daughter was worse than wasted. And I can't help thinking of the male patients who picked up on this therapist's unethical behavior. How many of them were turned off through loss of respect and through resentment over an adult taking advantage of a girl their age?

Another young woman and her family were hurt by sex in a different way. She met a man who was in an adult unit, located near the adolescent unit, at the hospital where they both were in treatment. They became infatuated with each other, and after their release from treatment, she became pregnant by him. She and her parents are raising the baby. The outcome of her treatment was that it had served to connect her with the wrong crowd again.

A similar story involves drugs. This is one that happens far too often. Two guys who met each other in treatment became buddies, exchanged phone numbers, and got together and did drugs after their release. Down the drain went two families' gallant efforts, high hopes, intense prayers, and more than $60,000 (the cost of treatment for the two). This last episode was not the fault of the treatment center; it's a natural hazard with which all programs must contend.

## Consider these important elements when you choose a program.

Since you never dreamed you'd be in a position of trying to figure out which treatment program would be best for your child, you didn't know to prepare yourself to make such a choice. And since this is one time when you really can't afford to learn from trial and error, you need to be aware of some important elements to evaluate. Here's some inside information.

### In treatment programs, psychiatrists are captains of the ships.

While your child is in treatment, psychiatrists may have more authority over your son or daughter than you do. Some treatment centers require parents or guardians to sign release forms.

Psychiatrists, if they so choose, have the legal means to overpower the parents' desire to take the child from their care. They have this power if they decide their patient is in danger of harming himself or herself or someone else.

Psychiatrists have another effective method for persuading parents to leave the child in their care. If parents remove their child from treatment without the psychiatrist's permission, the psychiatrist can declare it an AMA withdrawal—against medical advice. Some insurance companies won't pay the bill if a patient is withdrawn AMA. This can turn out to be a powerfully persuasive factor when the family already owes thousands of dollars to the hospital. In such a case, parents are faced with paying huge bills for the privilege of removing their child from what they had decided is an unhealthy establishment. Requesting a transfer to another medical institution would be an easier way to get the child out of the undesired unit.

This is a very serious matter. You need to know about the policies concerning withdrawals and transfers, you must read and understand what you're signing, and you'll be wise to do any negotiating you're going to do before they lock the door between you and your son or daughter.

A good psychiatrist can be a helpful ally. A bad psychiatrist has the position and power to harm your family.

### Psychiatrists may charge more for in-patient care.

Several parents who have been through treatment programs with their children have mentioned the $150 fee that some psychiatrists charge for each hospital visit with the patient. These visits are sometimes as brief as ten minutes.

Medical attention is vital during detox or during severe episodes of rebellious behavior; otherwise, parents have indicated that such visits are routine, accomplish little, and are too expensive. One parent said, "We paid $150 times thirty days— $4,500—to the psychiatrist during our child's hospitalization. He didn't do anything more than check up on our son's progress each day, and his visits never lasted longer than ten minutes. Our son wasn't on medication, he wasn't having physical problems, and the masters-level counselors did all the therapy. We feel taxed and depleted."

### Primary therapy is often provided by masters-level therapists, not by doctors.

I've observed—and many parents have reported to me—that the most helpful experiences have been with masters-level counselors who had recovered from behavioral problems or addictions. These people can be effective counselors because they've been there, they know what it's like, they know how to talk the talk, they can't be as easily manipulated, they are more alert to insincere gestures of recovery, they understand and care deeply, and they are living examples of the fact that recovery is possible. Counselors who have recovered from a life-dominating problem know both worlds— the world of bondage and the world of recovery—and they know how to get from the former to the latter.

Based on my experiences in a counseling center, I would not enter my child into a treatment center that didn't have a counselor who had recovered from what my child needs to recover from, unless there was simply no other alternative.

### The treatment center has to provide a loving environment to be successful.

Successful therapists do not counsel only on an intellectual level. If they are to be successful, they have to genuinely like their counselees, and they must counsel from the heart outward. Treatment centers that are all business, all clinical, devoid of a loving environment and personal interest in patients, do not succeed well enough to justify their existence.

### Don't be unduly impressed with resort-type facilities.

The buildings or the grounds will not change your child. The people who work with your child will be the deciding factor as far as the center is concerned. Pay attention to the people and . . .

> their beliefs
> their values
> their attitudes
> their love (they have to like your child
>     or they won't be able to help him or her)
> their approaches
> their concepts
> their programs
> their competency
> their insightfulness
> their spiritual maturity

Don't judge a facility by its architecture and equipment; judge it by the quality of its therapists and doctors. Glance at all the things they show you, but gaze long and intuitively at the people who work there.

Actually, centers and units can be *too* plush. They can be so fancy and resortlike and so much fun that it's better to be inside than outside. Balance is required. The center should be nice enough for you to feel satisfied that your child will be comfortable there (this will help you deal with the guilt you may be feeling for putting him or her there), but not so resortlike that it acclimates the child to too much to give up.

### "Selling the program" may be everyone's responsibility.

Don't be surprised when everyone knows how to talk impressive talk. In some treatment program settings, marketing is presented to employees as everyone's responsibility. They are schooled in how to impress you with their "product." In some of those corporations, staff members have to make a marketing contact each week. I was targeted by those marketeers until I became weary with the sales pitches (and the system) and stopped granting appointments.

While we're on the subject of marketing, I'd like to remind you that you are the consumer. You have the right to shop, to call the Better Business Bureau, to ask questions and judge answers. Never think it would be out of order for you to question highly educated therapists and doctors. They are close to being your last hope for rescuing and preserving your child. To whom are you going to turn if they don't turn out to be okay? Will you be able to get your son or daughter into another program? Will he or she agree to go? Will you have enough money to try another program?

Go ahead and diplomatically ask questions and judge answers. The stakes are too high for you not to investigate. If someone becomes irritated with you, then that should clue you in on what it would be like if your child were to become a patient there and you were to request information about the procedures.

A program director told me that if program officials resent being questioned, they probably aren't comfortable giving you the information you seek. They may feel the answers won't be beneficial to their purpose of admitting new patients.

### The treatment center may be "allergic" to Christian considerations.

Most professional therapists don't include God, and when God is excluded, rehabilitation itself is handicapped (and needs rehabilitating). I don't think there are many atheists among these professionals, and they aren't rejecting God; they're simply ignoring the issue. But the result is the same as if they are atheists. If God is left out, He's out of the picture and that's that, whether it is from rejection or *ignorance*.

If a therapist sidesteps something clients feel is vital to them—their faith—and tells them he or she prefers not to deal with it, he or she sets aside a big part of them. As an in-patient therapist expressed it: "Patients can feel that a part of them has been rejected by their therapist."

One of the main problems for secular therapists with including God is that God-talk, as they call it without warmth, is not considered to be scientifically sound. There is professional peer pressure against it. One day a counselor who was fired from a secular counseling agency immediately came by my office for companionship and support. He told me the reason for his dismissal: He had talked God-talk again after he was warned not to a couple of times.

We started taking interns at our office because aspiring Christian counselors who are in secular training settings are generally not esteemed by their professors and fellow students. We provide them with support, esteem, and abundant opportunity to grow as counselors without feeling pressure to keep their faith under wraps.

I know how they feel. I've gotten negative responses when I've attended various seminars sponsored by nonreligious psychological groups. I'm not exaggerating when I say that secular counselors have actually turned away from me upon learning that I am a Christian counselor.

In all fairness, I need to say that not all secular counselors are against God, and I wouldn't want you to stereotype them and approach them as if they are. Some are Christians themselves, some are tolerant of Christians, and some don't mind you having a "crutch."

The l-l-lo . . . the l-los . . . the losses . . . the losses of ignoring and excluding God from therapy are so great that I stutter even contemplating them. When God is left out, the Creator is ignored while therapists are trying to help His creation, the Redeemer is ignored while they're seeking to redeem people, the Savior is ignored while they're trying to save people, the Prince of Peace is ignored while they're trying to relieve people of confusion, and the Counselor is ignored while they're trying to impart wise counsel.

Counselors who are averse to the Christian faith don't teach kids to live toward heaven, to standardize their moral code and values according to the life of Jesus Christ, to deal with their guilt and anger through forgiveness, to escape from their self-destructive lifestyles through Easter, or to reconcile with their families through the

Lord's Prayer—"Forgive us our trespasses as we forgive those who trespass against us"—and much more.

Then why even go to a secular setting for help? Because the urgency and the desperateness of your situation may leave you with very little choice. Here are situations that can force it on you . . .

- if your child is in danger of committing suicide
- if your child is out of control
- if your child's presence is endangering others
- if your child needs detoxing from chemical abuse
- if your child has lost touch with reality
- if your child has gotten in trouble and he or she is going to be sent to a rehab unit or sentenced to a reform school
- if this is the only way you can get your child away from the wrong crowd that has stepped up its pace of destroying him or her

In almost all these cases, you are not deciding to put your child into a treatment center; you are only cooperating with the inevitable natural consequences of his or her erroneous lifestyle.

If you are forced into a situation where you have to use a secular setting and non-Christian counselors, arrange weekly visits with a Christian counselor or a pastor to keep your child in touch with the Christian truth. But be sure the Christian counselor or pastor is knowledgeable and experienced in helping strong-willed kids and/or substance abusers. Otherwise he or she may be a liability to treatment.

One treatment center counselor told me that she had had several bad experiences with pastors. One example she gave was a pastor who came into their unit to see a teenage boy. He said, "I came to find out one thing: Were you involved in stealing the hubcaps at the church three weeks ago?" His suspicious approach negated his healing touch, and the child experienced a setback in treatment. And the treatment team lost respect for that pastor.

### But substance abuse programs have a religious touch.

Substance abuse treatment centers almost always include a "higher power" concept. Why do they do this when there is so much negativism about God-talk in the field of psychology?

First, that's all that works! Only religious programs are effective. All professional counselors know this, and they have to cooperate with it since nothing else works.

Second, the "higher power" god is more palatable to them because it's an easygoing god. It's a god designed by the worshiper, so to speak. It is there to love and to help, but not necessarily to command a moral lifestyle in harmony with Jesus Christ.

Be aware that I'm not intending to be hypercritical of substance abuse programs that use the "higher power" concept since we Christians have not ministered sufficiently in this area. We have practically failed people who have become overpowered and enslaved by the desires of this world.

Also, the "higher power" concept serves as a warm and welcome alternative to an angry god bent on revenge as the Christian God is too frequently thought of. Chemical abusers are not repelled by an uncondemning and helping "higher power" who makes few demands, which can be a starting point for them. Many of them grow beyond their entry-level concept of God into a beautiful, committed relationship with Christ.

## How do you choose a treatment center?

You start looking early. You don't wait until the tremors become a fullblown earthquake. If you wait until the decisive trauma hits, you may very well be under too much pressure to be thorough.

First, the ideal way to find a good treatment program is to be referred by someone you trust, someone who basically agrees with the concepts and principles of this book. Perhaps your counselor or family doctor knows of a good one, has referred other families to it, has tracked those families, and is pleased with the results.

Ask your counselor or doctor if you can talk to some of those families. The response will be, "I'm sorry. That's confidential I can't release those names and phone numbers."

You respond, "I understand, but would you do me this favor? Would you call a couple of those families, tell them what I need, give them my name and number, and ask them to call me?" This is a way to secure references without violating confidentiality. This is an acceptable request, and if your counselor or doctor won't make a couple of phone calls for you, something's wrong.

Parents who have had great experiences in treatment programs are deeply grateful, and they love to share the healing. When they call, ask them for other names, or ask them to have other families call you who went through the same program or other programs.

Each time you talk to parents, ask them if they know of any parents who didn't like the program you're considering. If they do, try to get their names and phone numbers. If they won't give you phone numbers or don't know them, try to get names and cities where they live. Perhaps you can locate them through directory assistance. If they won't give you names because of the confidentiality issue, ask them if they'd do you a favor, locate the people, and ask them to phone you. Hearing from those who were unhappy with programs and finding out about specific complaints give you a more complete picture.

Ministers are also great sources for referrals. Other families in your church have likely had problems similar to yours, and your minister can ask them to get in touch with you. You can learn volumes of vital information from their 20/20 hindsight. Plus, they'll likely become supportive of you and form a special friendship with you; they understand the pain you're going through.

Other good sources for referrals are juvenile probation officers and judges who handle juvenile cases and are known to be solid Christians. They see hundreds of kids throughout the year. Many of these kids are referred to Christian (or, at least, effective) treatment centers. These officials, more than many other individuals, may know the reputation of treatment programs. To find out how to get in contact with them, call your county courthouse and ask how to reach the juvenile probation department.

Principals and school counselors are also in positions to know of other families who have needed the help that you need. They, too, can call a few families and ask them to phone you to help with your decision.

Children's Protective Services, police personnel who deal with juveniles, social service agencies, and employee assistance groups within large companies can help you by contacting families and asking them to call you.

And don't neglect to check with pastors, physicians, and social workers who live in the same community as the treatment program you're considering but aren't employed by them. Professionals working nearby have the closeness to know things that rarely make it to outsiders. You can get more mileage out of this effort by asking them if they know of anyone you could contact who used to work for the facility.

Some facilities will allow parents who are considering their unit to visit an open parents' meeting within the facility. This is an excellent way to see the therapists in action and meet parents currently involved with the facility. You can visit with them before and after the meeting and ask them for their phone numbers.

When you talk to these families and they describe treatment programs and personnel to you, you'll be able to decide which ones are in harmony with what you're looking for.

So, what are you looking for? You know more than you may think. Here's a list of what you probably already know to watch for:

- You want a place that's clean and attractive without a disorganized appearance.
- You want therapists who have their lives founded and integrity based firmly on the Rock instead of sand.
- You want therapists who are loving and approachable, who can establish rapport with your child. They should be men and women your child can admire and enjoy. If the therapists are all business, all clinical, they won't reach your child. They *must* start at the emotional level and then move to the reasoning level.
- You want therapists who look competent by the way they dress and conduct themselves.
- You want gifted therapists who know what they're doing (with credentials and experience).
- You want therapists who are open and courteous, not distant.
- You want a program that has already established a good reputation for helping and healing adolescents.
- You want an environment that does not include R-rated movies, unmonitored TV viewing, pornographic reading material, vulgar talk, and profane language—a wrong-crowd environment.

*Important note:* Cursing will be a part of the scene due to new admissions, but there is no justifiable reason for program officials to do it. They are to model self-control and maturity to the young people. Patients who have been in the program for a while should begin to mature beyond talking vulgarly as well. A mother recently made a comment to me about this: "Everyone needs to realize that these kids enter treatment with bankrupted moral values. As they get well, their family values return."

Now, add what I'll give you to what you already know, and you'll be pretty well set to shop intelligently. You shouldn't be too awestruck by medical settings to be a thorough investigator.

If you're too emotionally drained to take on this challenge, call in a new and fresh recruit. Ask your pastor, a relative, or a family friend to move in and help you gather information and make a decision.

Second, call the facility and request to speak with someone who can answer questions about the program. If the policy is for you to go in for an appointment, that's understandable. The mood you want to project during your interview will be one of information gathering and not of scrutinizing and being suspicious. Be diplomatic and courteous in your manner. You might do well to preface your questions with an introductory statement something like this . . .

*I have several questions I want to ask you, but please understand that I'm not trying to be difficult. I am faced with one of the biggest decisions I've ever made in my life, and I want to do everything I can to make the correct one.*

While you're guarding your approach, observe how the officials respond to you. If they act as if you probably couldn't comprehend anything technical, if they don't seem to be open with you, if they're being secretive (holding too many things confidential), if they say it's not a good time for a tour . . . generally, if things seem strained or strange, they may very well be. If you feel that something is not quite right, don't discount the reliability of your intuition (even though you're sitting in the midst of impressive surroundings where you may feel you're not "in the know" enough to question things). Either get it resolved or turn away.

I want to help you equip yourself for your investigative assignment. Here are the kinds of questions to ask. Write down the answers as they are given to you since you may be in too much emotional pain to remember well and keep things straight.

### 1. How well can you monitor the welfare of your child during the separation from you?

- Do you forbid parental contact with children during the initial assessment or detoxification period?
- If so, how many days? (normally five to seven days)
- During that time, who can we call to monitor the progress of our child?
- After that time passes, how much contact are we allowed with our child?
- Will our child be allowed to place phone calls to us?
- Are we allowed occasional visits during the week if we feel it becomes important?
- What are your policies concerning passes and home visits?
- Will we be called if something goes wrong concerning our child? (a sickness, physical injury, a serious relationship problem, etc.)
- Will we be called if your program doesn't seem to be working for our child? Will you be that open with us?

**2. How protective are they of their therapeutic community (to recover, your child has to have complete separation from family enemy #1—the old wrong-crowd friends)?**

- Will our child be allowed to make calls to friends?
- Will our child be allowed to receive calls from friends?
- After your initial assessment and/or detox period, who may visit our child?
- Will we be allowed to forbid certain people to visit our child?

**3. How are patient populations housed?**

- Will our child be placed on a unit with people who are psychotic?

With this question, you are asking if your child will be integrated with severely disturbed and potentially dangerous people. You don't want this for several reasons: It's dangerous. It's scary. It can be traumatizing. It doesn't provide a comfortable and positive environment for improving. And it can injure self-esteem and self-image. Your child can begin to feel classified with mentally-ill people. Understand that I am not prejudiced against the mentally ill; I want them to receive help, too. But I know it's not healthy for these two populations to be mixed.

**4. How much will you be involved in therapy and how much will be expected of you?**

- Does the program involve parents in the healing process?
- If so, when does that begin and of what will it consist?

**5. How much parental authority are you giving up or retaining?**

- Will we be asked to sign papers that give you more legal right to the custody of our child than we will retain?
- If we were to decide to withdraw or transfer our child from your program, what process would we have to go through to have our child discharged or transferred?

*Important note:* You must realize that rejecting a treatment program and removing your child from it can be like taking away good medicine if your child likes the program and is making progress there. It could be traumatic to him or her to be forced to leave trusted counselors and new friends. Rejecting a treatment program is very serious and should be done only if there are serious reasons for doing so. (Please read the comments on how to monitor your child's progress in treatment later in this chapter.)

*Another important note:* Disagreements with the treatment center staff should be handled between you and the staff without your criticizing them to your child. Your child needs to build respect for them and needs to learn to honor their authority; cutting them down to him or her will inhibit the trust he or she is developing for them, the trust that is vital for recovery.

- How much notice do you require?
- Have your psychiatrists or psychologists used legal measures to prevent parents from withdrawing their child?

**6. How do you discern the basic posture of the therapists and the institution?**

Ask something like this:

*I know you can't give me a specific answer until you've had some sessions with my child, but generally speaking, why do kids misbehave (or have emotional problems or do drugs)? Is it mostly an inherited thing? Is it mostly the way parents raise them? Maybe a fouled-up family system? Is it a mental problem? Is it the way society is today? Is it a religious problem?*

If they answer, "Well, it's all of the above," press for a more specific answer.

- What is your philosophy of why kids have problems? (Don't be embarrassed to stop them and ask them to put it into layman's terms for you.)
- How do you bring about change for the better?
- Would it be all right with you if our son's (or daughter's) present counselor consults with your therapists about the treatment plan once each week? That would be permissible, wouldn't it?
- I know you can't be specific because there are so many things to be considered, but can you give us an approximate idea of what progress we can hope for in our child when treatment is completed?

**7. How do you gain information about the competency and character of therapists and the institution that will be working with your child?**

- Is your facility accredited and by whom?
- Who will actually be doing therapy with our child?
- What are their backgrounds? What degrees do they hold?
- Where did they do their internships? How long have they been doing their specialization? Do you have therapists on staff who have recovered from the same problem that our child has?
- What kind of therapeutic techniques will be used with our child?
- What is your success rate? How is your success rate figured?

*Important note:* Don't be too impressed with a good success rate until you know how it's being figured. Success rate percentages are juggled all sorts of ways. For example, a treatment center that quotes an 80 percent success rate may be figuring it this way: If the patient stays in treatment for forty-five days, if he "works the program," if his family participates in the program with him as per instructions, if he comes to three months of weekly aftercare appointments, if he stays in group therapy for two years, they are 80 percent successful.

An honest 50 percent success rate for treating chemical abusers is not a disqualifying success rate. Informally, among themselves, Christian treatment center directors speak of the one-third rule: About one-third of their patients will go back to using chemicals after their release from treatment and continue using; about one-third will return to chemicals briefly but will quit again, remembering what they learned and experienced in treatment; and about one-third will not relapse into drugs after treatment. This means that they have an overall success rate of 67 percent.

- How many visits will our child have with a psychiatrist or psychologist?
- How many individual therapy sessions will our child have per day?
- How many group sessions will there be per day?
- May we have a copy of the daily schedule?

## 8. How are kids disciplined within the institution?

- May we have a copy of the patient handbook that you give new patients? (You'll not need to ask the following questions if the information is covered in the handbook.)
- May we have a copy of the rules that you expect kids to live by while they're here in treatment?
- May we have a copy of how consequences are structured when patients misbehave?
- And may we have a copy of the improvements needed for kids to move to higher levels?

## 9. How do you discern if Christian principles will be integrated within the healing process or depreciated?

- Does your program have a spiritual aspect?
- Are spiritual matters integrated into the program?
- Is spiritual counseling available?
- Is a chaplain on the health team?
- Are your therapists Christians?
- Can our child be assigned a Christian therapist? (This may be possible even if it's not a Christian institution.)
- If so, from what Christian perspective do they come?
- May we request a counselor who is a Christian?
- Our family belongs to the _____ church. Will there be any devaluation of our church preference?
- May our child have a pass to attend church with us after a couple of weeks or so?

## 10. How can you be sure that educational needs will not be neglected?

- How do you provide for educational needs?
- Is your school accredited, and will there be any problem with our child reentering his or her present school?

## 11. How are kids from the wrong crowd managed?

- Some kids are probably admitted who don't want to be here. How do you keep their defiant attitudes and manipulations from spreading to the other patients and spoiling their potential for improvement?

*Important note:* This is one of the main liabilities from which substance abuse treatment centers and misbehavior treatment centers suffer. They do not require kids to want to change to be admitted. Consequently, the admissions office is perpetually introducing the wrong crowd into the therapeutic community. Poor management here destroys any potential for recovery. Remember that the wrong crowd is family enemy #1.

I mentioned this concern to a supervisor of a treatment center. Her response is worth your consideration. She said it is true that the wrong crowd is constantly being introduced, but that can be good for the kids who want to change. She gave me three reasons. First, it keeps the unit consistent with the real world that they will be reentering in a few weeks. The wrong crowd will be out there, and there will be temptations. They need to practice saying "no" and strengthening their ability to say "no." Second, recovering kids get to see how bad off they used to be. And third, recovering kids are reminded that negative behavior doesn't work well enough to be worthwhile as they see the uncooperative and defiant kids receiving discipline.

But a treatment center that admits only those who demonstrate a genuine desire for receiving help is highly preferable.

### 12. How can you make sure there will be no sexual impositions?

- Don't take this personally, but we've heard some troublesome stories about sexual misconduct in other facilities. What precautions have you taken to be sure nothing happens between patients and patients or between personnel and residents?
- Who supervises kids at night, and how closely are they supervised?
- How are boys and girls separated? By a wall? Locked door? On different wings? (It's better if they are separated by a locked door in case supervision breaks down.)

### 13. How can you get access to the facility?

- Would it be possible to have a tour of the facility today?

*Important note:* Press a little; give them a reasonable explanation of why you'd like your tour while you're there. If you get to tour when they aren't expecting a tourist, you get a better view of how things actually are on the unit, precisely what you need to see.

### 14. How do you assess the costs?

- What is the basic cost of the program?
- How much will it cost us, considering our particular needs?

*Important note:* If you have insurance, treatment center personnel will call your insurance company for you, and they will ask what portion of in-patient treatment costs are covered by your plan. Have them ask what are the limits per year. Some plans will cover only a certain number of days of in-patient treatment per year. If and when you use it all up, you are on your own for the rest of the year.

*Very important note:* I have sat in on meetings where the treatment team discusses patients. I've heard them talk about how many insured days are left for certain patients. They were talking about how much time they had to help these persons resolve their problems before funds dried up and they would be having to turn off their efforts. Also, I've heard it said that the center is getting in the red financially and if any therapists had someone who needed psychological testing, biofeedback, or whatever, they needed to get it scheduled.

When you are spending your insurance company's money, you are spending *your own money* because that's all the money available to you for helping your child. Don't sit back and say, "Well, it's covered by insurance." *You are your insurance company's primary auditor* for being sure your portion of insurance money is being invested wisely in the recovery of your child.

If you have insurance but don't have the financial ability to pay what the insurance doesn't pay, ask:

- Can you put us on a payment plan for paying the part we have to pay?
- How do you handle payment plans?

*Important inside information:* If your insurance plan pays 80 percent of in-patient treatment costs, the treatment center will likely not want to lose the opportunity to receive that income. For example, if a twenty-eight-day program costs $30,000, the center will receive $24,000 guaranteed from your insurance company. With that amount insured, the center can easily afford to work with you for the remainder.

If you don't have insurance, and you will have to pay everything by yourself, ask:

- Do you have any reduced-fee beds?

*Important inside information:* When representatives from these treatment programs speak at my staff meetings, they always talk about their humanitarian side, how they give back to the community. They always mention that they have a limited number of reduced-fee or free beds for those people who honestly can't pay the full costs of treatment. They use these provisions in their publicity efforts, and it's perfectly fine to request this kind of help. Be aware, though, that a lot of people will be seeking the few reduced-fee beds, and you'll be in the position of convincing them to grant your family this highly desirable privilege. Also understand that we in the counseling field are used to too many freeloaders trying to talk us out of our fees. You are not one of those, but you'll need ways to assure them that you aren't, without insulting them by projecting that you suspect that they may be wondering if your needs are genuine. Perhaps a call from your counselor, physician, or school principal will help them know that your needs are real.

*Important note:* Whether you have insurance or not, some Christian groups have excellent treatment programs that are on a sliding-scale basis or on a free-will offering basis. Some of these programs are the best in the nation. Check for openings in those before placing your child into a secular setting.

How close do they need to be to where you live? Within flying distance is a good answer. You'd fly your child to a heart surgeon or a brain surgeon, wouldn't you? This isn't much different. And I'd urge you to be as generous as you can if the treatment is on a free-will offering basis. They are saving lives, and they need financial fuel for saving lives.

- Will there be "surprise" expenses that we wouldn't know to expect (intake evaluation, psychological testing, art therapy, recreational therapy, tutoring, fees from a medical director who isn't involved in doing therapy with your child but is paid to oversee the unit, etc.)?

### 15. How can you probe the honest personal feelings of the staff members to whom you talk?

The administrator of a successful treatment program suggested to "look them straight in the eyes and ask, 'Would you put your own child through this treatment program?' If they say they would, ask them for the reasons why they would."

## How do you monitor your child's progress during treatment?

Monitoring should come naturally because you should be involved in treatment on a weekly basis after the initial five- to seven-day assessment and/or detox period. You will be within the unit and see for yourselves.

In addition, you should receive weekly reports on the child. A daily report is asking too much (unless there is reason for special concern). If therapists were expected to prepare daily reports on each patient, they wouldn't have time to provide treatment.

And in addition, if your family counselor, the one you were going to prior to treatment, is allowed the privilege of consulting with the therapists of the treatment center on a weekly basis, you will have another means of monitorship. Referring agencies are treated respectfully by treatment centers; they appreciate their referrals.

Let me remind you of what you should do if at all possible. Do your investigation, select your treatment center, and then step out of your investigator's role and form an alliance of trust with your child's therapists.

It's likely going to be an emotional roller-coaster ride and your therapists will need your trust. Your son (or daughter) is likely going to have some mood swings. He may hate being in treatment. He may hate the treatment center. He may hate you for putting him there. He may be angry with his therapists for a time. He may love them more than you for a time. He may decide that he loves you after all, and then he may turn against you again. You'll need to be able to trust your therapists during such times.

If your son (or daughter) doesn't want to be in treatment, he knows which buttons to push to alarm you about the facility. If you don't like cursing, he'll report cursing. If you're worried sick that there might be a sexual imposition, he'll tell you about someone who is acting strangely toward him. If he knows you're bothered by divorce, he'll tell you that three out of the five nurses are divorced. If he thinks he can get out of treatment by being sweet to you, he'll turn on the charm and act as if the program has worked wonders and he's already rehabilitated. You can expect some manipulative efforts if your child does not want help.

You'll have to evaluate your child's complaints and your concerns by assessing the intuitive feelings you get from the therapists, the way family counseling is being conducted, and the way things are going in the parents' meetings.

## How important is aftercare?

Therapy in the treatment center is only one phase of the healing process. After-care is the next vital phase. Without adequate aftercare, the gallant efforts that you, your child, and the treatment center have put forth can fade away.

Aftercare means following up on the progress that was made in the treatment center after release and continuing the healing process. Some centers provide their own aftercare in a weekly alumni program, which includes individual therapy and group therapy. Others refer to other agencies. Aftercare programs could include additional residential treatment, such as a wilderness program or a halfway house, a day hospital, or out-patient therapy.

Begin your selection process for aftercare as soon as your child is admitted into a treatment program. There is sometimes a waiting list for aftercare; by starting immediately, you will get on the waiting list early. Also, the aftercare program waiting to admit your child will provide you another way to monitor what's going on in the treatment center. The aftercare therapists there can call the treatment center and check on how things are going.

Experience tells me that the safest and most therapeutic aftercare programs involve both individual and group therapy *every week*. The group is vital; it provides positive peer pressure and companionship for sticking to the change.

*Warning:* General counseling agencies won't be able to provide adequate aftercare unless they have a specialist in dealing with "uncivilized" behavior or chemical problems on their staff. Don't take a heart problem to an eye, ear, nose, and throat specialist, so to speak.

*Warning:* Parents have a hard time staying true to aftercare. The treatment program was intense, the child is better, the child is so much better that you can't imagine how he or she could "backslide," the pressure is off, and it's hard to follow through.

But you must *follow through!* Your child is just *one disagreement away* from misbehaving, *one phone call* away from making contact with the wrong crowd, and *one sip, snort, puncture, or swallow away* from getting back into chemical abuse! The final battle is won or lost in aftercare!

I have seen enough failures that I become disheartened when parents tell me that their child is doing so well that they've dropped out of aftercare against the advice of their counselor. Their optimism is sitting on potential quicksand, I warn them. Sometimes they hear me; sometimes they don't.

To select an aftercare program, you will need to go through an investigative process similar to the one outlined for choosing a treatment center.

## There is hope!

Our agency helped a lovely Christian couple seek to rescue their beautiful blonde seventeen-year-old daughter from drugs and the wrong crowd. Counseling for the teenager and her family was provided by one of our therapists, and the parents participated in our Parenting Within Reason support group each week.

The girl's involvement was more serious than could be dealt with in outpatient counseling, so she was admitted to a Christian inpatient treatment program. She was there thirty-nine days at a cost of $37,000.

Mom and Dad, knowing that the wrong crowd is family enemy #1, decided that they would separate for the semester to keep their daughter from having to return to the community and to the tantalizing temptations of her old friends. Mom picked her up at the hospital, moved out of state with her, and placed her in a new school to finish her senior year.

Sadly, after a few months she slipped back into drugs and drinking. Her parents grieved. They had done all they could possibly do, and their daughter was back on a course of destroying herself with chemicals. They felt the clammy fingers of despair getting a grip on their hearts.

Dad sent her a graduation card, and here is what he wrote in it:

Sweetheart, you're on the road to heaven, but you're going the wrong way.
To get there you've got to go right and stay straight. I love you, Dad.

Mom decided to move back home. The daughter became afraid. She asked her mother if she could come with her. She said, "If I stay here with no support at all, I don't know what will happen to me."

She came back with her mom, and the family reunited. She returned to our office for aftercare counseling. Again, she has succeeded in putting down drugs. She gains strength today from what she experienced and learned at the treatment center. She believes she will be free from drugs the rest of her life. Her new boyfriend is drug free, too. She no longer sees anything attractive about her old crowd. She told me, "All they do is get drunk or stoned. That's all they care about. I can't stand watching them do that."

Her parents couldn't be happier. They say it's been worth everything.

Jesus agrees. He authored salvation and resurrection. It's God's will that your son or daughter rise from the dying. I wish you and yours a successful rescue and recovery operation and a joyous Easter—our all-season season.